T0339880

ETHIOPIA AND THE UNITED STATES

ETHIOPIA AND THE UNITED STATES

HISTORY, DIPLOMACY, AND ANALYSIS

Getachew Metaferia

Algora Publishing
New York

Library of Congress Cataloging-in-Publication Data —

Getachew Metaferia.
 Ethiopia and the United States: history, diplomacy, and analysis / Getachew
Metaferia.
  p. cm.
  Includes bibliographical references and index.
  ISBN 978-0-87586-645-1 (trade paper: alk. paper) — ISBN 978-0-87586-646-8
(hard cover: alk. paper) — ISBN 978-0-87586-647-5 (ebook) 1. United States—Foreign
relations—Ethiopia. 2. Ethiopia—Foreign relations—United States. I. Title.

E183.8.E8G47 2009
327.73063—dc22
                                    2009002127

Front Cover: "Obelisk at Axum and the Washington Monument," by Helina Getachew
Metaferia, 2008.

Printed in the United States

To those, living or dead, who have been victimized by flaws in foreign policy and human shortcomings, intended or otherwise.

Ethiopia has always held a special place in my own imagination and the prospect of visiting Ethiopia attracted me more strongly than a trip to France, England, and America combined. I felt I would be visiting my own genesis, unearthing the roots of what made me an African. Meeting the emperor himself would be like shaking hands with history.

— Nelson Mandela. From *Long Walk to Freedom: The Autography of Nelson Mandela*

Acknowledgement

I wish to acknowledge Ethiopians and Americans who have been involved in building relations between an old and a new nation through formal diplomatic channels and informal people-to-people public diplomacy efforts. Government officials and functionaries, as well as private citizens, have served as their respective countries' official and unofficial ambassadors. American citizens who have worked in Ethiopia and loved it have been bridge builders between peoples. Ethiopians who have lived in the US and loved it have cultivated solid relationships with Americans and have fostered a positive image of their country. They have all played significant roles in bringing the two countries closer, be it at state or at public levels.

I wish also to acknowledge the following persons and organizations for their particular contributions:

My wife, Dr. Maigenet Shifferraw, for her unfailing support and her critical comment on the manuscript, and my daughters Tigist and Helina, son Kaleb and niece Messeret Taye, and my brother-in-law, the late Matiwos Shifferraw, who was supportive of my scholarship. Helina's imaginative work on the cover picture depicts the 1700-year-old obelisk at Axum, northern Ethiopia, and the 224-year-old Washington Monument. I am grateful to my family for their support of all my professional endeavors and in the consummation of this book;

The librarians at the Carter Presidential Library in Atlanta, Georgia and at the National Archives at College Park, Maryland;

Fantahun Tiruneh, reference librarian, the Library of Congress, Tewodros Abebe, Assistant Archivist, Howard University, and Theodros Dagne, Specialist in African Affairs, US Congressional Research Service, for their assistance in my queries and research;

Morgan State University for providing me with funds to conduct research at the Carter Presidential Library;

Dr. Max Hilaire, Chair of Department of Political Science at Morgan State University, for his continuous support; and

Many respected individuals and friends provided me with documents, gave interviews, commented on this work, and extended their support. The list could be longer, but space allows me to mention the following only:

Catherine E. Byme, former Director for African Affairs at the National Security Council; Professors Mario D. Fenyo of Bowie State University; the late Dejazmach Zewde Gabre-Sellassie; member of Ethiopian Parliament and professor at Addis Ababa University, Dr. Merera Gudina; Dr. Tekola W. Hagos, formerly advisor to Ethiopia's Minister of Foreign Affairs; Ato Abate Kassa; Ambassador Kassa Kebede; Ato Mulugeta Lule; Ambassador Ayalew Mandefro; Professor Dr. Tesfatsion Medhanie of the University of Bremen, Germany; Dr. Birhanu Nega, elect mayor of Addis Ababa in 2005; my former teacher, colleague, and friend, Professor Sulayman S. Nyang of Howard University;

member of Ethiopian Parliament and professor at Addis Ababa University, Dr. Beyene Petros; former Minister of Information, and currently Ph.D. candidate, Dima Noggo Sarbo; former US Ambassador to Ethiopia David H. Shinn; Gayle Smith, former Special Assistant to President Clinton; Professor Theodore M. Vestal of Oklahoma State University and Ato Gebeyehu Woldemariam, chair of Association of Former Ethiopian Airlines Employees in North America (AFEAENA);

Professor John and Bonnie Ward of Topeka, Kansas, for being my host family when I first arrived in the US;

Jo McFarlane for editing this work and Camille Acker for providing constructive suggestions;

Amha Merse Hazen for providing me with his computer expertise; and

The editors and staff of Algora Publishing for their continued support and for bringing this book to fruition.

Getachew Metaferia

ACRONYMS

ARDUF	Afar Revolutionary Democratic Unity Front
ACRI	African Crisis Response Initiative
AGOA	African Growth and Opportunity Act
AU	African Union
AFS	American Field Service
AAEJ	American Association of Ethiopian Jewry
AFEAENA	Assoc. Former Ethiopian Airlines Employees in North America
CIA	Central Intelligence Agency
CPJ	Committee to Protect Journalists
CUD	Coalition for Unity and Democracy
DFLSG	Democratic Front for the Liberation of Setit and Gash
DFLS	Democratic Front for the Liberation of Somalia
DoD	US Department of Defense
DV	Diversity Visa
EALG	Ethio-American Lobby Group
EAL	Ethiopian Airlines
EACF	Ethiopian-American Constituency Foundation
ECA	Economic Commission for Africa
EDU	Ethiopian Democratic Union
EHRCO	Ethiopian Human Rights Council
ELF	Eritrean Liberation Front
EPDA	Ethiopian Patriotic Democratic Alliance
EPDM	Ethiopian People's Democratic Movement
EPLF	Eritrean People's Liberation Front
EPMG	Ethiopian Provisional Military Government
EPRDF	Ethiopian People's Revolutionary Democratic Forces
EPRP	Ethiopian People's Revolutionary Party
EWPD	Ethiopian Women for Peace and Development
EU	European Union
HOA	Horn of Africa
IANSA	International Action Network on Small Arms
ILO	International Labor Union
IMF	International Monetary Fund
IUC	Islamic Union Court
MAAG	Military Assistance Advisory Group
MDA	Magen David Adom
MFN	Most Favored Nation
NACEJ	North American Conference on Ethiopian Jewry
NATO	North Atlantic Treaty Organization
NCP	National Congress Party
NDA	National Democratic Alliance
NFD	Northern Frontier District
NIF	National Islamic Front
NMRC	National Medical Research Center
NSC	National Security Council
OAU	Organization of African Unity
OALF	Oromo Abo Liberation Front

ODM	Orange Democratic Movement
OLF	Oromo Liberation Front
ORH	Operation Restore Hope
SNF	Somali National Front
SPLA	Sudan People's Liberation Army
PCV	Peace Corps Volunteer
PFDJ	People's Front for Democracy and Justice
PMGE	Provisional Military Government of Ethiopia
SSDF	Somali Salvation Democratic Front
SAP	Structural Adjustment Program
TFG	Transitional Federal Government of Somalia
TGE	Transitional Government of Ethiopia
TPLF	Tigre People's Liberation Front
TWA	Trans World Airlines
UDEF	United Ethiopian Democratic Forces
UIC	Union of Islamic Court
UN	United Nations
UNMEE	United Nations Mission in Ethiopia and Eritrea
USAID	United States Agency for International Development
USIA	United States Information Agency
WPE	Workers Party of Ethiopia
WSLF	Western Somali Liberation Front
WTO	World Trade Organization

GLOSSARY

Abyssinia	The ancient name of Ethiopia
Abune	Bishop of the Ethiopian Orthodox Church ranking below the Patriarch
Agazi	A special military force of Ethiopia
Amharic	Ethiopia's national language
Bete Israel	"House of Israel," Ethiopian Jews; also used to be known as Falasha
Blata	A learned person (also means "youth")
Blatengeta	A title bestowed on a learned person, higher than *blata*, usually reserved for government officials
Derg	Provisional Military Committee. *Derg* means "committee" in Amharic.
Dejazmach	A civilian title for a field commander: Commander of the Gate
Ferenji	Foreigner, European
Kebele	District
Kelbash	Amharic term for a revisionist, a counter-revolutionary
Kentiba	Mayor
Kilil	Ethnic-based delineated region under EPRDF government
Lij	Title for sons of the royal family and nobility (also means "child")
Madrasa	Islamic religious seminary
Nakfa	Eritrean currency, named for a place in Eritrea
Negadras	Head merchant, a financial officer
Ras	A high-ranking government official (also means "head"), equivalent to a British duke
Selfi natsenat	A Tigrigna term for independence movement
Schema	Ethiopian traditional dress
Woizero	Amharic term for married women, "lady"

The Horn of Africa (HOA)

TABLE OF CONTENTS

PREFACE

In this book, I reflect on the history of Ethiopia's relation with the United States in the 20th century, examine current political conditions in Ethiopia and in the Horn of Africa, and analyze the likely direction of the relationship between Ethiopia and the United States. The book is based on primary sources, archival and de-classified government documents, interviews with government officials, and personal observation.

The diplomatic relationship between Ethiopia and the United States, initiated by a private US citizen, has continued for more than a century. The first tangible outcome of the relationship was the signing of a trade agreement in 1903. For the US, it was the first contact with this sovereign African country that had a long and rich history. For Ethiopia, although it had long contacts with other countries, it was the first formal interaction with a newly emerging powerhouse. Each expected the furthering of own national interests. The two countries were fascinated with each other and that helped in the blossoming of diplomatic relations.

Ethiopia and the United States have benefited from each other and, as would be expected of two sovereign states, have also experienced frustrations. The diplomatic relationship between the two is carried formally by diplomats, although private citizens have played some roles. A new phenomenon in the relationship between the two is the role of the Ethiopian diaspora in the US that has gained visibility and political acumen and is playing a positive role in the relationship between the two — the sending and the receiving countries. These new actors in the field of diplomacy seem to be a harbinger of the future which points to globalization and an increased human mobility.

The diplomatic relationship between the two countries has been influenced by the personalities of individual political actors, domestic political environment, and global dynamics. World War II, the ensuing Cold War, and the current post-9/11 state of affairs have had a bearing on the relationship between the two countries. Both countries continue to maximize their own interests. The United States, however, is a dominant global power while Ethiopia is a poor developing country. In this unequal power relationship, the US has exerted its hegemonic power through economic, political, and military strength to influence Ethiopia's domestic and foreign policies to maximize US national interest. Ethiopia has benefited from the assistance received from the US after World War II. The successive governments in Ethiopia, however, have ruined some of the institutions that were built and human capital that was developed, and have contributed to the malaise the country currently faces. The US has also contributed to the sorry situation in Ethiopia by supporting and abetting unpopular governments and failing to listen to the people.

Rectifying such a situation and pursuing progressive, not conventional, foreign policy would cultivate the Ethiopian people's support for the United States and ensure a mutually advantageous long-term US national interest.

In the following pages I examine the history of diplomacy between Ethiopia and the United States between 1903 and 2008 and analyze the effects of that diplomacy. I also reflect on changes in diplomatic policies that could best affect the future of both countries.

CHAPTER 1. INTRODUCTION

Historically, Ethiopia — the country that was once known as Abyssinia — had trade exchanges and religious connections with a variety of Asian, European, and Middle Eastern countries. The Ancient Greeks, the Byzantine Empire, Portugal, Russia, and the Holy Lands of Jerusalem and Mecca were familiar with Ethiopia. Ethiopia continued to maintain its independence in the modern era, except for a five-year occupation by fascist Italy (whom it expelled in 1941), and even during the European "scramble for Africa" remained the torch bearer of independence for Africans on the continent and those in the diaspora.

In 1896, Ethiopia, in the Battle of Adwa, defeated Italy in its attempt to include her in its intended colonization of East Africa. Ethiopia gained importance and European countries expressed increased interest in establishing diplomatic relations. In spite of its isolationist posture, in 1903 the US had established trade with Ethiopia which eventually led to diplomatic relations. This relationship with the oldest independent state in Africa marks the first formal US overture towards an independent African country.

The US interest in Ethiopia was based on the knowledge of Ethiopia's past glory; expected economic opportunities for American businesses from an African "El Dorado," as it was touted by American media of the time; and prospects for researchers. The US, as an emerging power, saw benefit in forging diplomatic relations with an independent African country that had long attracted the attention of European countries and increasingly gained international importance. The US foreign policy regarding Ethiopia nonetheless has been determined by the isolationist and the idealist posture of the US and by the Cold War political realism.

The fact that the US was not a colonial power and had no history of antagonism toward Ethiopia, unlike a number of European countries, encouraged Ethiopia's emperors to establish ties with the United States. Both Emperors Menelik II and Haile Selassie I played pivotal roles in the Ethio–US relations until 1974 when a military regime replaced Emperor Haile Selassie, adopted socialism as a state philosophy, and opposed the US, whom it believed to have worked against Ethiopia's interests.

3

Ethiopia hoped to benefit from US technology in its own development and nation building. For more than half a century, the two countries remained allies, except during the short-lived Italian occupation during World War II and the seventeen years of a military regime in Ethiopia during the Cold War. The US is actively involved in the development of Ethiopia because of its geographic location, which has served the US national security interest. Ethiopia also supported the US at the UN, was the only non-NATO country that fought on the US side during the Korean War, and remained a strong ally during most of the Cold War period.

The longstanding complexity of the relationship between Ethiopia and the US began to intensify in the post Cold War era and post 9/11 has accelerated even more. After the demise of the military regime in 1991, a new government supported by the US assumed power. Similar to what transpired in Emperor Haile Selassie's times, the US is supporting a regime that is increasingly losing support from the people. This regime pursues ethnic-based politics and is regarded as undemocratic by its critics both at home and abroad. The US has adopted a double standard and a contradictory foreign policy. On one hand, it claims to promote democracy and good governance; on the other, it shores up undemocratic regimes. In the fight against what the US calls international terrorism, Ethiopia's current government has allied itself with the United States. Ethiopia has sent its troops to Somalia, claiming to fight terrorism. Ethiopia, bogged down in unpopular war, finally pulled out of Somalia in January, 2009, without gaining tangible results.

While such a track record in diplomatic relations between Ethiopia and the US is important, this relationship must be subjected to critical analysis. Despite US financial, technical, military, and material assistance, Ethiopia remains one of the poorest countries in the world. US assistance to Ethiopia has been insufficient to tackle the gravest challenges: the increasing powerlessness and marginalization of the people, poverty, and economic development that benefits the masses. While the successive Ethiopian governments must take the lion's share of the responsibility, the global system that works against the interest of countries such as Ethiopia contributes to the situation.

Ethiopia's record in economic development, human rights and human security and in institutional and human capital development remains unimpressive. Ethiopians have been rendered powerless by their successive governments and are losing ground in health, education, and the sustainability of natural resources in the global political economy. Shifting, unstable governments remain unaccountable and abject poverty is not addressed. There are few opportunities for people to give their best to their country.

Furthermore, the US post-Cold War policy of globalization and neo-liberal economic policy, which the Ethiopian government also claims to subscribe to, has not benefited the poor. US foreign policy makers seem to be disinterested in Africa generally; institutional competition and short-term tactical interests also have a wide bearing on US policy towards Ethiopia. Ethio–US relationship, in the post Cold War era, is mired in such contradictions.

Despite the historically strong relationship between the two, Ethiopia was abandoned by the US during World War II and again when Somalia attacked and occupied Ethiopia's territory in 1977–1978. Ethiopians also believe that the US was a party to the secession of Eritrea in the hope that its national interest in the region would be well served. Unfortunately, the US interest in the region is even more at stake now than it had before the dismemberment of Ethiopia. The government in Eritrea is noted for its human rights abuses, antagonizes its neighbors, and has left Eritreans increasingly insecure.

Notwithstanding the stifling political conditions, Ethiopians are increasingly aware of their rights and strive to protect them whenever opportunities avail themselves, such as during the students uprisings of the 1960s that led to the overthrow of the monarchy in 1974 and the May 2005, elections that, for the first time in Ethiopia's history, galvanized voters to endeavor to change government through democratic process. In the 2005 election, the current government was declared the winner, yet the results were contested by opposition parties and international observers. The US, however, continued supporting the government. Indeed, it behooves the US to examine critically its foreign assistance and the effectiveness of contributions intended to better the lives of the people. Ethiopia also has to make a critical self-examination as it enters its third millennium. The vicious cycle of poverty, the depletion of its human resources must be addressed, and adequate solutions sought.

This book examines the history of the diplomatic relations between Ethiopia and the US from 1903 to 2008, considers the problems that both countries face, and reflects on changes in diplomatic policies that could promote the best future of both countries. Some events are analyzed for their impact on the topics rather than exclusively on their chronology, and therefore they may be cited in more than one context.

Chapter 2 examines Ethiopia and the world. Ethiopia fascinated the Greeks, the Byzantines, and the Portuguese and other countries. Ethiopian leaders also interacted with the early kingdoms of Europe, Russia, and the Middle Easterners.

Chapter 3 is about US contact with Ethiopia. An African-American businessman, William H. Ellis, an admirer of Emperor Menelik II, visited the Emperor and suggested that Ethiopia enter into a trade treaty with the United States. Robert Peet Skinner, a US consul at Marseilles, France, influenced the State Department to establish commercial relations with Ethiopia. In spite of initial hesitation, Robert P. Skinner eventually convinced US officials, including President Theodore Roosevelt, to dispatch a mission to Ethiopia. Eventually the US decided to open channels with Ethiopia to benefit American businesses and researchers. Skinner was instructed to proceed to Ethiopia and a Treaty of Amity and Commerce with Emperor Menelik was signed on December 27, 1903. Emperor Menelik was looking for an ally that would counter European powers of the time and had no colonial agenda in his region. He hoped that the US would assist him in the development of his country. Relations between the two countries continued for more than a century, except during the Italian occupation of Ethiopia (from 1936 to 1941) and the socialist military regime (from 1974 to 1991.)

Chapter 4 discusses the concerns of the two countries during the reigns of Emperor Menelik's successors: Empress Zewditu Menelik, Lij Iyasu Michael, and Regent Teferi Mekonnen (the future Emperor Haile Selassie.) One concern was the racism in the United States. The US government tried to shield the first Ethiopian delegates to the US in 1919 from racism, and to some extent they succeeded. The delegation stayed at the Waldorf-Astoria in New York and at the Hotel Lafayette in Washington, DC, where the Ethiopian flag was unfurled over the national capitol. That was inspirational to African-Americans. However, during the subsequent visit of Ethiopian delegates, in spite of advice by US emissaries in London and in Addis Ababa, Crown Prince a.k.a. Regent Teferi complained about the treatment his officials received in the United States. In 1927, an Ethiopian writer published an article in Amharic about race relations in the United States.

Another situation involved a third party, Britain. The Ethiopian government desired to build a dam on the Blue Nile. An American engineering company, J.G. White, contracted to build the dam. That was opposed by the British government as its interest in the region would be affected. The British newspapers sensationalized the situation. The Italians and the French were also opposed to the US role in Ethiopia. The contract was aborted because of a previous treaty, signed between Ethiopia and England in 1902, that required Ethiopia to consult with Britain regarding the use of the Blue Nile River.

Another issue was Ethiopia's interest to purchase US-made weapons and contract military instructors. Ethiopia wanted to build a national defense force. The purchase of weapons was limited by the General Act of Brussels of 1890, and a treaty between Britain, France, and Italy which restricted the "importation of arms and ammunitions" into Ethiopia. When Italy eventually attacked Ethiopia in 1936, it was ill equipped.

Chapter 5 focuses on the Italian invasion and the US reaction. The Italian invasion was a prelude to World War II and the interruption of Ethio-US relations. Ethiopia was the first nation to be attacked by the Axis force, Italy, and the first to be liberated with the assistance of an Allied power, Britain. The Ethio-US relationship was once again established after Italy was expelled from Ethiopia. The Cold War between the US and the USSR commenced after World War II. Security interests once again compelled both countries to gravitate towards each other. Emperor Haile Selassie was a close US ally in the region. The US also assisted Ethiopia in its development efforts.

Chapter 6 covers the relation between the two countries during the reign of Emperor Haile Selassie from 1941 to 1974. The US foreign policy establishments, the State Department, the Central Intelligence Agency (CIA), and the Department of Defense (DoD) were interested in Ethiopia. The three institutions did not always work in unison. They competed and contradicted each other. That affected Ethiopia in different ways.

Chapter 7 looks at US contributions to Ethiopia's development and the political situation during Emperor Haile Selassie's reign (1941–1974). The building of Ethiopia's institutions of higher education, and of Ethiopian Airlines, and the role of the Peace Corps Volunteers, are discussed. The military regime and the current Ethiopian government are accused of undermining some of these institutions on political grounds.

Chapter 8 is about the fall of Emperor Haile Selassie's government, the rise of the military regime and the US role. The aging Emperor Haile Selassie's request to President Nixon to upgrade the national defense of Ethiopia went unanswered. The USSR, on the other hand, armed Ethiopia's antagonistic neighbor, Somalia. By 1974, Somalia had better military hardware. Emperor Haile Selassie's government was overthrown in 1974 because of the general dissatisfaction in the country. A military junta, called the *Derg*, assumed power. It charged the US with working against Ethiopia's interest, summarily executed Emperor Haile Selassie's high ranking officials, and shifted Ethiopia's alliance from the US to the USSR. In typical Cold War politics, Ethiopia was allied with the USSR and Somalia with the United States. Somalia violated Ethiopia's territory and its troops penetrated deep into Ethiopia. Ethiopia's army was also engaged against the royalist force of Ethiopian Democratic Union (EDU) and the forces of EPLF and TPLF. It also fought the Ethiopian Peoples' Revolutionary Party (EPRP), a Marxist opposition party. The border war with Somalia (1977–1978) was finally reversed by the USSR and its allies, Cuba and South Yemen. The military regime was finally overthrown by the joint forces of the EPLF and the TPLF in 1991.

Chapter 9 describes Ethio–US relations after the military leadership was overthrown. The issue of the emigration of the Bete Israel had its origins in the military regime and the Reagan administration. The new Transitional Government of Ethiopia (TGE) becomes party to this initiative to resettle Ethiopian Jews in Israel, and initiative was first proposed by the Reagan administration before the military was overthrown. The US sponsored the London Peace Conference; leaders of liberation fronts and representatives of the Ethiopian government participated. The conference was aborted as the *Derg* becomes marginalized and the two major rebel groups, the TPLF and the EPLF, contrived the conference to their advantage. Some argue that the Conference, mainly due to the US, failed to ensure the unity of Ethiopia and opened the way to the precarious situation the region currently finds itself in. US officials argue that their main purpose was to avoid chaos in Ethiopia. New powers were finally installed in Addis Ababa and Eritrea while Ethiopians remained onlookers only.

Chapter 10 analyzes the situation on the ground prior to the secession of Eritrea in 1993 and the roles of some important political actors, personalities and institutions, especially during President Jimmy Carter's administration.

Chapter 11 looks at Ethiopia's role as a regional gatekeeper. African Renaissance leaders, the leaders of Ethiopia, Eritrea, and Uganda, were expected to play a significant role in the region as bulwarks against Islamic fundamentalists and in assuring a new dawn of democracy in their respected countries. That did not happen. Ethiopian and Eritrean leaders have taken their countries to a devastating war, are intolerant of critical views, have dismal records on human rights, and have contributed to regional instability and human insecurity.

Chapter 12 assesses current US policy towards Ethiopia regarding economic liberalization and free press. The US supports Ethiopia now as the latter has prescribed to economic liberalization and political democratization. The US supports Ethiopia through the African Growth and Opportunity Act (AGOA). While the Act has helped open up the US market to Ethiopia's goods, some of the projects funded under the Act do not appear to be providing the long-term benefits promised to Ethiopia, namely alleviating poverty and overcoming the marginalization of Ethiopia in the global political economy. Another example of policies that have not fulfilled their promise is the effort to dismantle the VOA–Amharic radio program. The program has served well both its audience in Ethiopia and US public diplomacy. Yet US officials aligned themselves with the government of Ethiopia that strove for the termination of the program. The government is accused of intolerance of the press that criticizes it. International organizations such as the Committee for the Protection of Journalists (CPJ) and Human Rights Watch have been on record pointing out the government's shortcomings and as an enemy of the free press.

Chapter 13 speaks to Ethiopian diaspora. Its number has increased since the 1970s when Ethiopians started to immigrate to the US as political refugees and others opted to remain in the US because of human rights abuses in Ethiopia. The Ethiopian diaspora in the US, the largest Ethiopian concentration outside of Ethiopia, has become economically and socially active. It is trying to influence US policy towards Ethiopia, such as through passage of H.R. 2003 in the US Congress. This bill, among others, requires denying visas to Ethiopian officials accused of human rights abuses. Members of the Ethiopian diaspora supported opposition parties that challenged the government during the May 2005 elections. (The opposition won but the govern-ment stayed in power.) The remittances sent to Ethiopia by the diaspora provide a much needed shot in the arm of Ethiopia's economy. The government, although it likes the infusion of funds, disdains the diaspora's concern over human rights.

Chapter 14 provides an overview of regional politics and the Horn of Africa dy-namics, the triangulation between Ethiopia, the US, and the HOA countries; the May 2005 election in Ethiopia; the war between Ethiopia and Eritrea; and Ethiopia's in-volvement in Somalia with the support of the US.

The last chapter reflects on the present conditions and the immediate future, pro-viding a summary and conclusion.

Chapter 2. Ethiopia and the World: A Historical Perspective

Ethiopia has a long history and a rich culture. Ethiopia's presence in the memory of the outside world dates back to the Hellenic period, before AD 300. The Greek historian of the fifth century B.C., Herodotus, among other classical Greeks, mentioned Ethiopia in his writings. He gave prominence to the Ethiopian character of justice and magnanimity.[1] Ethiopia also "occupies a more prominent place in the Homeric poems than does Egypt ... and his own kindred tribesmen, the Dorians and Hellenes themselves...."[2] According to the *Iliad*, their gods retired, recuperated, and feasted among the "blameless Ethiopian."[3] It was because of the early Greeks interest in Ethiopia that William Leo Hansberry, called father of African Studies at Howard University, 1922–1959, commented that "no student bent upon determining the real position of Ethiopia in world history can afford to ignore the gleams of light shed upon the subject by the greatest luminary of world history, Homer."[4] Classical Greeks were interested in Ethiopia and there were cultural, religious, and trade interactions between the two. The Greek language was spoken by the Axumite emperors and the Orthodox religion tied the two countries.[5]

Portugal, a superpower of the post-classical period, presumed the legendary Christian Kingdom of Prester John was in Ethiopia.[6] The news of the existence of a Christian people also raised the interest of scholars and religious groups in countries such as Germany, beginning in the 12th and 13th centuries, in the belief that the

---

1 William Leo Hansberry.1991. *Africa and Africans as Seen by Classical Writers*, Joseph E. Harris ed., Washington, DC: Howard University Press, p. 83.

2 Ibid., p.84.

3 W.E. Burghardt Du Bois. 1946 &1965. *The World and Africa*, New York: International Publishers, p. 119.

4 W. H. Hansberry, ibid. p. 84.

5 Theodore Natsoulas. 1977. *The Hellenic Presence in Ethiopia: A Study of a European Minority in Africa (1740–1936)*, Athens: Greece.

6 Elaine Sanceau. 1944. *The Land of Prester John: A Chronicle of Portuguese Exploration*, New York: Alfred A. Knopf. Also refer to William Leo Hansberry.1981. *Pillars in Ethiopian History*, Joseph E. Harris, ed., Washington, DC: Howard University Press, pp. 110-150.

---

origins of these Christians might be linked with biblical peoples. A German, Hiob Ludolf (1624–1704), started a program of Ethiopian Studies in Frankfurt, Germany, during the Reformation movement directed against the supremacy of the Pope, and published the first Amharic grammar. Hiob Ludolf, assisted by his Ethiopian teacher, Abba Gregory, was the first European to write the history of Ethiopia.[1]

It was reported that in 1165 Pope Alexander III and Emperor Emanuel Comnenus of the Byzantine Empire received letters from the Ethiopian emperor. Emperor Yekuno Amlak also dispatched an emissary to the Byzantine emperor, Michael VIII Palaiogos in 1275, and the group visited Venice, Bologna and Rome.[2] Father Francisco Alvarez, chaplain and narrator of the Portuguese mission in Ethiopia (1520–1527) gave a detailed account of the country and its relationship with Portugal.[3]

The Portuguese arrived with a 400-man army to support Ethiopia's Emperor Lebne Dengel (1508–40) and his successor and son Gelawdeows, against an invading Muslim Somali leader, Ahmad ibn Ibrahim, known in Ethiopia as Gragn Mohammed. The Turks supported Gragn Mohammad in his fight against the Christian kingdom of Ethiopia but he was defeated in 1541. This amounts to the first international conflict in the region that involved the superpowers of the era. The Portuguese support of Christian Ethiopia eventually led to an alliance against Muslim control of the Holy Land. They also managed to convert Emperor Susinios of Ethiopia to Roman Catholicism in 1632 in order to solidify their alliance. This conversion cost him his throne, as Ethiopians, members of the Eastern Orthodox faith, rose against Susinios. Such an array of contact, cooperation and conflict between Ethiopia and Europe, as well as the geopolitics of the period, indicates the level of international relations between Ethiopian and European potentates. As a result of its long interaction with other countries, Ethiopia has developed its own consciousness, its own national psyche.

Meanwhile, in the 18th century, individual Europeans, such as the Scotsman James Bruce (1769), were interested in Ethiopia in their quest to discover the source of the Blue Nile, and to explore Africa for Europeans. James Bruce also announced to the Western world the existence of Ethiopian Jews, who used to be called *falasha* or new comer. Africa remained for a long time uncharted territory, mysterious and mystical. Lack of knowledge about Africa led some Europeans to see all of Africa and all Africans through the same lens, developing a pejorative attitude that is still prevalent among some non-Africans, with no recognition of Ethiopia's (and other African civilizations') long history, rich culture, civilization and equal status with Europeans.

Ethiopia has had a special relationship with Alexandria, Egypt, since the 14th century. The Egyptian Coptic Church used to provide Ethiopia with the *Abun*, the head of the Ethiopia Orthodox Church, until Ethiopia terminated this relationship and started to have its own native *Abun* in 1959, establishing its religious independence. The Egyptian *Abun* were foreigners who had tried to maintain their religious dominance, and their political independence from Egypt remained questionable.

Such questions influenced the psyche of Ethiopian rulers to the extent that Emperor Theodros (1855–1868)[4] had the shoes of European visitors washed at the port of

1 Ministry of Information. 1973. *Ethiopia Today: The Arts*, Addis Ababa, Ethiopia: Commercial Printing Press, p. 9.

2 Leo Hansberry.1965. "Ethiopian Ambassadors to Latin Courts and Latin Emissaries to Prester John," *Ethiopia Observer*, vol. 4, no.1.

3 Francisco Alvarez. 1881. *Narrative of the Portuguese Embassy to Abyssinia During the Year 1520-1527*, translated by Edward John Stanley, London.

4 Svan Rubenson. 1966. *King of Kings Tewodros of Ethiopia*, Addis Ababa, Ethiopia.

Mitswa (Massawa) before they boarded their ship home, to prevent them from taking any soil sample that they could analyze to determine what minerals were available in Ethiopia. Foreigners (*ferenji*), especially Europeans, were kept at bay. Nevertheless, Ethiopian leaders were willing to adapt European instruments of modernization as long as they did not undermine Ethiopia's culture or power structure.

This desire to introduce European technology led to the conflict between Ethiopia and Britain in the 1860s. When the British refused to help Emperor Theodros develop Western technologies, especially weapons, he felt disrespected by the Europeans and detained them. He committed suicide to avoid capture by the British force that was dispatched from India, under the command of Sir Robert Napier, to free the detainees. The British, supported by other forces hostile to Theodros, blasted his fortress at Makdala.[1]

Ethiopia had two major encounters with Egyptian forces. The first was at the Battle of Gundet in November, 1875, under the command of Rateb Pasha. In the second battle, at Gura, in March 1876, 20,000 Egyptian soldiers were involved. In both wars Emperor Yohannes IV (1872–1889) and his illustrious general, Ras Alula Engeda, successfully repelled the Egyptian invaders and Emperor Yohannes consolidated his power.[2] Ras Alula, is called the "Lion of Gura" for his bravery.[3] He was the governor of *Mereb Mellash* (Eritrea) and founded Asmara, the capital of Eritrea.

The Egyptians were assisted by American mercenaries. The American officers were Col. William Dye, Ratib Pasha's Chief-of-Staff and Brigadier-General W.W. Loring, the one-armed confederate veteran.[4] Other Americans were Col. Charles W. Field of Virginia; Lieutenant-Colonel Derrick of Virginia; Major Luesh; Major Robert Schuyler Lamson; Surgeon-Major W.W. Wilson of Ohio; Captain David Essex Porter and Captain Irgenus, both from Montana; Surgeon-Major Johnson of Tennessee; Col. Samuel H. Lockett of Alabama and Lieutenant-Colonel C.J. Graves of Georgia.[5] The American presence in Ethiopia, in the service of the Egyptians, was the first of its kind reported. Egyptian rulers Muhammad Ali (1769–1849), an Ottoman pasha of Egypt, known as the father of modern Egypt, and his grandson, Khedive Ismail (1863–1879), wanted to control the Nile Valley and the Red Sea coast. Emperor Yohannes was mortally wounded on March 10, 1889, fighting the Mahadist army in Metemma bordering Sudan.[6] The Mahadis were followers of al-Mahdi of Sudan who tried to impose Islamic laws.

Ethiopia's experience with foreigners has proven the need for dependable allies.

After Emperor Menelik defeated Italy at the Battle of Adwa in 1896, Ethiopia became a regional power and a country to be closely watched. The European presence

---

1 For the history and incidence at Makdala, refer to Philip Marsden. 2007. *The Barefoot Emperor: An Ethiopian Tragedy*, Harper Collins Press. Also see Darrell Bates. 1979. *The Abyssinian Difficulty: The Emperor Theodros and the Magdala Campaign, 1867-68*, New York, NY: Oxford University Press.

2 Richard Pankhurst. 2001. *The Ethiopians: A History*, Malden, MA: Blackwell Publishing, pp. 166-168. Also refer to Edward Ullendorff, 1965, *The Ethiopian: An Introduction to Country and People*, London: Oxford University Press, p. 90.

3 Haggai Erlich. 1996. *Ras Alula and the Scramble for Africa*, Lawrence, NJ: The Red Sea Press, Inc. p. 12.

4 Pierre Crabites, *Americans in the Egyptian Army*, 1938, London: George Routledge & Sons, Ltd., p. 191. Also Zewde Gabre-Sellassie, 1975, *Yohannes IV of Ethiopia – Political Biography*, Oxford University Press, pp. 63-7.

5 Pierre Crabites, ibid., pp. 187–196.

6 Haggai Erlich, pp. 134-35.

in Ethiopia increased. Italy, Britain and France had long been in the region, through the colonization of Ethiopia's neighbors. Others, like Germany and Belgium, were also colonial powers in Africa and their emissaries were posted in Ethiopia to protect their interests and kept an eye on the activities of other European countries. The role of the Legations of these countries in Addis Ababa was mainly political.

Russia's presence in Ethiopia, though Russia was not a colonial power in Africa, was based on the religious ties that existed between the two countries, both followers of Eastern Orthodox Christianity. Their churches influenced the monarchs of their respective countries. Russia's interest in Ethiopia dates back to 1784 when the Russian government sent an official request to the patriarchies in Antioch and Jerusalem to translate 285 Russian words into Ethiopian languages. Eventually, Kharkov University, founded in 1805 in Ukraine, introduced the regular study of Amharic in 1829.[1] Russia's most significant contribution to Ethiopia's development was through the staffing of Balcha Hospital (named after an illustrious hero at the Battle of Adwa) in Addis Ababa. A few Ethiopians also received technical training in czarist Russia. One prominent Ethiopian, who took military training in Russia and represented Ethiopia at the League of Nations, was acquainted with the last Russian czar, Nicholas II, and served both Emperors Menelik and Haile Selassie. This was Tekle Hawariat Tekle Mariam.[2] The Russian Legation in Addis Ababa was the only one that provided free hospital services, physicians, and pharmacy, and trained Ethiopian nurses. Thus Russia's relationship with Ethiopia, unlike that of other European countries, was substantial and largely devoid of colonial agenda. When the USSR was invited by Ethiopia's military regime in the 1970s to replace the United States during the Cold War because of the fierce rivalry between the superpowers, the USSR saw it as a reuniting of former allies and historic friends.

Ethiopian rulers, beginning with Emperor Menelik, have also been interested in a diplomatic relationship with the United States. The US had not been antagonistic to Ethiopia and had no overt colonial design.

When the US made its diplomatic overture to Ethiopia, the European powers resented it and regarded it as a newcomer to the international arena, especially in African politics. Only in Liberia, home to freed slaves from the United States, did the US ties seem natural and unavoidable. European emissaries in Ethiopia tried to discredit the US in the eyes of Ethiopians. They resented its establishing a Legation in Addis Ababa.[3] Russia was not happy, either, about the budding relation between Ethiopia and the United States.

Thus, in general, Ethiopia is an African country that was respected before the advent of the large-scale international slave trade, colonialism, neo-colonialism and today's globalization that has increasingly exploited and marginalized the entire African continent. Ethiopia, as a sovereign state, had dealt with foreigners, successfully maintained its culture, and protected its national interests for an extended time.

---

1 D. Bashiron. 1958. "Ethiopian Philology in Russia," *Ethiopia Observer*, vol. 2, no. 3, p. 123.

2 Tekle Hawariat Tekle Mariam. 2005. *Yehiwete Tarik* (Autobiography), Addis Ababa: Addis Ababa University Press.

3 C.L. Hussey. March 4, 1904. *Report on the U.S. Diplomatic Expedition to Abyssinia*, Office of Naval Intelligence, Register No. 167, pp. 5-6.

CHAPTER 3. UNITED STATES CONTACT WITH ETHIOPIA (1903–1919)

Ethiopia's diplomatic relationship with the United States is comparatively recent. Because of distance and the American isolationist posture from 1776–1941,[1] there was no official contact between the two for a long period. The US concentrated on internal economic development, territorial expansionism to the west, and industrialization. However, individual US citizens went to Ethiopia for a variety of reasons. In the late 19th century, Henry M. Stanley, a special correspondent for *New York Herald*, accompanied the British expedition under Sir Robert Napier (1868) and witnessed the fall of Makdala and the death of Emperor Theodros.

Some African-Americans and Afro-Caribbeans who profess Ethiopianism have historically looked up to Ethiopia. Its long history and culture and the divination in the Old Testament that "Ethiopia shall soon stretch forth her hands unto God" (Psalm 68, verse 31) has made Ethiopia attractive especially to diaspora Africans. Ethiopia is known and romanticized by some Americans. After the Battle of Adwa, in 1896,[2] for example, a young Haitian, Benito Sylvian, arrived at Emperor Menelik's court in 1897 and became the Emperor's *aide-de-camp*. Similarly, Dr. Joseph Vitalien, from the French colony of Guadeloupe, visited Ethiopia and remained there to serve as Emperor Menelik's personal physician. He helped found two early hospitals in Ethiopia: the Ras Mekonnen Hospital in Harar (1903) and the Menelik II Hospital in Addis Ababa (1909).

William H. Ellis, an African-American cotton grower in Texas, later a Wall Street stockbroker, and an admirer of Emperor Menelik, visited Ethiopia in 1899. Ellis received permission to grow cotton in Southern Ethiopia and establish a textile factory. In the diplomatic arena, Ellis convinced Menelik to enter into a Treaty of Amity and

---

1 President James Monroe charted the American isolationist policy, which is referred to as The Monroe Doctrine of 1823.

2 Refer to Paulos Milikias and Getachew Metaferia, ed. 2005. *The Battle of Adwa – Reflections on Ethiopia's Historic Victory Against European Colonialism*," New York: Algora Publishing.

Commerce with the United States.[1] That served as an impetus for forging an official relationship between the two countries[2]

The American Consul at Marseilles, France, Robert Peet Skinner, in January 1900, during the administration of President William McKinley, suggested that the State Department dispatch a commercial mission to Ethiopia, similar to the trade mission scheduled to visit China.[3] In his letter to David J. Hill, Assistant Secretary of State, Skinner stated that "there is a field for study and commercial expansion in Africa that is deserving of consideration ... and our people know next to nothing of the situation and possibilities in Abyssinia."[4] Skinner suggested that in Abyssinia the US maintained "not even the semblance of official representation, although there exists a vast population, politically independent, and capable of absorbing our products."[5]

The McKinley administration had a foreign policy of sponsoring democracy and involvement in international politics. In his speech just before he was assassinated, McKinley stated that "isolationism is no longer possible or desirable." Skinner grasped this opportunity and pushed for diplomatic relations between Ethiopia and the United States. Skinner believed that "[Ethiopia] remained the one spot upon the globe where a powerful government exercised authority over some millions of subjects recognized as free and independent, and had absolutely no point of contact with our own."[6] Skinner wrote several letters urging the State Department to establish contact with Ethiopia but the responses were not positive. Thomas W. Cradler, Third Assistant Secretary of State, for example, responded to one of Skinner's letters and stated that it was not advisable for the State Department "to make any recommendations to Congress upon the subject."[7]

After three years of persistent proposal and efforts, Skinner sent a letter to the Department of State on May 13, 1903, urging that a special mission be dispatched to Ethiopia, "a country destined to play a large part in the future of Africa."[8] Skinner also met with President Theodore Roosevelt in Washington, D.C. and presented his case. Francis B. Loomis, Assistant Secretary of State, sent a confidential letter to Skinner in which he stated that "after careful consideration of the matter, you are hereby instructed to proceed to Abyssinia, at a such a time as you may deem best, for the purpose of investigating and reporting upon commercial conditions in that empire ... The negotiation of a treaty with Abyssinia and your appointment as a diplomatic agent have not yet been decided upon, but it is probable that your recommendations on these subjects will be acted upon favorably."[9]

---

1 Eric Rosenthal. 1938. *Stars and Stripes in Africa*, London, p. 244.

2 For some background on William Ellis, refer to Negussay Ayele. 2003. *Ethiopia and the United States*, www.Ocopy.com pp. 42-45.

3 Donald W. Kilhfner. 1968. "The United States and Ethiopia, 1903–1915," M.A. Thesis, Howard University, p. 55.

4 Department of State. January 6, 1900. *Consular Letters from Marseilles*, vol. xviii, no. 93. Also refer to Frank J. Manheim. 1932. "The United States and Ethiopia: A Study in American Imperialism," *Journal of Negro History*, vol. 17, no. 2, p. 142.

5 Frank J. Manheim, ibid.

6 Robert P. Skinner. 1906. *Abyssinia of To-Day*. London: Edward Arnold, Publisher to the Indian Office, p. 94.

7 Department of State, *Instructions to Consuls*, vol. 171, p. 35, letter No. 61, dated February 6, 1900. Also refer to Frank J. Manheim, ibid., p. 143.

8 *Consular Letters from Marseilles*, vol. XIX, letter no. 99, as quoted by Frank J. Manheim, ibid., p. 146.

9 *Instructions to Consuls*, vol. 187, letter no. 178, dated Washington, June 4, 1903. Quoted by Frank J. Manheim, ibid., p. 147.

On June 4, 1903, the Department of State advised Consul General Skinner to proceed to Abyssinia. Skinner was also advised that "upon receipt of this instruction, and prior to July first, you will draw upon the Secretary of State for $2,000 from which to pay the actual and necessary expense of the journey etc."[1] In July, Assistant Secretary of State Loomis informed Skinner that it had been decided to enter into negotiation with the Emperor Menelik for a "Treaty of Amity, Reciprocal Establishments and Commerce."[2] It was reported that President Theodore Roosevelt was interested in the treaty. Skinner and his party left Marseilles for Naples, Italy, on October 25, 1903, and there boarded the US gunboat S.S. Macias at Naples. The mission proceeded to Beirut, where it took on board US marines commanded by Lieutenant C.L. Hussey, and sailed for Djibouti.

Consul Skinner[3] and his American party arrived in Addis Ababa on December 18, 1903. A 5,000-man guard of honor greeted Skinner, who later described the scene as "bewilderingly beautiful." Captain George C. Thorpe and 19 Marines pitched their tents at Emperor Menelik's palace courtyard, which they named "Camp Roosevelt," and raised the US flag of forty-five stars and thirteen stripes. Thus was formed the first American diplomatic mission to Ethiopia, and its guard.[4] Skinner, however, was housed at the palace of Ras Wolde Giorgis, the Emperor's cousin.

Emperor Menelik's counselor of state, a Frenchman, Leon Chefneux, chaperoned Consul Skinner in the absence of Alfred Ilg, who was in Europe at the time. Alfred Ilg and Chefneux had arrived in Ethiopia in the 1870s and were close to Emperor Menelik and assisted in the development of Ethiopia. Ilg was an engineer who eventually became a foreign affairs advisor and counselor. Emperor Menelik's hospitality, the elaborate court routine, and its modernity impressed the Americans. Skinner's initiative gained support and on December 27, 1903, a Treaty of Amity and Commerce, which comprises seven articles, was signed between Emperor Menelik and Robert P.. Skinner. The treaty regulates commercial relations between the two countries and also accorded Ethiopia the status of "Most Favored Nation"(MFN).[5]

Paving the way for the eventual diplomatic relationship of Ethiopia and the United States, the terms of agreement that was signed between Emperor Menelik and Consul Skinner in 1903 states that the two parties will:

> Article I. Provide for citizens "to travel and to transact business through the extent of the territories of the two contracting Powers" and for citizens to obey the laws and submit to the courts of the country in which they were located.
>
> Article II. Provide for the security of person and property of those engaged in trade in either country.
>
> Article III. The two countries grant citizens of each other all the advantages accorded to other Powers.

---

1 G. Pabst, Jr., "Official Relations Between the United States of America and Abyssinia," May 14, 1925, p.4 in Record of the Department of State Relating to Political Relations Between the US and Ethiopia, 1910–1929, US National Archives, box # M412,1.

2 Frank J. Manheim, ibid., p. 147.

3 For more information on Skinner, refer to Negussay Ayele, pp. 45-51.

4 Bernard C. Nalty. September, 1959. "Guests of the Conquering Lion: The Diplomatic Mission to Abyssinia, 1903." Washington, D.C.: Marine Corps Historical Reference Series, no. 12.

5 For Consul-General Skinner's mission to Abyssinia, refer to *US Bureau of Manufactures*, May, 1904. US Bureau of Statistics, Department of Commerce and Labor. Monthly consular reports, no. 284, pp. 339-347.

Article IV. Provide to Americans the use of telephones, postal service and other means of communication on the same terms as other foreigners in Ethiopia.

Article V. Provide for reciprocal exchange of official representation.

Article VI. Provide for the treaty to remain in effect ten years with renewal of or modifications possible upon one year's prior notification.

Article VII. Provide for the treaty to become effective after ratification by the United States government and notification of ratification given to His Majesty Menelik II, King of Kings of Ethiopia within one year of the treaty's signing.[1]

Refer to Appendix I for the treaty between the two countries.

The Americans had arrived with a treaty proposal already prepared in Amharic, and the negotiations took nine days; a day short of what had Skinner expected. The treaty was written in Amharic and French, and the final English version was translated from the French version. The Amharic version of the treaty had been drafted by Professor Enno Littman of Princeton University, an archeologist and professor of Semitic languages, whom Skinner acknowledged as probably the only man in the US who was familiar with Ethiopia's national language. Littman, originally from Germany, had led an expedition team to Ethiopia in 1906; they unearthed the tomb of Emperor Kaleb of the Axumite kingdom who ruled in the fourth century.

It would be interesting to examine some of the provisions of the above treaty, especially Article I. At the time of the signing of the treaty, the Jim Crow laws that legitimized the segregation of the races in the American South were in effect. Those laws would apply to black Ethiopians if they attempted "to circulate and to transact business in all liberty" in those states. Or possibly as "foreign blacks" Ethiopians conducting business in the US might have been able to circumvent Jim Crow laws.

Ethiopian merchants who arrived in New York's Wall Street in 1808 faced racial segregation for the first time when they attempted to worship at the First Baptist Church. When they were told to sit in the back of the church, they were surprised to discover color-based segregation in the house of worship and walked out. African-American worshipers walked out with them and established their own church. That was how the Abyssinian Baptist Church was established in Lower Manhattan, before it moved to its current location in Harlem, in 1922, under the leadership Rev. Adam Clayton Powell. (In commemoration of the bicentennial anniversary of the church, 161 members of the church and a few others, under the leadership of Rev. Calvin O. Butts III, made a pilgrimage to Ethiopia in September 2007, which coincided with the celebration of the Ethiopian millennium.)[2]

Besides signing a treaty with Emperor Menelik, Skinner gathered information regarding commercial resources in Ethiopia that could be beneficial to the United States.[3] Skinner estimated the population of Ethiopia to be 10 million, with a daily increase of purchasing power and wants. There seemed to be opportunities for Ethiopia to supply agricultural goods to the American market and the opportunity for US

---

1 Donald W. Kilhfner, ibid., pp. 78–79. Also see US Department of State, 1904, *Foreign Relations of the United States*, Washington, DC, Government Printing Press, pp. 298-300.

2 For the history of the Abyssinian Church refer to the webpage of the Church http://www. abyssinian200.org

3 Robert P. Skinner, "Our Mission to Abyssinia".

government agricultural researchers to use seeds from Ethiopia to experiment in the US with growing marketable products for the United States.[1]

Skinner brought gifts to Emperor Menelik, including a signed portrait of President Theodore Roosevelt and the president's book on *North American Big Game* and a magazine rifle of the latest model with a burnished barrel and gold-plated mountings; the Emperor immediately experimented with it. A typewriter sent by the manufacturer impressed the Emperor, who inquired how such a machine could be adapted to Amharic.[2] The Italian company Olivetti, founded in 1908, later fulfilled the Emperor's desire to have a typewriter with Ethiopian alphabets, developed by an Ethiopian engineer Ayana Biru. The US Department of Agriculture also sent the Emperor a "well-selected lot of American garden seeds"[3] which the Emperor distributed to farmers.

Emperor Menelik sent gifts to President Theodore Roosevelt through Skinner. The gifts included two lion cubs, a hyena, and two elephants' tusks. The two lion cubs and the hyena were kept at the Washington Rock Creek Zoo, the current National Zoo.[4]

In addition, all the Marines who accompanied Skinner received decorations from Emperor Menelik. The golden medal, bearing a profile of Emperor Menelik, hung from a ribbon decorated with the green, yellow, and red Ethiopian flag. It was reported that one of the marines, Captain Joseph Rossell, made the mistake of wearing the medal at the marine barracks in Washington, DC while a Masonic convention was meeting. Captain Rossell was "mobbed by a phalanx of Masons, each of whom addressed him as 'Potentate' and insisted upon shaking his hand. Red, yellow, and green, it seems, are also the colors of the Shriners."[5]

Recognizing Ethiopia's potential for American entrepreneurs, President Theodore Roosevelt sent Emperor Menelik a special invitation to attend the World's Fair in St. Louis in 1904. The objective of the Fair was to provide "an opportunity to exchange ideas and information, and to see the latest advances in arts, sciences, inventions, agriculture, and helped propel the world into the Industrial Revolution."[6] Emperor Menelik was interested in the visit and wanted his wife, Empress Taitu, to accompany him. He requested and received a formal invitation by the US government and had royal honors accorded him. Menelik also requested that the US provide a warship for his return voyage.[7] However, Emperor Menelik's visit to the US failed to materialize.

Emperor Menelik also accepted the invitation for Ethiopia to participate at the Louisiana Purchase Exposition and promised to send a "commission of distinguished and representative men" in order to expand the commercial relations of the Empire. The Exposition (also held in St. Louis, Missouri, in 1904) was in celebration of the

---

1 Richard Guenther. February, 1904. "Trade Opportunities in Abyssinia," US Bureau of Manufactures, US Bureau of Statistics, Department of Commerce and Labor. Monthly consular reports, no 281, pp. 333-335.

2 Robert Skinner. 1906. *Abyssinia of Today: An Account of the First Mission sent by the American Government to the Court of the King of Kings (1903–1904)*. London: Edward Arnold Publishers to the Indian Office, pp. 119-120.

3 Ibid., p. 121.

4 Bernard C. Nalty. 1903. *Guests of the Conquering Lion: The Diplomatic Mission to Abyssinia*, Marine Corps Historical reference Service, No. 12, Historical Branch, G-3, Washington, DC: US Marine Corps, 1959, p. 2.

5 Ibid., p.8.

6 Refer to the 1904 St. Louis World's Fair Webpage http://ftp.apci.net-truax/1904wf/

7 Robert P. Skinner.1963. *Abyssinian Scrapbooks*, U.S.N. Academy, Reel 2900.

Centennial of the Louisiana Purchase. The exposition was said to be "without a peer in history" and second only to the Declaration of Independence in its importance.[1] This indicates the importance the US gave to Ethiopia and hoped to benefit from the resources it provided. According to Skinner, the US Department of Agriculture was interested in the "seeds of the more important crops peculiar to Ethiopia, a number of which may be found valuable in the exploitation of the uncultivated western lands of the United States."[2]

A formal diplomatic relationship with the US government, which was limited to trade, was thus forged in 1903. Between 1903 and the outbreak of World War II, several treaties were signed and the US had emissaries posted in Ethiopia as did several European countries. The original treaty, which expired on March 7, 1914, was renewed as stipulated in Article VI of the treaty. (Refer to Appendix IV for a copy of the Treaty.) The treaty has subsequently been altered and absorbed by the many that have followed.

Robert P. Skinner aptly expressed the Ethio–US relationship at the time. He wrote, "Probably for the first time in the modern history of Ethiopia has a foreign mission visited the country upon an errand of peace and amity bringing no vexed question of territorial integrity or national honor to decide, and neither asking nor granting anything to which both sides could not accede."[3] The fact that Americans came to Ethiopia not seeking territories impressed Menelik. Emperor Menelik was reported to have said that other nations come to Africa like sons to their fathers, say-ing, "Father, are you going to make a will, and leave us something?" He added that America was alone without land in Africa and wanted none. She only wanted liberty to trade.[4]

In his book that gave account of his mission to Ethiopia, Skinner wrote of being impressed by its people and rulers. During his long journey from Djibouti to Addis Ababa, Skinner wrote that his goods were not stolen and that good old-fashioned honesty was the rule in the empire of the king of kings. According to Skinner, "The Abyssinians are an extremely ceremonious people, possessed of an innate courtesy which in many aspects is most admirable."[5]

Upon his return to Marseilles in 1904, Skinner suggested that he be designated as the agent to Abyssinia while residing in Marseilles. He would then be authorized to receive and transmit the views of the two governments, especially as the situation did not at that time require the appointment of a permanent diplomatic representa-tive in Ethiopia. Skinner also stated that "our present trade interests in Ethiopia are greater than those of any of the three Powers now legislating for that country."[6]

ETHIOPIA AND THE US: ARCHITECTS OF A NASCENT DIPLOMACY

The US was a latecomer to Ethiopia, as several European powers had their emis-saries already posted in Addis Ababa. Emperor Menelik II, despite the antagonism of the European powers, was open to the US and saw it as a counter force to the Euro-

---

1 http://Washingtonmo.com/1904/index.htm

2 Robert P. Skinner, ibid.

3 Robert P. Skinner. 1904. *Our Mission to Abyssinia*, Washington, D.C.: Government Printing Office, p. 4.

4 Richard Pankhurst. 1972. "William H. Ellis–Guillume Enriques Ellesio: The First Black American Ethiopianist?" *Ethiopia Observer*, vol. 15, no. 2, p. 89.

5 Robert P. Skinner.1906. *Abyssinia of To-Day*, p. 26.

6 Ibid.

peans, especially to Britain, France, and Italy, as he was suspicious of their ulterior motives and their colonial history in Africa. Russia also led a campaign against US influence in Ethiopia out of a concern that the US might get a toe-hold in the Red Sea region. Western technology and medicine, which he wanted to introduce to his country, fascinated Menelik, as an enlightened leader, despite the resistance he faced from the nobility and the Church. Menelik hoped that the US would assist Ethiopia in its efforts to modernize the country. The diplomatic relationship between Ethiopia and the US was thus on course to be established. The Europeans were unsuccessful in undermining the budding Ethio–US relationship.

The US Senate ratified the 1903 treaty (Articles I–VII) on March 12, 1904, and it was signed by President Theodore Roosevelt on March 17, 1904. The treaty was claimed to be the most picturesque document of its kind to be placed before the US Senate foreign relations committee. It promised to "provide for trading posts and telegraph and other means of transportation in Menelik's provinces."[1]

William H. Ellis, a.k.a. Guillaume Enriques Ellesio, who frequently visited Menelik and wanted to assist in Ethiopia's development, was interested in delivering the copy of the treaty to Ethiopia. The US State Department, however, according to an article by Richard Pankhurst, was reluctant to entrust the mission to a black man. The treaty was entrusted to Kent J. Loomis, brother of Assistant Secretary of State Francis B. Loomis, who offered to travel to Ethiopia at his own expense (to hunt lions and find adventure). Naturally Ellis was disappointed at not being chosen as the bearer of the treaty to Menelik. As Ellis was familiar with the country, had developed an acquaintance with Emperor Menelik, and was the first American to greet Robert P. Skinner in Addis Ababa in 1903, he asked to accompany Kent Loomis to Ethiopia. On their voyage to Ethiopia, a mishap befell Loomis, who disappeared on June 20, 1904, from the steamer Kaiser Wilhelm II and was later found dead. Loomis was reported to be often inebriated, which condition was suspected to be the cause of his demise. Ellis, by default, becomes the bearer of the treaty to Emperor Menelik.[2]

In general, Ethiopia had a great allure for US businessmen, and newspapers reported the country to be an "El Dorado" possessing "wealth beyond power of calculation of human beings."[3] However, the US still clung to its isolationist foreign policy which sought to avoid any "entanglement" in international politics. That policy was beginning to unwind, however, and the US initiated the use of its armed forces abroad between 1901 and 1921 in order to protect its interests.[4] At the same time, some Americans were interested in Ethiopia because of its unique history,[5] and missionaries were also interested in Ethiopia, hoping to convert Ethiopians to Western religions.

The US legation was eventually opened in Addis Ababa on December 19, 1906, after Frank R. Mower was appointed as the first Consul General that August. The position of Consul General, a rank lower than that of a minister, displeased Emperor Menelik. General Mower resigned on January 3, 1907, only two weeks after he was confirmed and assumed his post. One reason he gave for his resignation was that he

1 Robert P. Skinner.1963. *Abyssinian Scrapbooks*, U.S.N. Academy, Reel 2900.

2 Richard Pankhurst. 1972. Ibid.

3 Robert P. Skinner. 1963. Ibid.

4 Eugene R. Wittkopf, Jr. and J. M. Scott. 2003. *American Foreign Policy*, Belmont, CA: Wadsworth/Thomson Learning, pp. 30-34.

5 David Shinn. 1971. "A Survey of American-Ethiopian Relations Prior to the Italian Occupation of Ethiopia," *Ethiopia Observer*, vol. 14, no. 4, pp. 297-311.

agreed with Emperor Menelik that the position needed to be raised to ministerial level.[1] The British representative was then in charge of American affairs. Writing from Leghorn, Copenhagen, where he was transferred, Mower said that a Legation should be established in Ethiopia.

In September 1907, Edward Vialle was appointed American Vice-Consul General in Addis Ababa and served there until Spring 1908; he left his post because of illness. The British again looked after the American interests in Addis Ababa. Mr. Guy Love was appointed Deputy Consul General in Addis Ababa and after some days Mr.. Hoffman Philip was appointed as Minister Resident and Consul General on June 14, 1909.

The US-Ethiopia relationship thus begun, albeit with low-level diplomacy on the part of the US, indicative of a lackluster attitude toward an African country. The relationship eventually gained momentum in response to both the global political condition and a shift in US foreign policy. In 1910, the US President proclaimed that Ethiopia's government was friendly and "imposes no terms or restrictions on US product ... [and that it] imposes no export duty or prohibition upon the exportation of any article to the United States that unduly discriminates against the United States...." [Refer to Appendix III, Proclamations of 1910.]

The relationship between Ethiopia and the US, during the reign of Emperor Menelik II, may be summarized as follows:

- In 1903, a Treaty of Amity and Commerce was signed between Ethiopia and the US,
- 1906, American Consul General served in Addis Ababa,
- 1906-1909, a Vice Consul was in charge of the US mission to Ethiopia,
- 1909, the Mission was run by a Resident Minister and a Consul General,
- 1910-1913, a Vice Consul General ran the office, and
- In 1913 US mission was temporarily closed and the British Legation in Addis Ababa looked after American interests.[2]

The Ethiopia and US treaty, signed by Skinner in 1903, was renewed in 1914 as required under the treaty of 1903. (Refer to Appendixes I & IV.)

The US Mission to Ethiopia was closed during Woodrow Wilson's first term in office, coincident with the death of Emperor Menelik II in 1913, who had suffered a massive stroke. The architect of modern Ethiopia, Emperor Menelik had been instrumental in establishing the relationship between Ethiopia and the US as he undertook the modernization of his country and the protection of its sovereignty. The treaty was successfully renewed by John P. Ward.[3]

Ethiopia's interest in friendship with the US continued under Menelik's successors. A commercial treaty was signed on June 27, 1914, in Addis Ababa, between "His Royal Highness, Prince Lidj Yassou [Lij Iyasu], Successor of Menelik II, King of Kings of Ethiopia and the United States of America" to regulate and develop commercial relations between the two countries. Ratification of the treaty was advised by the US Senate on September 15, 1914 and the US President ratified the treaty on September

---

1 Donald W. Kilhfner, ibid., "The United States and Ethiopia, 1903-1915."

2 US Printing Press. 1927. *Foreign Relations of the United States*, vol. 2, p. 584.

3 Frank J. Manheim, "The United States and Ethiopia: A Study in American Imperialism," p. 150.

19, 1914. Lij Iyasu was notified of ratification on December 20, 1914. The treaty was proclaimed on August 9, 1920.[1]

As Emperor Menelik had no surviving sons, Lij Iyasu, the Emperor's sixteen-year-old grandson, was named successor. Lij Iyasu was born in 1897. He was the son of Ras Michael of Wollo and Emperor Menelik's daughter Woizero Shewa Rega. Ras Michael was a Muslim who converted to the Ethiopian Orthodox religion.

Lij Iyasu's reign lasted from 1911 to 1916. In 1916, Ethiopia's council of ministers found Iyasu unfit to lead the country, staged a coup d'état, and replaced him with Menelik's daughter Empress Zewditu, who reigned from 1916 to 1930. Lij Iyasu had liaisons with different women and was starkly different from his predecessors. Iyasu spent most of the time in Ethiopia's peripheries and married daughters of the local leaders such as the daughters of Ras Mengesha Seyoum of Tigre, Ras Hailu Tekle Haimanot of Gojam, Dejazmach Kumsa of Wollega, King Aba Jiffar of Keffa, Nega-dras Abokar of Yefat, and Chiefs of Adal, and Yefat.[2] Ethiopian Orthodox Christians would not support a polygamist ruler.

The Ethiopian nobility and the Church accused Lij Iyasu of converting to Islam. Iyasu for his part told Negadras Hasib Ydlibi, one of the foreigners in the service of Ethiopian rulers, born in Manchester, England, of Syrian extract, that he had not changed his faith and he would never think of doing so. However, Lij Iyasu said that Ethiopians were all his subjects and as he was "in the country of Muslim subjects [he] might favor them," as he had done with the Oromos when he was in their country. He said that he would like to make his "country a happy family" and that he aimed to "unite [his] people regardless of the question of religion."[3]

In international relations, Lij Iyasu was inclined towards the Central Powers that consisted of the Ottoman Empire and Germany on the eve of World War I. The support for the former was because of religion, as he claimed descent from the Prophet Mohammad,[4] and for the latter because it had not historically tried to undermine Ethiopia's sovereignty, unlike the members of the Allied Powers, Britain, France, and Italy, who had surrounded Ethiopia through their colonies. The Allied Powers protested Iyasu's support of Turkey during the First World War (1914–1918) in September 1916.[5]

Abune Mathewos, an Egyptian head of the Ethiopian Orthodox Church, excommunicated Lij Iyasu, who was soon deposed in favor of both Empress Zewditu Menelik and Regent Teferi Mekonnen. Teferi Mekonnen was known for outmaneuvering his rivals, mostly Emperor Menelik's courtiers,[6] and Lij Iyasu. Iyasu took refuge with

---

1 It was reported that the six-year delay in the proclamation of the treaty by the US was a result of an administrative oversight. Refer to Edward W. Chester. 1974. *Clash of Titans: Africa and U.S. Foreign Policy*, Maryknoll, NY: Orbis Books, p. 174. Also refer to Library of Congress. 1978. *The United States and Africa: Guide to U.S. Official Documents and Government-Sponsored Publications on Africa, 1785–1975*, Julian W. Witherell, compiler, p. 40.

2 Richard Pankhurst. 2001. *The Ethiopians: A History*, Malden, MA.: Blackwell Publishing, pp. 202-208.

3 May Ydlibi. 2006. *With Ethiopian Rulers: A Biography of Hasib Ydlibi*, Bahru Zewde, ed., Addis Ababa, Ethiopia: Addis Ababa University press, p. 250.

4 Edward Ullendorff. 1965. *The Ethiopians: An Introduction to Country and People*, London, UK: Oxford University Press, pp. 94-95.

5 Bahru Zewde. 1991. *A History of Modern Ethiopia, 1855–1974*, Athens, OH: Ohio University Press, p. 127.

6 Richard Pankhurst. 2002. *The Ethiopians: A History*, Malden, MA: Blackwell Publishing Ltd. P. 214.

---

the Dankals, in the Afar region, but he was captured. He died under dubious circumstances prior to the Italian occupation of Ethiopia in 1936. If he had been found alive, the Italian invaders might well have used him against Emperor Haile Selassie to discredit him and challenge his legitimacy.

It appears that Lij Iyasu had sought to get closer to the United States. In his letter to President Woodrow Wilson Iyasu addressed the US president as "his Excellency, my great friend, Woodrow Wilson." American officials in Addis Ababa believed that Lij Iyasu received advice and assistance through the German and Turkish representatives in Addis Ababa. A confidential letter to the Secretary of State from John Q. Wood, American Consul General in Addis Ababa, dated April 18, 1914, reported that "The Prince, a boy of 18 years, is ... without absolutely any idea of his duties..."[1] The Ethiopian leadership also found Iyasu unfit to be king.

Thus the overthrow of Iyasu represented a convergence of domestic and international concerns. This move probably averted the consequences Ethiopia would have faced by joining the Central Powers, who ultimately lost the war.

Regent Teferi Mekonnen, who later becomes Haile Selassie I, participated in the overthrow of Lij Iyasu and was named Crown Prince.[2] Empress Zewditu Menelik was a symbolic leader and Crown Prince Teferi Mekonnen was the Regent to the Empress.

Immediately after Teferi was installed as Crown Prince, he sent a letter to "His Excellency Doctor Woodrow Wilson, President of the United States" on January 12, 1917, and assured President Wilson that the friendship between the two countries "will expand and endure in the future."[3] Crown Prince Teferi also wanted to resume direct diplomatic relations between the two countries,[4] closely ally his country with the US, and follow its pattern of modernization. Empress Zewditu wrote a letter to President Woodrow Wilson conveying her government's wish to enhance the trade relationship established between their two countries by her father, Emperor Menelik. The Empress also expressed approval of the US effort to establish world peace[5] and the effort of President Wilson to create the League of Nations.

In 1918, Negadras Afework Gebre Iyesus headed a trade mission to the US for Empress Zewditu Menelik. Later, a treaty between the US and Ethiopia was signed between His Majesty King Teferi on behalf of Her Imperial Majesty, Zewditu, Empress of Ethiopia.[6]

Regent Teferi wanted European, and especially American, advisors, but while the US Department of Commerce depicted Ethiopia as "an almost virgin field for

---

1 Record of the Department of State Relating to Political Relations Between the US and Ethiopia, 1910–1929. The National Archives and Record Service, General Service Administration, Washington, DC, 1962, 711-84-711.842/181, box # M412,1, p. 2.

2 Refer to an account by Tekle Hawariat Tekle Mariam, *Yehiwete Tarik (Autobiography)*, who participated in the deposition of Lij Iyasu, pp. 288-324. Tekle Hawariat received military training in Russia.

3 Negussie Ayele, *"Ethiopia and the United States,"* p. 63.

4 There was no US diplomat in Ethiopia from 1910 to 1928. The British legation in Addis Ababa and the US Consul in Aden looked after the US interest.

5 Dawit Gebru. 1985. *Kentiba Gebru Desta ye Ethiopia Kirse*, p. 145.

6 Crown Prince Teferi Mekonnen was chosen as Regent on September 27, 1916. He served in that position until the death of Empress Zewditu on April 2, 1930. On November 2, 1930, Teferi Mekonnen was coroneted Emperor Haile Seals I. He was deposed in 1974.The documents consulted for this book uses freely the titles of "Ras" King," "Regent," and "Crown Prince". These titles were used from 1916 to1930. In 1928, Teferi Mekonnen becomes King.

productive work," the State Department advised Americans that it would be hard to secure the salaries normally attached to the position of advisor. Nevertheless, some Americans did elect to work in Ethiopia.

In December 1925, President Calvin Coolidge dispatched Consul General Ralph J. Totten to Ethiopia to express the need for reestablishing a consulate there, and the Ethiopian government responded favorably. President Coolidge's effort was in contrast to his first message to the US Congress in December 1923, when he called for renewed isolationism, and earlier, the Department of State had been unable to secure funds to establish a Legation in Ethiopia. The organized labor party was energetically opposed the appropriation of funds to establish a legation in Ethiopia[1] and Secretary of State Elihu Root opposed the appointment of a Minister to Ethiopia. It was reported that Secretary Root commented in a letter, "I never could see anything for a minister in Abyssinia to do. I need all the money I get for use in the places where it counts."[2] In the end, the US withdrew its Minister from Ethiopia and entrusted its interest to the British legation until 1927.[3]

On the other hand, there were advocates for a high-level US engagement in Ethiopia because of the profitability Ethiopia provided the US commercial sector. One such advocate spoke thus:

> Our cotton goods trade has always been an important one; Abyssinia is able to supply hides, coffee, and articles of lesser importance such as honey, beewax, ivory, civet, etc.... The mineral resources are the richest — gold, silver, copper, iron, coal, sulfur, oil and potash. The presence of oil seems assured, while potash is abundant near the Italian frontier. The Virginia–Carolina Chemical Company and the Anglo–American Oil Company are materially interested in Abyssinia. It would be better to be on the ground when those under developed resources were proved actually to exist in commercial abundance — and not wait until the European powers have established themselves to our exclusion. As a precautionary measure as well as a means of investigation, a legation would be of the utmost importance.[4]

Diplomatic relations between Ethiopia and the US have not always been cordial. In addition to the normal influences of differing philosophies and policy outlooks, the shifting definition of national interest and global and regional politics, the relationship between Ethiopia and the US has also been influenced by the perception each had of the other and the role played by other dominant countries, such as Britain. Needless to say that the US was unsure as to how to deal with an independent black African country while its own black citizens were denied their share of the American dream of equality and dignity. The following chapter illuminates these problems.

---

1 The National Archives of the United States, box # M411, roll 3.
2 Edward W. Chester, *Clash of Titans: Africa and U.S. Foreign* Policy, p. 174.
3 Ibid.
4 The National Archives of the United States. 1923. M-412, p. 10. Wondwossen Hailu, "Origins of American Imperialism in Ethiopia." 1971. *Challenge*, Journal of the World Wide Union of Ethiopian Students, New York: The Ethiopian Student Union of North America, p. 13.

CHAPTER 4. CONCERNS BETWEEN ETHIOPIA AND THE US (1919–1936)

Issues that have direct bearing on the diplomatic relations between Ethiopia and the US may be primarily bilateral but also have wider ramifications. Following are some issues that have been of concern to both countries.

ETHIOPIANS AND RACISM IN THE UNITED STATES

Ethiopian traders ran into discrimination in the US in the 19th century, and this contributed to the establishment of the Abyssinian Baptist Church in New York City.

On June 10, 1919, the London-based Consul General telegraphed the US Secretary of State, Robert Lansing, and advised him on the appropriate hospitality that the State Department must accord to an Ethiopian delegation that was about to visit the United States. The Consul General stated that the honorable Abyssinians, with their traditional cloth and fine features, were different from American Negros. Despite their skin color and hair texture, they belong to the Semitic race and had to be treated like white men. The Consul General wanted to make sure these sensitive people would not face any discrimination in their hotels or during their meetings with government officials, and he said the Secretary of State must arrange for special preparations.[1]

The goodwill delegation included Dejazmach Nadew Aba Mebrek, a.k.a. Aba Wello, who later was promoted to Ras, head of the mission; Kentiba Gebru Desta; Ato Heruy Wolde Selassie, who later was promoted to Blatengeta; and Ato Sinke. They arrived in New York from London on July 11, 1919. The delegation stayed at the Hotel Waldorf-Astoria, where they occupied suite No. 16, rooms 209 to 215.[2] They also met with the African American delegation of Harlem and invited them to assist

---

1 Translated from an Amharic book by Dawit Gebru, 1985, *Kentiba Gebru Desta ye Ethiopia Kirse*, Addis Ababa: Bole Printing House, pp. 141–142.
2 A report by *The Chicago Defender*, July 12, 1919. "Representatives of foreign government on way to White House; mission secret," p. 1.

25

in Ethiopia's development. At the time, blacks were *de jure* second-class citizens and the lynching of blacks was the order of the day.

In New York, R. D. Jones, a member of the International League of Darker Races (established on January 2, 1919, to organize an African-American delegation to the Paris Peace Conference) met the delegation. R.D. Jones was also a reporter for an African-American newspaper, *The Chicago Defender*. He asked the head of the delegation, Dejazmach Nadew, the delegation's views about lynching in the United States. Dejazmach Nadew, responded that: "[They] dislike brutality, burning at stake, lynching of any nature, and other outrages heaped upon your people [blacks in the United States]." When asked for any advice that the delegation had for African-Americans, Dejazmach Nadew answered, "to fight on, don't stop."[1] Their visit in New York included touring the Irish Catholic cathedral, the Jewish synagogue, and Metropolitan Baptist church in Harlem.[2]

Dejazmach Nadew, in his parting message to African-Americans said:

> On the part of the Ethiopian Empire we desire to express the satisfaction we have felt on hearing of the wonderful progress Africans have made in this country. It gives us great confidence in the Government of the United States to know that through the independence given you by America, you have increased in number and developed in education and prosperity. We want you to remember us after we have returned to our native country.[3]

The delegation also travelled to Washington, DC, and discussed the furthering of their country's relationship with US officials. In Washington the group stayed at the Hotel Lafayette, across from the White House, for a formal meeting with President Woodrow Wilson. The delegation brought gifts from Empress Zewditu for both President and Mrs. Wilson. The visit of the Ethiopians, dressed in their white *shema*, with their national flag of green, yellow, and red, flying over the national capitol, inspired racial pride in African-Americans.

Despite the fact that the delegation had been housed in luxury hotels and had received VIP treatment, they were uncomfortable about race issues in the United States. When they travelled to Detroit, Michigan, to visit General Motors, they were escorted by US officials, [Captain Morris, from U.S.Army, was the chaperon], who had been advised by the State Department to shield them from racial segregation. They also visited Chicago, Yellowstone National Park, and San Francisco.

Dejazmach Nadew's exposure to Western countries contributed to his enlightened administration as the governor of Illubabor province. He built stone-cobbled streets and made Gore one of the major cities in Western Ethiopia, according to unpublished autobiography of Ras Imiru Haile Selassie.[4] After Addis Ababa was occupied by fascist Italy in 1936, Emperor Haile Selassie designated Gore a temporary capital of Ethiopia. (But Gore fell under the invading Italian force, as had Addis Ababa.)

Subsequently, Ethiopians on official business could not escape racism in the United States. Dr. Martin Workeneh confided to the US envoy in Addis Ababa, Addison E. Southard, that Crown Prince Teferi was very much hurt at the reception of Blatengeta Heruy Wolde Selassie, who had been sent to America to purchase mu-

---

1 "Representatives of foreign government on way to White House; mission secret."Report by
  The Chicago Defender, under a headline "Abyssinian Mission Arrives in U.S." July 12, 1919, p. 1.
2 *The Chicago Defender*, July 12, 1919, p. 1.
3 Roi Ottley. 1943. '*New World A-Coming' Inside Black America*, New York: Arno Press.
4 Imeru Haile Selassie. 1937. *Ye Ras Imeru Haile Selassie ye Hiwot Metsaf*, (Ras Imeru Haile Selassie's
  Autobiography, 1885–1928, no. 1,) Ponza Island, Italy, p. 137.

nitions in 1922. He was refused admission into the better hotels and theaters, and public institutions, and was deprived of even the ordinary courtesies. This seemed to be much different from the experience of the Ethiopian delegation that visited the US in 1919. Ethiopians, never colonized, faced racism in the US and were unable to comprehend it.

An article appeared in the Amharic newspaper *Berhanena Selam* (*Light and Peace*) on June 16, 1927, in which Zauda Bayanna [Zewdu Beyene] wrote about racial discrimination experienced by Blacks in the United States.

He speaks of two different kinds of people, whites and blacks, and observes the following:

> That the Blacks were first taken to America by an English man who sold them there more than 308 years ago. That they have increased to about 12,000,000 and that they were liberated by the President called Abraham Lincoln. That the Blacks who are living in the Southern States of America suffer a great deal of oppression from the Whites, that the life of the Whites and Blacks in America is quite different and that the living of the Blacks there is like cats and dogs. That the Whites have theaters and lectures in many towns but the Blacks are not permitted to attend the theaters or lectures. That there are doctors, lawyers and teachers among the Blacks, but whenever the Blacks want to spend their holidays in the big theaters and hotels, they are not allowed entering. If a Whiteman murders a Blackman, and Judge and Assessors make delays by saying that they will judge the case either today or tomorrow. However when the (murderer) attends the Court, he will be examined and the judge will then say that he should be imprisoned for two years. They also say that if the murderer's conduct proves to be good while in prison, he will be released after two years. Thus the blood of the Black is shed like the blood of a dog. On the other hand, if a black happen to murder a Whiteman, he will be brought to Court immediately and will then be sent to prison where he will stay for two or three months after which time he is hanged. That the children of the Whiteman, whether they be clever or ignorant are given the best work and the hard and the dirty works to the blacks. If employment is scarce, the blacks do not get any work however clever they are, and in some places the blacks who have been working for several years in a certain place is dismissed and his work given to a white. This shows that the whites are supporting each other. The white asks what is the use of such an independence for the Blacks, as they only hear the news in papers of what is going on the theaters or in big buildings and not allowed to go into the big hotels whilst half-casters are allowed to do so. That even the half-casters are too proud to speak with the Blacks for fear of being dispised [*sic*] by the Whites.

> That a certain Englishman went on a visit to America and on his return to England wrote in a newspaper that America herself was a very good country, but that he was very sorry for the White Americans who are living with the Blacks and who are therefore not happy in their life.[1]

The above description of race relations shocked most Ethiopians. The US Vice-Consul, James Loder Park, wrote to the State Department on July 26, 1927, about the "advisability of preparing the public for an appropriate reception, free from certain natural color prejudices, which might conceivably have unfortunate and undesirable results."[2] Although this was an acceptable diplomatic advice, the social condition,

---

1 Copied from a letter of 1-8-58 from W.H. Anderson to the State Department. National Archives at College Park, MD, Box# M411, roll 3.

2 Ibid., Box #M411, roll.3.

embedded for a long time, and the legally condoned racial segregation in the US, took a long time to address.

In 1958, the Africa Bureau was established in the State Department in response to the deep-rooted discrimination in the United States. Segregation in the US was used not only against blacks living in the US but also against black African diplomats who, soon after their countries gained independence, represented them in the United States. According to an officer in the Africa Bureau, the Bureau was to remind "Washington of the importance of America's living up to its ideals. Rhetoric overseas about freedom and equality under the law rang hollow for Africans and other non-whites around the world as long as state-sanctioned racial discrimination existed in America."[1]

African leaders have criticized the US for social inequalities and unjust treatment of fellow blacks in the United States. An Ethiopian diplomat (Dejazmach Zewde Gabre-Sellassie), a guest of the US government in the 1950s, was appalled by segregation and discrimination in the United States. He was unable to get a haircut in a hotel few blocks from the White House. Returning from the independence ceremony of Ghana in 1957, Vice-President Nixon commented that the US could not talk equality to the people of Africa and Asia and practice inequality in the United States.[2]

US domestic politics moved toward harmony with the positions it promoted abroad when Secretary of State Dean Rusk urged Congress to pass the Civil Rights Act of 1964. The Act outlawed racial discrimination in public accommodations.

THE US AND THE POLITICS OF CONSTRUCTING A DAM

In May 1927, Regent Teferi gave a statement to the American press and invited investors. Dr. Workeneh Martin, Ethiopian Envoy Extraordinary and Minister Plenipotentiary to the Court of St. James in London, was being sent to the US to negotiate, among other issues, a $20 million contract to construct a dam at Lake Tana with J.G. White Engineering Corporation of New York.

J.G. White Engineering Corporation saw the possibility of constructing a dam on the Blue Nile as an opening to further lucrative projects in Ethiopia, a country with vast untapped resources. When Henry A. Lardner, Vice President of J.G. White Engineering Corporation, left for Ethiopia to negotiate the construction of the dam, his firm understood that it was important to observe the customary presentation of gifts to Ethiopian officials. Not to do so would be seen as a premeditated discourtesy. The Ethiopian officials, who saw the engineering firm as a wealthy entity, expected it to bring high-quality gifts to the Ethiopian royalty. The State Department suggested gifts in the sum of $1,000 but the corporation wanted more expensive gifts as it had to compete with Europeans, especially the British and the Italian firms, who were anxious to build the dam and were willing to pay handsomely for the privilege.[3]

The US Legation in Addis Ababa also advised the State Department that giving gifts were the custom for all foreign visitors to Ethiopia, whether there on business

1 Gregory L. Garland. September, 2008. "Ideals in action: Africa Bureau marks 50th anniversary," *U.S. Department of State Magazine*, p. 13.

2 Refer to Getachew Metaferia. 2002. "African American political empowerment: Impact on United Sates policy towards Africa." A reprint in *American Government and Politics: A Multicultural Perspective*, Alice M. Jackson and Maurice C. Woodard, Boston, MA: Pearson Custom Publishing, p. 151. Also refer to The American Assembly, Columbia University. 1958. *The United States and Africa*, New York: Columbia University Press, p. 22.

3 A letter to the US Secretary of State from Addison E. Southard, March 22, 1929. National Archives Microcopy #411, roll. 4.

or for pleasure. Earlier, Americans who had attended the coronation of Prince Regent Teferi on October 7, 1928, for example, had presented the customary gifts. Empress Zewditu was presented with basset (a fine toiletry product) and Regent Teferi with a motion picture for entertainment after dinner (Teferi was known to enjoy films) and a Winchester Model 1910 .401 caliber self-loading rifle. It should be noted here that the tradition is not a one-way gesture of goodwill. When King Teferi sent Dr. Workeneh Martin to the US in 1927, he sent gifts to the US president. This, according to Southard, was a "traditional and inflexible idea of Ethiopian courtesy."

Henry A. Lardner, representing White Engineering and its president, Gano Dunn, arrived in Addis Ababa on April 24, 1929, and met with Regent Teferi on April 26 and with Empress Zewditu on April 28, 1929.

Britain and Italy tried to derail the agreement. Both countries had long-standing geopolitical and economic interests in Ethiopia. The US Legation in Addis Ababa reported to the State Department that there was an "Italian intrigue and duplicity in opposing American as well as other national efforts to participate in the economic and social development of Ethiopia."[1] Southard's memo to the State Department reported that the Italians were not only trying to get information about the proposed agreement but were claiming to have special access to Ethiopian authorities and encouraging the Americans to use them as a conduit. Italian intelligence tried to secretly obtain a copy of the contract. The Italian Minister in Addis Ababa, Mr. Cora, gave a dinner in honor of Mr. Lardner on May 17, 1929, and asked about the content of the contract. The memo to the State Department, dispatched on the same day, mentioned that it was "very canny on the part of the Italians indirectly to endeavor to persuade the White Corporation that their influence is essential to a successful outcome of present negotiations."[2]

The British, on their part, endeavored to obtain concessions from the Ethiopian government in northern Ethiopia, including Lake Tana, in order to gain control of the entire Blue Nile from its source to its mouth in Egypt.

The right to control Lake Tana remained a British permanent desire, as the Nile River affected the development and security of the British colonies of Egypt and the Sudan. In order to ensure water flow from Lake Tana, Great Britain had signed a treaty with Ethiopia in 1902. This Anglo–Ethiopian Treaty recognized the rights of Britain in the headwaters of the Nile.[3] According to that treaty, "His Majesty, Emperor Menelik II King of Kings of Ethiopia, pledges himself to the British Government not to construct, or allow to be constructed, work of any nature on the Blue Nile, Lake Tana or on the Sobat, which would arrest the flow of said water into the Nile," as the source of the Blue Nile was "so vital to the prosperity of Egypt and the Sudan and indeed to their very life."[4] The idea of building a dam on Lake Tana, the source of the Blue Nile, infuriated Great Britain.

---

1 Addison E. Southard's report of May 31, 1929, to the US State Department, Microcopy #411, roll. 4.

2 Ibid.

3 David Mathew.1974. Reprint, *Ethiopia: The Study of a Polity 1540–1935*. First print, 1947, London, UK: Eyre and Spultiswoode, Westport, Connecticut: Greenwood Press, p. 240.

4 Haile Selassie I, *My Life and Ethiopia's Progress, 1892–1937*, vol. I. Translated and annotated by Edward Ullendorff, *The Autobiography of Emperor Haile Sellassie I, King of Kings and Lord of Lords*, 4th printing, 2007, Chicago, Jamaica, London, Republic of Trinidad and Tobago: Frontline Distribution International, Inc. p. 128.

The British interest in the Horn of Africa remained both economic and strategic.[1] During World War I, for example, the British held imperial ambitions of establishing a protectorate over Ethiopia as the country offered both commercial opportunity and a climate conducive to settlement.[2] That ambition persisted in the minds of some colonial-minded British officials after World War II, when Emperor Haile Selassie had British assistance in his return to Ethiopia from his exile in Britain.

The agreement to build a dam on the Blue Nile was both an economic and geopolitical struggle between the US and Britain. In this game, Regent Teferi preferred the US as he was suspicious of the Europeans and preferred to free himself from the European tutelage. The British, the French, and the Italians closely monitored what happened inside Ethiopia and with its imports and exports. Further, the British tried to invoke the 1902 agreement. The British claimed that "[T]he cotton fields in the Sudan and Egypt are the property of the British capitalists, and are irrigated by the Lake Tana in Ethiopia."[3] In the Sudan, the Gezira area had exported cotton since the 1920s and earned the British good money.

The flow of the Blue Nile water was a sensitive issue for Britain at that time as it is today for Egypt. British newspapers sensationalized the issue. Some of the most dramatic headlines[4] were:

"U.S. Stealing a March in Abyssinia," *Westminster Gazette* November 4, 1927

"Abyssinia's Deal with the United States," *Daily News* November 4

"Egypt's Water in Peril," *Daily Express* November 4

"Stranglehold on Nile Water," *Daily Chronicle* November 5

"Egypt Alarmed," *Daily Mail* November 7

Because of the 1902 treaty, construction across Lake Tana was postponed and J. G. White revised the contract and conducted two surveys.

As the war between Ethiopia and Italy was about to erupt, the plans were halted. Ethiopia proposed to the US to send military instructors and supplies for national defense.[5]

In the meantime, normal diplomatic relations between the two countries was resumed after the US Congress approved the position of Minister Resident and Consul General in Ethiopia. Accordingly, Addison E. Southard was appointed as Minister Resident and Consul General and assumed duty on March 1, 1928.[6] The US took the initiative in seeking to open its legation in Addis Ababa.[7] [Refer to Appendix V for list

---

1 Theodore M. Vestal. 2002. "Consequences of the British Occupation of Ethiopia During World War II, Barry J. Ward, ed. *Rediscovering the British Empire*, Malabar, Florida: Krieger Publishing Company, p. 44.

2 Vestal, ibid.

3 Ellen Horup. 1936. "Ethiopia: Member of the League of Nations?" A reprint of articles published in *Politiken*, Copenhagen, p. 6.

4 Letter to the U.S. Secretary of State, Washington, DC., from Ray Atherton, Charge' d' Affairs ad interim, Addis Ababa, Nov. 8, 1927. National Archives at College Park, MD, M411, roll 3.

5 Regarding political relations between the US and Ethiopia, 1910–1929, refer to US Department of State record, Washington, DC: National Archives, 1966, reel 1, Microcopy M412.

6 Addison E. Southard was not new to Ethiopia. He served as American Consul in Aden, Yemen, looked after American interest in Ethiopia, and reported to the State Department about personalities and conditions in Ethiopia. Southard also authored "Abyssinia: Present commercial status of the country with special reference to the possibilities for American trade," 1918. Published by US Bureau of Foreign and Domestic Commerce, special consular reports, no. 81.

7 John H. Spencer. 2006. *Ethiopia at Bay: A personal Account of the Haile Selassie Years*, Hollywood, CA: Tsehai Publishers, p. 104.

of US emissaries to Ethiopia.] Ethiopia inquired about buying one airplane and two tanks from the US War Department.

ETHIOPIA'S INTEREST IN RECEIVING US-MADE WEAPONS

The Ethiopian government was interested in equipping its budding army and sent an unofficial representative to the US, Ato Paulos Manamano, for the purpose of purchasing weapons. Paulos Manamano served as Ethiopia's Consul General in Jerusalem during the reign of Empress Zewditu. According to the US Legation in Addis Ababa, Ras Teferi was induced by some sources to believe that American airplanes and tanks were superior to European ones. Ras Teferi was willing to pay cash in advance for American weapons if the US War Department was willing to sell. In addition, Ethiopia was willing to employ American trainers.[1] This of course alarmed the British, the French, and the Italians, who did not want to see Ethiopia gain meaningful development that they would not control. Ethiopia, on the other hand, wanted to harness its own physical resources for its own development and build its own army for defense and security independent of the European powers. Ethiopia's suspicion of the colonial powers was justified when Italy, in violation of the League of Nations covenant, attacked Ethiopia in 1936.

On November 5, 1928, the US State Department responded through Southard that the War Department had no surplus airplanes and tanks to sell to Ethiopia, and it was required by law to sell only surpluses to foreign governments.[2] Such a response suited the British, who were opposed to Ethiopia's possession of weapons from sources outside of Britain. Even so, on November 14, 1928, Secretary of State J. Reuben Clark, Jr., assured Ethiopia through Southard that "while the Department does not encourage the exportation of arms and ammunition to any country, there are no legal restrictions on the exportation of those commodities to Ethiopia."[3]

Ethiopia remained a victim of the geopolitics of the time. Even Eritrea, which was part of Ethiopia, was colonized by the European powers. As a result, Ethiopia was landlocked, surrounded by colonies of European powers who opposed any arms shipment to Ethiopia. In Britain the *Westminster Gazette*, in its January 18, 1929, edition, aroused the British public against importation of arms into Ethiopia. Hence, like the proposal to build a dam on the Blue Nile, the idea of arms importation to Ethiopia from the US resulted in rancor and antagonism from the European powers.

In 1928, Ethiopia had only one tank, presented, it is said, by the Italian government and operated by a non-commissioned officer of the Italian army who served at the Italian legation in Addis Ababa. Another version of this story states that Ethiopia's first two tanks were gifts to Regent Teferi from the King of Italy's cousin, the Duke of Abruzzi.[4] These tanks were also said to be operated by an Italian, DeMartini, but employed by the Ethiopian government. DeMartini also trained Ethiopians how to operate a tank.[5] Five other tanks were bought and brought over from Europe. In 1929, Ethiopia had four two-passenger airplanes: one a gift from the German gov-

---

1 A memo by Addison E. Southard, US Consul General and Minister Resident, September 14th, 1928, US National Archive, Box #M411, roll 3.

2 Edward W. Chester, ibid., p. 204

3 Ibid.

4 Mersie Hazen Wolde Kirkos. 2008. *Ye Haignaw Kefle Zemen Mebacha, (The Dawn of the 20th Century), Addis Ababa, Ethiopia: Addis Ababa University Press,* p. 333.

5 Ibid.

ernment and three from the French government, each with only a 450 horsepower engine.

Two broader topics are broached here. One is the international agreement that governs arms trafficking in Africa. The agreement served to block the delivery of any arms to Ethiopia except those from Britain, France, and Italy. Another is the cultural taboos in Ethiopia, which in this case cast a dubious eye on the notion of airplanes and the flying of humans in this modern machine.

The traffic in arms in Africa was governed by the General Act of Brussels, Article 8 to 14, signed on July 2, 1890, by the US and some European powers. The Act called for the repression of the African slave trade and the restriction of importation into, and sale within, a certain defined zone of the African continent, of firearms, ammunitions, and spirituous liquors. The restriction of the sale of arms was intended to control "the pernicious and preponderating part played by fire-arms in operations connected with the slave-trade as well as internal wars between the native tribes...."[1] The prohibition applied to territories located between 20th parallel north and the 22nd parallel south, and extending westward to the Atlantic Ocean and eastward to the Indian Ocean.

The General Act of Brussels was reinforced, in regard to Ethiopia, by an Agreement of December 13, 1906, between Great Britain, France, and Italy. The three countries bound themselves to exercise "a rigorous supervision over the importation of arms and ammunitions" into Ethiopia.[2] There is some ambivalence on this point. Article 28 of the Geneva Convention, for example, excluded Ethiopia from the special zone described in Article 12 of the Convention. Yet Article 6 of the Geneva Convention of 1919 placed Ethiopia under the special zone.

Then, Regent Teferi Mekonnen, faced resistance to the arrival of the first airplanes in Ethiopia. According to Addison E. Southard, the Church and Empress Zewditu Menelik were opposed to the arrival of a man flying in the air. They believed that that would mark the beginning of the end of the country's independence. The Empress later consented to the arrival of the airplanes. Fortunately, Teferi Mekonnen the *de facto* leader, was a man of foresight. According to Southard, who reported everything that went on in Ethiopia, the Church saw the arrival of the airplane as a "devilish influence" on Ras Teferi and held secret church services for several days. The situation indicates the reactionary tendencies of the Church and the resistance it posed to Teferi's introduction of modern technology, just as Emperor Menelik had faced in his efforts to modernize the country.

Nevertheless, an airplane, a gift from the French government, flew out of the French colony of Djibouti and landed in Addis Ababa on August 18, 1929, at 1:30 P.M. German airplanes, however, which had been purchased for use in Ethiopia, were not allowed by France to fly out of Djibouti. The planes were transported by rail, assembled in Akakai, outside of Addis Ababa, and flown to Addis Ababa.

One Ethiopian author, however, provides a different version of the situation. After Haile Selassie was crowned king, he dispatched Blatengeta Wolde Mariam to Europe to negotiate for the purchase of airplanes and purchased three from a French company, Pâtés. A pilot and a mechanic, Messrs. Maye and Pikaperm, respectively, were hired.[3]

---

1 *American Journal of International Law.* 1909. Supplement vol. 3, p. 35.

2 Department of State, Division of Near Eastern Affairs, Nov. 13, 1928. National Archives, Box # M411, roll 3.

3 Merse Hazen Wolde Kirkos, ibid., pp. 368-372.

After Southard's appointment in 1928, several treaties were signed between Ethiopia and the United States. The Treaty of Conciliation was signed on January 26, 1929 in Addis Ababa. The Treaty of Arbitration was signed and ratified (by Regent Teferi, Heir Apparent to the throne and regent Plenipotentiary for Her Imperial Majesty, Zewditu, Empress of Ethiopia) on August 5, 1929. As these treaties with Ethiopia indicate, peace and conciliation appeared to be at the core of the US foreign policy.

After the death of Empress Zewditu Menelik on April 2, 1930, the US sent a special ambassador for the coronation of Regent Teferi Mekonnen as Emperor Haile Selassie I on November 2, 1930. The delegates, Ambassador Herman Murray Jacoby and Brigadier General W. W. Harts, were treated with great courtesy. All the great powers attended the coronation.

As Ethiopia entered a new era, after the coronation of Emperor Haile Selassie, fascist Italy was preparing to attack. In June 1935, Emperor Haile Selassie appealed to the League of Nations to rescue his country from the fascist invasion. His appeal failed to garner positive response. The US also failed to support Ethiopia. On May 5, 1936, the Italian force entered Addis Ababa. Ethiopians took to the jungles and fought the Italian occupation. After five years of occupation and the assistance of Britain in 1941, the Italians were finally expelled. Thus Ethiopia became the first country to be attacked by a member of the Axis powers and also the first to be liberated, with the assistance of an Allied power.

Chapter 5. The Italian Invasion of Ethiopia (1936–1941) and The US Response

The Italian attack heralded the demise of the League of Nations and the beginning of World War II. As Italy was poised to wage war on Ethiopia, President Roosevelt and Secretary of State Cordell Hull cabled a message to Benito Mussolini on August 18, 1935, calling on the two countries to resolve their disputes without resorting to armed conflict. Mussolini boastfully responded that as "Italy had mobilized a million men and had spent two billion lire," it was too late.[1] The US claimed neutrality despite fascist Italy's violation of international law by attacking Ethiopia, a member of the League of Nations, and the use of poison gas — one of the first uses of a weapon of mass destruction (WMD). The US abandoned all of its commercial interests in Ethiopia, treaties signed over the years, extraterritorial rights to its consulate and, at home, a segment of its population, African-Americans, who identified with Ethiopia.

Addison Southard served from 1928–1936 until the Italian invasion of Ethiopia. John Spencer, an American advisor to the Ethiopian government, witnessed the dubious stand of the US during the invasion. As Italian forces approached Addis Ababa, the US embassy was closed and its personnel evacuated. After the Italians deliberately fomented looting in Addis Ababa, US Secretary Cordell Hull dispatched a telegram to Benito Mussolini insisting that fascist forces enter the city to avert total chaos. Spencer mused that the Italians must have had a good laugh over the US simplemindedness.[2] The Italians were used to such preemptive attacks. According to historian Mario Fenyo, Mussolini, for example, instructed General Rodolfo Graziani to "initiate and conduct systematically a policy of terror and extermination" against Ethiopians.[3]

---

1 John H. Spencer, ibid., p. 206.
2 John H. Spencer, ibid., p. 66.
3 Abdul Karim Bangura. 2002. Mario Fenyo on the Third World. A reader, "Italians in Ethiopia," New York, NY: Writers Club Press, p. 46.

Benito Mussolini boasted of having murdered Ethiopians by the thousands,[1] in violation of the Geneva Protocols. According to the noted Ethiopianist Richard Pankhurst, the fascist Italian atrocities included "the use of mustard gas, the bombing of Red Cross hospitals and ambulances, the execution of captured prisoners without trial, the Graziani massacre, the killings at Dabra Libanos monastery, and the shooting of 'witch-doctors' accused of prophesying the end of fascist rule."[2] Two Ethiopian religious fathers were also murdered for refusing to collaborate with the Italians: Abune Petros was murdered in Addis Ababa and Abune Michael in Gore. The Graziani massacre was a three-day massacre (February 19–21, 1937) in Addis Ababa. An attempt on the life of Rodolfo Graziani, the fascist viceroy of Ethiopia, by two young Ethiopians from Eritrea (Abreha Deboch and Moges Asgedom) led to a holocaust that claimed thousands of lives of defenseless Ethiopians.[3]

The primary cause of the Ethiopian defeat, according to George Steer, was that "they had no arms, and were allowed none" and that the secondary cause was "Italian air supremacy, exploited eventually by the spraying of mustard gas."[4] The Italians used "an absurd excess of force" with vengeance and the situation was well depicted by an Ethiopian Ras who said that "They [Ethiopians] could not fight the heavens or the burning rain."[5] According to an Ethiopian scholar and a human rights activist, Mesfin Wolde Mariam, "Ethiopians saw for the first time the full force of Western technology in its most brutal form."[6]

During the Italian invasion of Ethiopia, US arms were not sold to either side. The US State Department terminated the Italian–American Treaty of Commerce and Navigation signed in 1871. Italy, however, did receive certain valuable commodities such as "food, fibers and petroleum products."[7] President Roosevelt forbade the export of war materials and chemicals to Italy for the manufacture of weapons. Secretary of State Cordell Hull (1933–1944) also ordered the cancellation of the Standard Vacuum oil concession between Emperor Haile Selassie's government and the company, though to no avail.[8] On the diplomatic front, a new Italian ambassador to the US, who was to present his accreditation from "The king of Italy and the Emperor of Ethiopia," was denied the presentation of his credentials.[9]

During the Italian occupation, African-American organizations were established to support Ethiopia and lobby both the League of Nations and the US government. Such organizations are the International Council of Friends of Ethiopia, under the leadership of Dr. Willis Huggins; United Aid to Ethiopia, and the Ethiopian World

---

1 Ellen Horup. 1936. "Ethiopia: Member of the League of Nations?" A reprint of articles published in *Politiken*, the "leading" paper of Copenhagen, p. 20.

2 Richard Pankhurst. 1999. "Italian fascist war crime in Ethiopia: A history of their discussion, from the League of Nations to the United Nations (1936–1949), *Northeast African Studies*, vol. 6, no. 1-2, p. 83.

3 Richard Pankhurst. 2003. *Sylvia Pankhurst: Counsel for Ethiopia*. Hollywood, CA: Tsehai Publishers, p. 58.

4 George Steer. 1937. *Caesar in Abyssinia*. Boston, Mass.: Little, Brown and Company, p.8.

5 Ibid.

6 Mesfin Wolde Mariam. June 18, 1991. Testimony at the US Congressional Hearing, "The political crisis in Ethiopia and the role of the US," p. 31.

7 Paul Henze. 2001. *The Horn of Africa from War to Peace*, New York: St. Martin's Press, p. 52.

8 *Ethiopia and the Horn of Africa Hearing Before the Subcommittee on African Affairs*, US Senate Ninety-fourth Congress. August 4, 5, and 6, 1976. Washington, DC: US Government Printing Press, p.15.

9 Paul Henze, ibid., p. 62.

Federation, under the leadership of Dr. Melaku Beyan from Ethiopia.[1] The US government seems to have capitulated to the Italian-American pressure to keep the US neutral despite the moral indignation some Americans felt in seeing a country whose sovereignty was violated and its citizens gassed.[2]

The US foreign policy reflected its continuing isolation policy and indecisiveness. The US refused Ethiopia's request to uphold the Kellogg-Briand Pact[3] and refrained from supporting Ethiopia. The US failed to side with the victim of aggression and denied a visa to allow Emperor Haile Selassie to enter the US and appeal to the American public. Eventually, the world witnessed the Second World War, the utter destruction of Europe, and the US involvement in the war.

When the Italians invaded Ethiopia, the US distanced itself from Ethiopia. On July 26, 1935, President Roosevelt remarked that the dispute between Ethiopia and Italy was of no concern to the United States.[4] Claiming to act under the Neutrality Law, the US failed to support a victimized country, failed to uphold the sanction imposed by the League of Nations against Italy, and refused to provide armaments to Ethiopian patriots; at the same time the US denied recognition of Ethiopia's occupation by Italy. On October 5, 1935, the US prohibited American citizens from traveling as passengers on vessels of either of the "belligerent" nations. This policy especially barred African American volunteers from serving in the war on the Ethiopian side.

In the summer of 1935, 20,000 African-Americans demonstrated in New York in support of the Ethiopian cause against fascist aggression. The war outraged and galvanized blacks throughout the world. As the historian John Hope Franklin noted, Ethiopia was seen by Africans in Africa and in the diaspora as "the sole remaining pride of Africans and Negros in all parts of the world."[5] Jomo Kenyatta, the future president of Kenya, commented from his exile in London that "Ethiopia was the sole remaining pride of Africans and Negros in all parts of the world" and that its invasion was taken as an insult to the black race.[6]

After Europe was ravaged by the Axis forces and the US joined the war, President Roosevelt declared that il Duce (Benito Mussolini), "head devil, should be surrendered together with his chief partners in crime."[7] President Roosevelt pressed for them to be treated as war criminals, brought to book, and punished for their crime against humanity.[8] Despite such strong words, the charge was not followed. Marshal Pietro Badoglio, Commander-in-chief of the Italian army in East Africa, ordered the use of poison gas. Marshal Rodolfo Graziani, Commander of Italian forces in Somalia, later governor-general of Italian East Africa and viceroy of Ethiopia, ordered the massacre of Ethiopians; but Britain opposed trying the Italians for war crimes committed against Ethiopia. There was a broader effort by western countries not to bring to justice fascist Italian war criminals for their crimes against an African country. Many

1 Edward W. Chester, ibid., p. 209. Also refer to Negussay Ayele, ibid..

2 Edward W. Chester, ibid., pp. 202-210.

3 This pact was signed in Paris between Frank Kellog, US Secretary of State, and Aristide Briand, Foreign Minister of France. It is also called the Pact of Paris or the General Treaty for the Renunciation of War.

4 John H. Spencer, *Ethiopia, the Horn of Africa, and the U.S. Policy*, note 19, p.8.

5 John Hope Franklin and Alfred A. Moss, Jr., 1994. *From Slavery to Freedom*, New York: McGraw Hill, Inc., pp. 433-434.

6 Jomo Kenyatta, September. 1935. "Hands Off Abyssinia," *Labour Monthly*, London, XVII, 9, p. 536.

7 Richard Pankhurst. 1999. Ibid., p.83.

8 Quoted from *The Times*, July 29, 1943, by Richard Pankhurst. 2003. *Sylvia Pankhurst*, ibid., p. 195

British Foreign Office officials were said to be "colonially-minded, and/or racially prejudiced. They considered Ethiopia, an African country, to be outside the confines of European statesmanship."[1] Some British officials were even supportive of Italians in Ethiopia. The Governor-General of the Anglo-Ethiopian Sudan, Sir Stuart Symes, was an opponent of Ethiopian independence, opposed the Emperor in Sudan, and was exceedingly pro-Italian.[2]

After five years of Italian occupation, Ethiopia gained its freedom with the assistance of the British, free French, Belgium, Indian, and South African forces, called the Gideon Force. However, US foreign policy towards Ethiopia had begun to shift. John Spencer, an American who was a foreign affairs advisor during Haile Selassie's rule, noted that Ethio–US relations had markedly declined by 1959. At that time, Secretary of State John Foster Dulles reversed US policy in the region, thereby exposing Ethiopia to the full blast of Arab hostility.[3] John Foster Dulles was known for his aggressive stance during the Cold War. His policy towards Ethiopia, however, was one of benign neglect and indifference. It also reflects the impacts of high level officials and vacillation in US foreign policy.

Yet Emperor Haile Selassie was interested in interacting with the US, as he distrusted the European countries. We will now examine that interaction.

Ethiopia and US Relations after the Italian Occupation

After Italy was ousted from Ethiopia in 1941, the relationship between Ethiopia and the US resumed. Emperor Haile Selassie continued counting on the US as a counterbalance to the European powers. Several treaties of cooperation were signed between the two countries beginning in the 1940s as the result of the commencement of the Cold War rivalry between the US and the USSR that continued for four decades. The national interests of both countries appeared to converge.

The relation between Britain and Ethiopia after the war had a significant impact on the relation between Ethiopia and the United States. The Anglo–Ethiopian Agreement of 1942, for example, recognized "Ethiopian independence but obliged the Emperor to make concessions that preserved and legitimized a very substantial degree of British control."[4]

After the war Britain, who had helped in the liberation of Ethiopia, remained influential in Ethiopia.[5] It controlled the country's telecommunications and air transport. British banks owned the Bank of Ethiopia, introduced its East African shilling (issued by the East African Currency Board), and pegged it to the British pound.[6] Britain even contemplated establishing trusteeship over all of Ethiopia. In 1943, when the British officials discussed that intention, the State Department op-

1 Richard Pankhurst. 2003. Ibid., p.194.

2 Ibid., p. 113.

3 John H. Spenser, ibid., p. 26.

4 Theodore M. Vestal. 2002. "Consequences of the British Occupation of Ethiopia During World War II," Barry J. Ward, ed. *Rediscovering the British Empire*, Malabar, Florida: Krieger Publishing Company, p. 44.

5 For the British assistance in the war against the fascist Italian occupation of Ethiopia and the role of the Ethiopian patriots who "kept the flame of revolt going," refer to David Shirreff, 1995, *Bare Feet and Bandoliers – Wingate, Sandford, the Patriots and the Part they Played in the Liberation of Ethiopia*, London and New York: The Radcliffe Press.

6 Max J. Wasserman, "The New Ethiopian Monetary System." August 1946. *The Journal of Political Economy*, vol. 54, no 4, p. 359.

posed the idea.[1] Yet, Britain categorized Ethiopia as an Occupied Enemy Territory Administration (OESTA) to be operated from Nairobi, the capital of its settler colony Kenya.[2] President Roosevelt was opposed to the British idea as it is inconsistent with the Declaration of the United Nations and the Atlantic Charter signed by President Franklin D. Roosevelt and Prime Minister Winston S. Churchill on August 12, 1941. That charter stipulated that no territorial gains were to be sought by the US and the United Kingdom (UK) and that all peoples had a right to self-determination.

Ethiopians, who believed that their country had not been colonized but occupied, and who had waged a guerilla war against the Italian forces, found the British posture puzzling.

The British also were keen to know Ethiopia's interactions with other countries. But when Emperor Haile Selassie met with President Franklin Roosevelt at Great Bitter Lake in the Suez Canal [on Roosevelt's way back from the Yalta conference with Winston Churchill and Joseph Stalin on February 13, 1945,] the meeting was kept secret from the British.[3]

This meeting would seem to indicate that Ethiopia was gaining in importance in US regional foreign policy. At the Yalta conference, the Emperor had submitted Ethiopia's foreign policy goals and asked for US political and technological support. The issues he wanted the US to consider included these:

- The necessity of access to the sea and, to this end, a request of US support for the return of Eritrea;
- The importance of Ethiopian control of the management of the railway to Djibouti and support to engage an American firm, J.G. White Corporation, for this purpose;
- the problems of the Ogaden, the report on discussions with the Sinclair Oil Corporation, and the promotion of American enterprise in Ethiopia;
- Ethiopia's wish to participate in drafting the United Nations Charter to replace the Covenant of the League of Nations, and in so doing to help others to profit from her own past experience under the League;
- Ethiopia's wish, as the first nation to enter the war against the Axis Powers, to play a role in the decisions taken at the peace conference; and
- A request to arrange the financing of greatly needed additional arms and transport, and communications equipment.[4]

Relations between Ethiopia and Britain were precarious and for a time affected Ethiopia's diplomatic relations with other countries, including the United States. Emperor Haile Selassie tactfully managed to ensure the sovereignty of Ethiopia. Weakened by World War II and at the waning stage of her hegemony, Britain had no will to pursue another adventure. The post-World War II era saw the ascendance of the United States in international politics and the beginning of the Cold War, i.e., superpower rivalry between the US and the USSR.

---

1 Statement of John Spencer, foreign policy advisor to Emperor Haile Selassie's government, at the Congressional Hearing of August 4-6, 1976, p.22, footnote 3.

2 Vestal, "Consequences of the British Occupation of Ethiopia During World War II," p. 46.

3 Statement of John Spencer at the Congressional Hearing, ibid., p. 21.

4 Dejazmach Zewde Gabre- Sellassie. 2003. "Ethio–American Business Relations, 1903-2003," a speech given to African-American business people in Addis Ababa. The author appreciates Dejazmach Zewde. for a copy of his speech. Also refer to Harold G. Marcus. 1994. *A History of Ethiopia*, Berkeley: University of California Press, p. 156.

ETHIO–US RELATIONSHIP DURING THE COLD WAR

The Cold War, the ideological rivalry between the US and the USSR, manifested in the developing countries. Ethiopia once again needed a dependable ally to help her develop her economy and protect her sovereignty. Though a founding member of the Nonaligned Nations, Ethiopia sided with the US in the bipolar global politics. [The notion of "nonaligned" is a misnomer, as virtually all the nonaligned nations were aligned to some extent with one or the other superpower.]

Emperor Haile Selassie, like Emperor Menelik, wanted to cultivate a close relationship with the US because he believed that the US, unlike most European countries, had no colonial aspirations. This may have seemed to be the case before World War II, when the US talked about isolationism and dismissed Africa as a European sphere of influence. That policy soon changed.

In an exchange of messages between President Franklin Delano Roosevelt and Emperor Haile Selassie in 1942, the US considered resumption of the diplomatic representation in Ethiopia that had been terminated during the Italian occupation (1936–41). In general, the various Ethio–US treaties and the extent of the US overseas involvement after World War II indicate a paradigm shift in the US foreign policy. It was a period when the US stretched its wings, cultivated allies, and committed to counter Soviet expansionism diplomatically, economically, and militarily in far-off places.

The US embarked upon a program of rehabilitation of Ethiopia. Promoted in part as an exercise to encourage those countries still under colonial occupation, the US in fact had an interest in the agricultural machinery left behind by the Italians, which it wanted to ship to other areas of the Middle East. It also wished to develop Ethiopia's potential as a source of foodstuffs for the war effort in Europe and the Middle East.

In May 1943, an Ethiopian envoy, headed by Lij Yilma Deressa, vice-minister of finance, attended the World Food Conference at Hot Springs in Virginia and also met with President Roosevelt. Lij Yilma signed a mutual aid agreement, the first post-war pact between Ethiopia and the United States. President Roosevelt also authorized that Ethiopia be qualified for lend-lease program, in which the US supplied Allied nations with war materials, signed on August 9, 1943. In the same year, Ethiopia appointed Blata Efraim Tewolde Medhin to be its first Resident Minister in Washington, DC. (Refer to Appendix VI for the list of Ethiopian ambassadors to the United States.)

In 1944, Emperor Haile Selassie gave the US a permanent home for its Legation in Ethiopia. The US had thus increased its ties with Ethiopia as the US global outreach increased after the war.

On January 20, 1949, in his inaugural address, President Franklin Roosevelt's successor Harry Truman stated the concept of a new US operations mission. He called for a program making the benefits of America's scientific and industrial progress available for the improvement and growth of the people of other nations. Beginning in 1949, the US and Ethiopia agreed to raise their diplomatic representation from legation to embassy, thus indicating the high level of diplomatic contacts that both countries intended to pursue. Ras Imru Haile Selassie, the Emperor's cousin, became Ethiopia's first Ambassador to the US and Mr. George Merrill became the first US Ambassador to Ethiopia. In 1950, the US Congress passed the Act for International Development and established US International Cooperation Administration (Point Four.) It was established to "...aid the efforts of peoples to develop their resources and improve their living and working conditions and to encourage the exchange of technical knowledge and skills."[1]

On May 15, 1952, Ethiopia signed a Point Four technical aid agreement and the US commenced its activities in Ethiopia in the 1950s under the directorship of Herman Kleine. Its activities included teacher education, vocational trade schools, agricultural research, extension and technical schools, crop and livestock protection programs, health programs, nurse education, malaria eradication, mapping and national archives and a Blue Nile basin survey. It also established several programs to assist Ethiopia in regional development, national airlines training and public administration. It was reported that by June 30, 1958, the US had spent $29 million in these projects.

In addition, the following are some of the treaties of cooperation signed and projects undertaken in the 1950s that depict the close relationship between Ethiopia and the United States:

- In 1953 a Treaty of Amity and Commerce, similar to the one in 1903, and a mutual defense assistance agreement were signed.[2]
- The Technical Cooperation Special Technical Service was signed in Addis Ababa on April 21, 1954. According to this agreement, the US would assist Ethiopia in economic development through the Foreign Operation Administration.
- The Technical Education Cooperation Program was signed on May 10 and was implemented on June 1, 1954.
- On May 11, 1954, the Technical Cooperation in Water Resource Development Program was signed.
- The Technical Cooperation Vocational and Industrial Craft Program were signed on May 18 and June 12, 1954 in Addis Ababa.
- On June 12, 1954, the Technical Cooperation Service Joint Fund for Eritrea was signed.[3]

While the Cold War was in progress, Ethio–US relations were enhanced considerably. As the US increased its involvement in global politics, the relationship between the two moved from trade treaty only to economic, military and development assistance and in diplomatic status from consulate to ambassador level.

In support of the US effort to contain communism, Ethiopia joined the UN force and participated in the Korean War in 1951, making Ethiopia the only non-NATO member in the Korean War.

As the American adviser John H. Spencer stated, "Through his reign, as automatically as a compass needle drawn towards the magnetic Pole, His Majesty [Emperor Haile Selassie] turned towards the United States." Spencer further stated that in retrospect he could not "be confident of correctly ascribing the reason for that steady and incontestable attraction."[4] The Emperor's attraction to the US was unique compared to other Ethiopians in authority, who "uniformly harbored profound and last-

---

1 US Congress. 1950. The Act of International Development Public Law 535, 81st.

2 In the mutual defense assistance agreement, the US agreed to furnish military equipment and training. It also standardized the operations of Kagnew communication facility in Asmara.

3 The above treaties were taken from US Government Printing Office, "Treaties between the United States and Ethiopia," 1914, 1929, and 1955.

4 John H. Spencer, US Congressional hearing of August 4-6, 1976 in Ibid., p. 102.

ing distrust towards the great powers"[1] as a result of having been betrayed during fascist Italian occupation.

In his first trip abroad as Emperor, Haile Selassie visited the US and, at the invitation of President Dwight Eisenhower, addressed a joint session of the US Congress on May 26, 1954. In his address, the Emperor stressed on the importance of Ethiopia's geographic location to the United States. Ethiopia received from the US the largest economic and military assistance of any nation in Africa, from 1953 until the overthrow of Emperor Haile Selassie's government in 1974.

Emperor Haile Selassie's itinerary included Princeton (New Jersey), New York City, Boston (Massachusetts), Ann Arbor and Lansing (Michigan), Chicago (Illinois), St. Paul (Minnesota), San Francisco and Los Angeles (California), Las Vegas (Nevada), New Orleans (Louisiana), Raleigh (North Carolina), and Stillwater (Oklahoma).[2]

Emperor Haile Selassie was the first head of state to visit Stillwater, Oklahoma, on June 18, 1954, home of the Oklahoma State University (OSU). OSU rolled out the red carpet. They hosted an elaborate black-tie banquet, unprecedented in the history of the university, in honor of the Emperor.[3] Ethiopia's connection to OSU started with President Truman's Point Four program. According to a contract signed in 1952, OSU was to assist Ethiopia in an agriculture development program, mainly through the establishment of the Agricultural Technical School at Jimma and the Imperial Ethiopian College of Agricultural and Mechanical Arts at Alemaya. OSU was to develop a system for the establishment of agricultural institutions in Ethiopia, similar to the US land-grant system.[4]

The partnership between OSU and Ethiopia lasted for 16 years, during which time 185 faculty and staff from the US worked in Ethiopia and 57 Ethiopians earned graduate degrees at the university.[5] The program was terminated under the military regime and was resumed later.

According to a Department of State publication, Ethiopia was "one of the countries of the free world receiving assistance under the United States mutual security program" and Ethiopia "contributed significantly to the position of the free world by its consistent cooperation with the West in the United Nations."[6]

In the 1950s, US assistance to Ethiopia was based on three agreements: a) the technical cooperation economic assistance signed in 1951, b) an accord for mutual defense assistance signed in 1953, and c) an agreement signed in 1957 to provide economic assistance.

The objectives of US assistance to Ethiopia were these:

1. to increase agricultural production;
2. to increase the number of trained Ethiopian teachers and to raise technical and educational levels in order to develop skilled manpower;

---

1 Ibid., 103.

2 US Department of State, "Visit to the U.S. by foreign Heads of State and Government, 1954," ‹www.state.gov/r/pa/ho/34905.htm›

3 Susan Simpson, staff writer, "Emperor's visit to school planted seeds of an alliance," July 1, 2007, NewsOK.com, http://newsok.com/article/3073545/?print=1

4 Ibid.

5 Ibid.

6 U.S. International Cooperation Administration, *Fact Sheet: Mutual Security in Action, 1959*, Department of State Publication 6801, Public Service Department, Bureau of Public Affairs, Washington, DC: US Government Printing Office, pp. 1-3.

3. to assist in improving the health of the population through training of public health workers, dissemination of health information, and provision of adequate health facilities;
4. to provide training in public administration and management; and
5. to strengthen Ethiopia's internal security and defensive capacity.[1]

There were some in the US who opposed a commercial and trade treaty with Ethiopia. The National Foreign Trade Council, founded in 1914, suggested earlier in 1952 that "the treaty with Ethiopia should be rejected because of the difficulty, in Ethiopia's present stage of development, of finding satisfactory grounds for an agreement."[2]

The State Department, however, argued that the "treaty with Ethiopia [was] a good treaty, that it was adapted to the situation of Ethiopia, that it contained a number of assurances that should be valuable to American diplomatic and Consular offices and to the Americans who do business in Ethiopia."[3] The State Department further stated that the US negotiation with Ethiopia was successful while other countries who tried to "make treaties with Ethiopia had not succeeded."[4] The success in negotiations between the two countries was due to the preference given to the US by Emperor Haile Selassie.

In the 1950s, different US institutions held different views of Ethiopia. US foreign policy was not clearly defined. Nevertheless, the Emperor had some pressing concerns; hence the need for closer alliance with the United States.

In the late 1950s and early 1960s, President Gamal Abdul Nasser of Egypt spearheaded the expansion of Pan-Arab and Pan-Islam movements that threatened the interests of Ethiopia, US, Israel and other non-Arab countries in the region. To counter such movements, the US designed the alliance of non-Arab states in the region that included Ethiopia, Iran, Israel, and Turkey. Such an alliance did not materialize on paper but consisted of a tacit understanding between these countries at that time. The relationship between Ethiopia and Israel, of which the US is a staunch ally, is also governed by geopolitical concerns. When a military regime that allied itself with the Soviet Union replaced the pro-US government of Emperor Haile Selassie in 1974, it was a major drawback for the United States.

The following chapter examines US security interests in Ethiopia and the roles played by US foreign policy institutions.

---

1 Ibid., p. 6.
2 Hearing before the Subcommittee of the Committee on Foreign Relations, United States Senate Eighty Third Congress, Washington, DC: US Government Printing Press, 1953, p.21.
3 Ibid.
4 Ibid.

CHAPTER 6. THE US AND ETHIOPIA UNDER EMPEROR HAILE SELASSIE

The Ethio–US relationship is based not only on the consideration of geopolitics but also on economic and social factors. Ethiopia attracts potential investors because it has one of the largest populations in Africa. From 10 million in 1903, as estimated by the American diplomat Robert P. Skinner, it had risen more than eight fold by 2008. This makes Ethiopia the second most populous state in Africa, after Nigeria, with untapped natural resources and a potential market for American goods (depending on the economic strength and purchasing power of the people.) US foreign policy makers, therefore, must consider Ethiopia's demography and potential for rewarding investors, given a favorable political environment and a conducive policy.

Besides the potential advantages that Ethiopia offers, it has a unique historical and geographical position in Africa as an independent country (except for the five-year Italian occupation) and for its proximity to the Middle East. Ethiopia does not have a European colonial legacy and does not come under any European country's sphere of influence. This lack of political entanglement helped make Ethiopia attractive to the US during the Cold War. Ethiopia was a safe area for the US and its leader, Emperor Haile Selassie, was a staunch US ally. Ethiopia supported the US cause not only on the diplomatic front at international organizations such as the UN, by voting along US lines, but also by dispatching its military, the Kagnew battalion, to Korea under the UN flag and US command in 1951. The Kagnew battalion that consisted 1,158 troops served with valor in South Korea from 1951–1954. Ethiopia lost 121 troops and 536 were wounded. That military undertaking was meant to check the Communist expansion. In the 1960s, Ethiopia once again put its troops under UN command, this time during Congo's civil war (1960 to 1965) for a peacekeeping operation. Such tangible undertakings proved to the US that Ethiopia was a dependable ally against Communist expansion, a participant in the peacekeeping mission, and a force for stability in the area.

After Emperor Menelik, the architect of the Ethio–US relationship, Emperor Haile Selassie ruled Ethiopia for almost half a century. He was a strong pro-American leader who, like Menelik, sought a durable friendship without a hidden agenda, and an ally who could be counted on. To Ethiopian leaders, the US seemed to fulfill such a desire. The fact that Ethiopia controlled the western littoral of the Red Sea, after Eritrea once again became part of Ethiopia, lent Ethiopia a geostrategic advantage that was beneficial to the United States. Ethiopia's command of such a strategic place and its close relation with Israel, a strong US ally, was assumed to ensure unwavering support for Ethiopia.

A political binding thread has historically tied Ethiopia and the United States, at least from the Ethiopian point of view. Ethiopia paid for this tie once, as many other nations in the region were opposed to such a friendship. Ethiopian intellectuals and students and some pan-Arab/Islam African states, such as Somalia, Libya and Egypt, continued to criticize Emperor Haile Selassie's pro-America and pro-Israel foreign policy in the 1960s. Egypt, under President Gamal Abdul Nasser, with his desire for the unity of the valley of the Nile under Egyptian hegemony, similar to his pan-Arab and pan-Islam design, encouraged some Ethiopian Muslims to agitate against the Ethiopian government. Egypt was also at the forefront in supporting Eritrean secessionists. The Egyptian government used Radio Cairo as a propaganda tool to destabilize Ethiopia in addition to arming and training secessionist Eritrean Liberation Front (ELF).

President Nasser was an officer in Sudan in 1941 and met Emperor Haile Selassie during the Emperor's return from exile. After Nasser became president, the Emperor did not support his regional design and interference in the affairs of Egypt's Arab neighbors such as Sudan and Libya. The Emperor also declined Nasser's invitations to visit Egypt. Besides supporting Eritrean secessionists, Radio Cairo's propaganda "reminded Ethiopian Muslims where their 'primary loyalty' lay," thus undermining Ethiopia's unity.[1]

Somalia's Radio Mogadishu also beamed programs that encouraged Somali irredentism in Ethiopia's Ogaden region. The two countries had a border war in 1964. Ethiopia felt encircled by countries whose interest was to weaken it and who left it without any committed ally.

The US demonstrated inconsistency in its foreign policy towards Ethiopia. Secretary of State John Foster Dulles (1953–1959) suddenly shifted his position at the Suez conference of 1956. The accommodation of Arab states, who had been in resolute opposition to Ethiopia on Eritrean and Somali issues, gradually emerged. That, according to John Spencer, exposed Ethiopia to the "wrath of Nasser."[2] There was a shift in the way Egyptian nationalists viewed Ethiopia. In the 1920s Ethiopia was seen as a "friendly neighbor." In the 1950s and 60s, militant Egyptian nationalists were contempt of Ethiopia and saw it as "uncivilized enemy and the brutal destroyer of the 'unity of the Nile Valley'."[3] This was the era of Egyptian militancy when Gamal Abdul Nasser came to power after overthrowing King Farouk on July 23, 1952.

Arab states, especially Syria and Libya, were supportive of the idea of Greater Somalia, including the Ogaden region which is populated by Ethiopian Somali speakers, and the secession of Eritrea. Libya, a member of the OAU, accused Ethiopia of

---

1 *Addis Tribune*. August 13, 1999. "Egypt and the hydro-politics of the Blue Nile River, Part II," p. 2.

2 Ethiopia and the Horn of Africa Hearing before the Subcommittee on African Affairs. US Senate Ninety-fourth Congress. August 4, 5, and 6, 1976. Washington, DC: US Government Printing Press, p. 17.

3 Haggai Erlich. 2002. *The Cross and the River, Ethiopia, Egypt and the Nile*. Boulder, Colorado: Lynne Rienner, p.5.

being an "imperialist" state faithless to African traditions. Libya, which had wanted to house the OAU headquarters, called for the removal of the OAU headquarters from Addis Ababa. At the OAU summit in 1973, Libya went to the extent of declaring Ethiopia an imperialist state opposed to the realization of Greater Somalia. Moscow joined the alliance in opposition to Ethiopia, who had been pro-US during the imperial period. Some faulted US Secretary of State Dean Rusk for strengthening Nasser's position by neglecting to heed the animosity of Libya and Moscow toward Ethiopia in the 1960s.[1]

The student movement of the 1960s in Ethiopia also accused the Emperor for his feudal rule, his economic neglect of the country and, above all, for being a lackey of the US and Israel.[2] In the 1960s, at the height of the Cold War, the world witnessed uprisings in several countries. There was general dissatisfaction among Ethiopians with the status quo, the US role in their country, and the West in general. Many espoused a Marxist ideology and idealized revolutionaries such as Che Guevara, leader of the Communist Revolution in Cuba, and Ho Chi Minh, leader of the Vietnamese independence movement. The USSR, a rival of the US, exploited the condition to further its own interests. This was at the height of the civil rights movement and anti-Vietnam protests in the US, the liberation of African countries, US intervention in Congo in 1964, and a general global reaction to the socio-economic conditions in many countries.

US foreign policy towards Ethiopia during the Cold War was based primarily on the consideration of the importance of the geopolitics of Ethiopia to the US national interest. Ethiopia, similar to other non-NATO allies such as Iran under Shah Pahlavi Reza, Turkey, and South Korea, was the beneficiary of the American military and economic assistance that initially had been targeted for Europe.[3] For example, Ethiopia was the beneficiary of the following assistance as stipulated by US government acts:

> The Mutual Defense Act was signed between the two in 1949 and the Mutual Security Act signed in 1951.

> In 1953, Ethiopia signed another mutual defense agreement with the US and, over the years received $350 million in economic assistance.[4] That assistance comprised technical support, capital goods, and food.

> The Foreign Assistance Act and the Foreign Military Act were signed in 1961 and in 1968 respectively.

> The International Security Assistance and Arms Export Control Act were signed in 1976 during the military or the *Derg* regime.[5]

> Ethiopia had also benefited from the lend-lease program, enacted in 1941, that brought wartime assistance to American allies during World War II and assist-

1 Baffour Agyeman-Duah. 1994. *The United States and Ethiopia. Military Assistance and the Quest for Security, 1953–1993.* Lanham, MD: University Press of America, p. 12.

2 For some of the above arguments please refer to Harold G. Marcus, Op.cit. For the history of Ethiopian student's movement, refer to Randi Ronning Balsvik. 1985. *Haile Selassie's Students: the Intellectual and Social Background to Revolution, 1952–1977.* Harold G. Marcus, ed. African Studies Center, Michigan State University, East Lansing, Michigan.

3 Baffour Agyeman-Duah. 1994. *The United States and Ethiopia. Military Assistance and the Quest for Security, 1953–1993.* Lanham: University Press of America, p. 12.

4 Edmond J. Keller.1985. "United States foreign policy on the Horn of Africa: Policy making with blinders on," Gerald J. Bender, James S. Coleman and Richard L. Sklar, *African Crisis Area and U.S. Foreign Policy.* Berkeley: University of California Press, p. 180.

5 Baffour Agyeman-Duah, ibid.

ed nations especially deemed to be vital to US security. The US even decided on lend-lease assistance to Ethiopia before Ethiopia requested it. This was announced on the first anniversary of Pearl Harbor in 1942.

Such are the mixed signals the US sends in its international relations. While there appears to be an overall security interest in having Ethiopia as an ally, some officials in the State Department over the course of events have failed to reflect that interest or, in the worse scenario, there was no coherent long-range strategic guidance for diplomats to follow.

ETHIOPIA AND US FOREIGN POLICY ESTABLISHMENTS

During the Cold War era, Ethiopia attracted the attention of US foreign policy makers and major institutions, especially the State Department (SD), the Central Intelligence Agency (CIA), and the Department of Defense (DoD). These three institutions saw Ethiopia in terms of the overall US national interest as well as from their parochial institutional interests. Their political outlook towards Ethiopia or towards Africa in general is hardly analytical and progressive, and policy changes, if at all possible, are at best incremental and status-quo oriented. Such bureaucrats are "playing it safe" so as not to jeopardize their positions and their likely promotions.

ETHIOPIA AND THE US STATE DEPARTMENT

The State Department took into account the diplomatic advantage and influence that Ethiopia had on other African countries, especially after their independence. As the former Foreign Minister of Ethiopia Ketema Yifru has pointed out, the African diplomatic corps followed Ethiopia's moves and took cues from Ethiopia while voting at the UN or the OAU. He also said that that was mainly because of the respect most African countries had for Emperor Haile Selassie and Ethiopia as a country that was at the forefront in resisting colonialism and supporting the struggle for decolonization in Africa and against apartheid in South Africa.[1] The Emperor was also instrumental in bridging the ideological divide between African leaders and ensured the birth of the first pan-African organization in Africa — the Organization of African Unity (OAU) in May 1963. Addis Ababa became the headquarters of the OAU and the UN Economic Commission for Africa (ECA). Addis Ababa thus became the ostensible capital of Africa, where more than 2,000 Africans from other parts of Africa resided and worked in OAU, ECA, ILO and other international organizations. That gave Ethiopia an enhanced position in African politics.

Ethiopia's influence in Africa continued until the 1990s, though it did not maintain the level of the 1960s. According to officials at the National Security Council (NSC), Ethiopia still has a considerable influence in Africa.[2] During the Cold War period, Ethiopia was seen by the US geopolitical strategists within the context of: a) the political dynamics of the Middle East, mainly the Arab–Israeli relationship, b) the Soviet Union's activities in the region, and c) the security of the oil route through the Red Sea. As Middle East oil has a considerable impact on the oil-based US economy, regional and domestic politics there are given great consideration. The security of oil tankers that travel through the Red Sea has both political and economic implications for the US and its allies. The region is one of the most politically volatile areas.

1 The statement is based on a discussion the author had with Ato Ketema Yifru in the US.
2 Interview with Gayle Smith, Special Assistant to President Clinton and Senior Director for African Affairs and Catherine E. Byrne, Director, African Affairs, NSC, September 12, 2000, the Executive Office Building, Washington, DC.

In what is known as the Carter Doctrine, President Carter stated that the US would intervene militarily if international oil supplies were threatened.[1]

Ethiopia is currently landlocked because of the secession of Eritrea and has no access to the Red Sea. As the Afar population of Ethiopia has a legitimate claim to that part of the region (the Red Sea), the situation seems to remain unresolved. Nevertheless, landlocked Ethiopia still has a geopolitical significance to the US. The Horn of Africa, which includes Somalia, is the eastern gate to Africa and the US is determined that no one, including terrorists, will use the area as a springboard to attack American interests in the region.

As Addis Ababa is the headquarters of African Union (AU),[2] the US has established a diplomatic mission to the AU similar to the one in Brussels, headquarters of the European Union (EU). The US role in Ethiopia has been enhanced and its embassy in Addis Ababa extended to manage broad-based activites. The track record of State Department officials is indicative of the lukewarm approach to Ethiopia, and interventionism in Ethiopia's domestic affairs, as I will eventually discuss. Ethiopia, however, has remained important to the State Department and foreign policy establishments after the end of the Cold War.

ETHIOPIA AND THE CENTRAL INTELLIGENCE AGENCY (CIA)

The interest in Ethiopia evidenced by the Central Intelligence Agency's (CIA) Africa Division became more intense as Addis Ababa increasingly became a diplomatic hub — ideal for monitoring events in Africa as well as those in the Middle East. Its geographic location made it even more attractive to the US geopolitical strategists when Ethiopia controlled the western Red Sea littoral. The US Naval Communications Unit (NAVOMMU) operated from Kagnew Station in Asmara.[3] Kagnew Station, which used to be the Italian radio station Radio Marina, was considered to enhance US communications capability when the US signed a 25-year treaty with Ethiopia in 1953.[4] Kagnew Station was created in the then War Department with a Disposition Form dated January 26, 1943, that ordered the "Establishment of a War Department Fixed Radio Station in Africa."[5]

The station provided valuable communications services such as the MYSTIC STAR — a presidential communications support system.[6] MYSTIC STAR, for that time, "assured a high-level mission of simultaneous secure voice and teletype circuits from the aircraft."[7] Ethiopia's location had made it attractive to the US intelligence

1 Peter Woodward. 2006. *US Foreign Policy and the Horn of Africa*, Brookfield, Vermont: Ashgate Publishing, p.26

2 The Organization of African Union, established in 1963, was renamed African Union in July 2002 OAU conference in Durban, South Africa

3 The US started operating from the Kagnew station as a result of a 25-year defense assistance agreement signed with Ethiopia in 1953.

4On the background of Kagnew station, see Jeffrey A. Lafebvre . 1991. *Arms for the Horn: U.S. Security Policy in Ethiopia and Somalia 1953–1991*, Pittsburg, PA: University of Pittsburgh Press, pp 55-58 and pp. 102-103.

5 John R. Rasmuson. 1973. *History of Kagnew Station and American Forces in Eritrea*, Asmara, Ethiopia, p. 39.

6 Memo for the Assistant to the President for National Security Affairs from Secretary of Defense Harold Brown. 1977. Carter Presidential Library, Declassified NSA Staff Material, Box, (March 21), 3/77.

7 Paul B. Henze memo for Z. Brzezinski. March 28, 1977. Carter Presidential Library, Box 1, 3/77.

community prior to the establishment of satellite-based communications and information gathering. Nevertheless, Addis Ababa remains an important city for gathering information by agents whose service would be hard to replace by technology.

In general, Kagnew was an ideal communication station. It provided unique features: its location in the tropics, its distance from the north and south magnetic poles and from the aurora borealis and magnetic storms. Kagnew is in a zone with a limited degree of seasonal variations between sunrise and sunset that reduces the need for numerous frequency changes.[1] In the 1970s, some 3,000 Americans with their dependents were attached to Kagnew. The station published a monthly letterpress newspaper and ran the first army-operated television station in the world.

Kagnew Station became a focus of symbolic attacks by Ethiopia's activist students, some Arab countries, and the predominantly Muslim Eritrean secessionist organization, the Eritrean Liberation Front (ELF). As indicated earlier, they were all fellow-travelers whose causes were opposition to Israel and the United States. Arab countries and the Arab League supported the Eritrean cause diplomatically, financially, and militarily in order to convert the Red Sea to an Arab lake by denying Ethiopia access. It became logical for the US to close Kagnew Station, as there was a high risk to its citizens. Eventually the CIA established a clandestine agreement with moderate Eritrean groups that could challenge or neutralize the Muslim-dominated and pro-Arab ELF and protect the US interest. In spite of fundamental changes, such as the closing of the Kagnew Station and the secession of Eritrea, Ethiopia remains important to the CIA.

ETHIOPIA AND THE DEPARTMENT OF DEFENSE (DoD)

The Department of Defense (DoD) Office for African Affairs is interested in Ethiopia and the Horn of Africa in general because of its strategic location. It has proximity to the Middle East oil fields, the sea oil routes, and the Red Sea passage to the Mediterranean Sea. The DoD found the area important enough to ally itself with the military of friendly and comparatively stable countries in the area, especially with Ethiopia. Generally, in the Horn of Africa, "the U.S. seeks regional stability and evolutionary developments in an area environment congenial to the U.S. goals."[2] Ethiopia, prior to the 1960s, was comparatively stable and the US was invited to conduct exercises with the Ethiopian military and navy, familiarize the US military with the environment and topography, and build camaraderie with the armies of a friendly nation. These forms of cooperation went on for just a short while, as Ethiopia increasingly became unstable because of internal and external forces and was no longer in a position to serve the immediate interest of the United States.

Unfortunately, in the face of undemocratic rule and abject poverty, the alienated and the disenfranchised had no patience for the "evolutionary development" the US claimed to favor and did not operate on schedule. The Emperor also bowed to the pressure from Arab countries and the majority of the OAU members and terminated official diplomatic relations with Israel on October 23, 1973 [the geopolitical reality necessitated that an unofficial and covert relationship continue.] This was unexpected, as the Ethiopian monarchs have claimed lineage to King Solomon of Israel through Queen Sheba of Ethiopia. The faithful Christian Ethiopians also worshiped

---

1 John H. Spencer, ibid., p. 23.

2 Presidential Review Memorandum/NSC-21, "The Horn of Africa" Carter Presidential Library, Vertical File, USSR-US Conference, 3/95, Briefing Book #I.

the "God of Israel," thus indicating both the historical and theological connections between the two countries.

In 1974, the world witnessed the overthrow of pro-US Emperor Haile Selassie. The *Derg* was radicalized by intellectuals who were the products of the students' movement of the 1960s. The military junta, who saw the US in a different light comes to power. The US terminated military-to-military relations and diplomatic relations between the two countries were mutually downgraded.

Thus in the mid-1970s, despite the cooperation and development assistance, the relationship between Ethiopia and the US started to cool. The US claimed not to be involved militarily in the "local controversy in the Horn of Africa" but only in economic assistance. That seemed to be far-fetched as Cold War politics meant the US was deeply involved in the Horn of Africa in many ways, and the distinction between military and economic would be hard to pin down.[1] The military regime (the *Derg*) became increasingly anti-US and pro-Soviet Union. The US Congress in 1976 pressured the Ford Administration to reduce US military aid to Ethiopia. The *Derg* questioned the quality of weapons that Ethiopia had been receiving despite the comparative preference Ethiopia was supposed to have been given in sub-Sahara Africa.[2]

Ethiopian officials, during Haile Selassie's reign, also complained that the US failed to provide sufficient military and economic assistance to withstand Soviet threats at a time when the Soviet Union supported forces that undermined Ethiopia such as Somali irredentism and Eritrean secessionism. These groups also received assistance from Arab countries and the Arab League. Nevertheless, quantitatively, at least, Ethiopia, over the years, was the recipient of the largest US economic and military assistance in sub-Sahara Africa.

As the government of Emperor Haile Selassie became increasingly unstable in the 1960s, the US moved its communication facility from Kagnew Station in Asmara to Diego Garcia, an island in the Indian Ocean. The Diego Garcia facility was opened in March 1973. The advent of space-based communication technology also made the Kagnew communication station less useful, if not completely irrelevant.

Emperor Haile Selassie was overthrown in 1974. The military government that replaced him, headed by Colonel Mengistu Haile Mariam, adopted a Marxist anti-West, especially anti-US [or what they called an "anti-imperialist"] ideology, and the country went to the abyss because of the military government's undemocratic rule, muddled policies and gross human rights abuses.

Finally, in the nearly 70-year relationship between the two countries, from 1903 to 1974, the pendulum swung from positive to negative. Colonel Mengistu Haile Mariam changed course only in 1991, when he made an overture to normalize relations with the United States — though just before his downfall.

As the relationship between the two countries deteriorated and the US looked for an alternative ally in the region, Ethiopia also needed a dependable ally that would help her withstand any real or perceived security threat. Ethiopia thus changed camp and allied with the Soviet Union. In a move typical of the Cold War era marked by the revolving door syndrome, the US left Ethiopia and moved to Somalia, an erstwhile enemy of Ethiopia, while the USSR was booted out of Somalia and found a red carpet in Ethiopia. There is no permanent ally, only a permanent interest. Both superpowers wasted no time in shifting alliance to protect and advance their national interests.

---

1 Robert G. Patman, ibid., p. 197. Also *New York Times*, February 13, 1970.
2 See Jeffrey A. Lefebvre, *Arms for the Horn: US Security Policy in Ethiopia and Somalia, 1953–1991.*

Given all the advantages of Ethiopia, and the development assistance it received from the US that could have propelled her to economic growth and development, she failed to live up to expectations. While the political system partially contributed to this failure, other exogenous situations such as destabilizing forces from Middle East and North Africa countries contributed. The continued war with secessionist forces in Eritrea ruined the economy and, together with the famine, tarnished its image, discouraged foreign investors, and frustrated its allies. Eritrean secessionists allied themselves with anti-Ethiopian Arab forces such as those in Syria, Pakistan, Iraq, the Palestinian Liberation Front (PLO), Libya, and Egypt.

Some in the West who claimed to be progressive also took the Eritrean war to be a struggle between progressive forces and a reactionary Ethiopia supported by an "imperialist" US and therefore lent their support to Eritrean secessionists in the 1960s. Eritrean disinformation assisted them in gaining supporters and influencing world opinion. Successive Ethiopian governments, however, failed to actively counter the propaganda or solve the problem peacefully, but only alienated Eritreans who were pro-Ethiopia.

The US backed a policy of stabilizing the area and maintaining the status quo by providing financial aid and military assistance to Ethiopia in the early 1970s. Emperor Haile Selassie continued to remind American officials that Ethiopia was the only country in the region that operated independently of the Arab line, shared the US interest in protecting the security of Israel and the Red Sea region.

While the lion's share of Ethiopia's foreign assistance comes from the US, thereby creating a position of clientism and dependency, Ethiopia tried to play one superpower against the other. Emperor Haile Selassie, especially during the waning days of his power, attempted unsuccessfully to use the USSR against the US by shifting towards the communists. However, the opposition to his rule became overwhelming and the status quo was altered through revolution.

We will now examine the US contributions to Ethiopia's development during Emperor Haile Selassie's rule and the Cold War period.

Chapter 7. US Contributions under Emperor Haile Selassie

In response to Ethiopia's pro-US stand and to promote its own national interest, during Emperor Haile Selassie's reign the US provided Ethiopia with financial and military assistance that was the largest in sub-Sahara Africa. In various fields, assistance to Ethiopia by the US government and committed American citizens remained significant in building its human resource and institutional capacity.

US Citizens in the Service of Ethiopia

US citizens have served Ethiopia well and some remained by her side during darker days, such as during the invasion by fascist Italy. Others contributed to Ethiopia's development after the Italian force was expelled. Their support for Ethiopia continued after they returned to the United States. Let us look at four Americans in particular.

Ernest Work, from Muskingum College in New Concord, Ohio, served as educational advisor to Emperor Haile Selassie in the 1930s. A professor of history, Ernest Work authored a book just before the Italian invasion of Ethiopia.[1] Writing about the Italo–Ethiopian war, he stated that "the intense rivalries among the European powers [are] exhibited in their insatiate grabbing of the black man's country."[2] Professor Work warned that "[I]f Italy is permitted to succeed in her present designs the black man's culture will be lost under a veneer of European imposition."[3] Dr. Melaku Beyan of Ethiopia, who attended Muskingum College, introduced Ernest Work to Emperor Haile Selassie. Melaku had his medical degree from Howard University, established the Ethiopian World Federation, Inc., in New York, published the *Voice of Ethiopia*

---

1 Ernest Work. 1935. *Ethiopia, A Pawn in European Diplomacy*, New York: The Macmillan Company.

2 Ibid., p. v.

3 Ibid., p. vi.

newspaper during the Italian occupation, and mobilized Americans, especially African-Americans, in support of the Ethiopian cause against fascist Italy.[1]

Another American, Everett A. Colson, who had experience in advising the governments of Haiti and Turkey, was also appointed as financial advisor to Ethiopia and served from 1931 to 1935. Colson's role in organizing the Ethiopian national bank and in planning currency reform earned him respect from Ethiopians but the British, French, and Italian legations in Addis Ababa attempted to interfere with his operations.[2] Colson also served as a consultant to the Emperor on foreign affairs during the Emperor's exile in London during the occupation by fascist Italy. At Colson's funeral, Emperor Haile Selassie eulogized him, saying that "though Mr. Colson's grave is in the United States, his loyal services remain engraved in the heart of his Imperial Majesty and the people of Ethiopia."[3]

George A. Blowers, who replaced the British C.S. Collier, was the first American employee of the Ethiopian government after Emperor Haile Selassie returned from exile. Blowers was the governor of the Bank of Liberia, created in August 1942; he introduced the first Ethiopian *birr* (paper currency), replacing the East African shilling that was introduced by the British. The State Bank of Ethiopia absorbed the Bank of Abyssinia which was founded in 1905 under the Egyptian charter.[4] Ethiopia had no government bank and the bank of Abyssinia operated as a branch of the National Bank of Egypt under British management.

Although the Bank of Abyssinia was largely moribund and capital depleted, the National Bank of Egypt insisted on a selling price of 190,000 pounds. "Ethiopia paid the price in two installments in time for the Bank of Ethiopia to open for business on 1 July 1931."[5] The US lent five million ounces of silver, under a lend-lease arrangement, to be returned to the US, ounce for ounce, within five to seven years,[6] for the minting of divisional coinage. This was also intended to replace the Maria Theresa *thaler* and the East African shilling. The US was also to assist in printing paper currency. Both the coins and the *birr* were prepared at the US Mint in Philadelphia[7] George A. Blowers' service became invaluable to the Vice Minister of Finance, Yilma Deressa, in these negotiations with the United States.

Another US citizen known for his service in Ethiopia was John Hathaway Spencer. Within months of establishing Ethio–US diplomatic relations, John H. Spencer was appointed as foreign policy advisor to the Emperor in 1936. Ethiopia appointed American bankers and advisors to make Ethiopia attractive to US investors, to seek political and military alignment with the US, and to assure independence from the European, especially British, tutelage. Spencer witnessed the fall of Addis Ababa in 1936. Spencer served as advisor to the Emperor during his exile in England and prepared the English version of the Emperor's speech at the League of Nations on June 30, 1936. After fascist Italy was ejected, he returned to Ethiopia and served as prin-

1 Getachew Metaferia, "Ethiopia: A bulwark against European colonialism and its role in the pan-African movement," Paulos Milkias and Getachew Metaferia, ed. 2005. *The Battle of Adwa; Reflections on Ethiopia's Historic Victory Against European Colonialism*, ibid., p. 208.

2 Edward W. Chester, *Clash of Titans: Africa and U.S. Foreign Policy*, ibid., p. 204.

3 Ibid.

4 Max J. Wasserman. August 1946. "The new Ethiopian monetary system," *The Journal of Political Economy*, vol. 54, no. 4, p. 359.

5 Zewde Gabre-Sellassie, p.4.

6 Ibid.

7 Testimony of John H. Spencer. *Ethiopia and the Horn of Africa Hearing Before the Subcommittee on African Affairs*, US Senate Ninety-fourth Congress, August 4, 5, and 6, 1976, p. 23

cipal advisor to the Ethiopian Ministry of Foreign Affairs (1943–1974). At the fall of Emperor Haile Selassie's government, he left Ethiopia. Spencer moved to the US and gave testimonies at the US congressional hearings on Ethiopia. He identified with Ethiopia and agonized over the secession of Eritrea and the introduction of ethnic-based politics in Ethiopia.

Dr. Spencer participated in rallies organized by Ethiopians in the US to pressure the government and influence policies towards the undemocratic governments in Ethiopia. In one such rally in New York City, he reminded participants that "[They] are the sons and daughters of the brave Ethiopians who defeated the invading Italians in the Battle of Adwa; your country is the oldest nation in the world next to China; you are the only black nation with your own script; you are the pride of black Africa."[1] Loved and respected by Ethiopians in the diaspora, he died in New York on August 25, 2005, at the age of 98. John Spencer was a voice for democracy and human rights in a country he called his second home. A eulogy by Ethiopians in the diaspora stated that Ethiopians had lost a precious friend and noted that he "will surely be remembered by Ethiopians at home and abroad as a generous defender of their famous land. He defended strongly Ethiopia's unity and condemned swiftly the concept of secession. He upheld the support of nourishment and detested the presence of destitution. Dr. Spencer vigorously supported equality and abhorred discrimination."[2]

US Involvement in Building Ethiopia's Institutions

In the 1950s and 1960s, the US assisted in building Ethiopia's institutions of higher education, modeled after those in the United States. For example the Business School at Haile Selassie I University, [renamed Addis Ababa University,] used not only American professors but also textbooks and materials that were used in the US universities and colleges. The same could be said of the Law School at Addis Ababa University, College of Public Health in Gondar, Alemaya Agricultural College in Harar, with ties to Oklahoma State University, and Jimma and Ambo agricultural high schools established with US assistance.

The Gondar College of Public Health was established by UN agencies (UNICEF and WHO) and the United States Operations Mission in Ethiopia and became operational in October 1954.[3] The US contribution to the establishment of Agricultural College came as a result of a cooperative agricultural education program between the Ministry of Agriculture and USAID. Article II of the agreement between the two countries specifies the objectives of the program:

> To promote and strengthen friendship and understanding between the people of Ethiopia and the United States of America and to further their general welfare.

> To aid the efforts of the people of Ethiopia to develop their agricultural and related resources, to improve their working and living conditions so as to further their social and economic progress.

> To facilitate the development of agricultural and mechanical arts education activities in Ethiopia through cooperative action.

---

1 Quoted by Abate Kassa. March, 1994. "The unmaking of the Great Ethiopian Airlines," *Ethiopian Register* vol.1, no. 2, p. 18.

2 Ethiomedia. August 29, 2005. "Dr. John H. Spencer (1907-2005). A message from Ethiopians in the Diaspora." www.ethiomedia.cm/fastpress/john_spencer.htm

3 Teshome G. Wagaw. 1990. *The Development of Higher Education and Social Change: An Ethiopian Experience*, East Lansing, Michigan: Michigan State University Press, pp. 82–83.

To stimulate and increase the interchange of knowledge, skills, and techniques in the field of agricultural and mechanical arts education.[1]

Such was the extent of the multifaceted cooperation between Ethiopia and the United States.[2] The above mentioned institutions in their own right produced qualified specialists in their respective areas; this trained and educated human resource unfortunately left the country *en masse* because of the stifling political conditions under the *Derg*. The loss of human resources was a gain for other countries such as the US who benefited from the training and expertise of diaspora Ethiopians — although many have faced status inconsistency, unable to find jobs that are commensurate with their training, skills, and expertise.[3]

PEACE CORPS VOLUNTEER (PCVs) CONTRIBUTIONS TO ETHIOPIA'S DEVELOPMENT

The contribution of the US Peace Corps to Ethiopia's modern education and development efforts is laudable. Ethiopia was one of the first countries to invite Peace Corps Volunteers (PCVs) and 279 volunteers arrived in September 1962.[4] The Peace Corps program in Ethiopia was one of the largest. Volunteers worked in rural development, education, law, and agriculture.[5] The program was closed during the military regime in 1977 and resumed in 1995 after the fall of the *Derg*, then the political situation forced the program to close once again in 1999. Close to 3,500 volunteers have served in Ethiopia.[6]

Most Peace Corps Volunteers have remained committed friends of Ethiopia and cherish their experiences there.[7] The program had become controversial in the 1960s as opposition was mounted against the PCVs by Ethiopian students. The students alleged that some PCVs were working for the CIA and undermining Ethiopia's national interests and its culture. Antagonism toward the Peace Corps program reflected the global trend of opposition to US interventions in Vietnam and African and Latin American countries.

Now the Peace Corps manages a website in which they announce their activities in Ethiopia and Eritrea.[8] During the centennial commemoration of Ethio-US relations at Howard University, titled "A Tale of Two Nations: Celebrating 100 Years

1 Ibid. pp. 79–80. Also refer to "Agreement for a Cooperative Education Program between the Government of the United States of America and the Imperial Ethiopian Government," Article II (15 May 1952), 1.

2 For US involvement in education-related projects in Ethiopia, refer to Paulos Milkias. 2006. *Haile Selassie, Western Education and Political Revolution in Ethiopia*, Youngstown, New York: Cambria Press, pp. 85–94.

3 Getachew Metaferia and Maigenet Shifferraw, *The Ethiopian Revolution of 1974 and the Exodus of Ethiopia's Trained Human Resources*, ibid.

4 The Peace Corps was established on March 1, 1961, by Executive Order 10924. It was authorized by Congress on September 22, 1961 under the Peace Corps Act (Public Law 87-293).

5 Peace Corps volunteers worked in Ethiopia from 1962 to 1977. Some PCVs worked in Ethiopia from 1995 to 1999 when the program was again terminated because of conflicts in some regions. The program was resumed in October 2007 with 43 volunteers. Included in this group, for the first time, are Ethiopian-Americans.

6 Refer to the Peace Corps website, www.Peacecorps.gov/index.cfm?shell=resources.media. press.view&news_id=1152

7 James W. Skelton, Jr. 1991. *Volunteering in Ethiopia: A Peace Corps Odyssey*, Denver, CO.: Beaumont Books.

8 Check the website of the PCVs who served in Ethiopia and Eritrea. www.ethiopiaeritrearpcvs. org

of Ethiopian-United States Relations," in March 2004, I witnessed volunteers who spoke fondly of Ethiopia. Clare Shea, who served in Gojjam province identified with that region and claimed that she is a Gojjame. David Levine, who served in the Gurage region, testified that he spoke in a Gurage accent.[1] He got emotional and said: "Let's go home and build our country." I personally was taught by PCVs in Gore, Illubabor province, and addressed the Returned PCVs of Washington, DC, on April 30, 1991. Most Peace Corps volunteers are young idealists and energetic. The US successfully and gracefully advances its own best interests when it can send out such selfless civilians, people who can identify with other cultures and are willing to learn from other people's experiences.

THE ETHIOPIAN AIRLINES (EAL)

When Emperor Haile Selassie returned in 1941 to Ethiopia from his exile in Great Britain, he began championing a national airline. His vision was for a world-class commercial airline that would fly the Ethiopian flag, a symbol of the sovereignty of Ethiopia.

The Ethiopian Airlines (EAL) was established by government proclamation on December 21, 1945, and began to develop its business plan. They started operation in the following year, supported by Ethiopian capital. With a loan from US Export–Import Bank and the International Finance Corporation, six C-47 planes were purchased from US large stocks of surplus planes at Payne Field, outside of Cairo, and were converted to DC-3s.[2] Trans World Airlines (TWA) provided management service, standard supervision, equipment procurement, and technical advice.[3] EAL commenced international flight to Cairo on April 8, 1946, and has the largest airlines network in Africa. It now provides service to 22 domestic and 42 international cities, connecting Africa, Asia, Europe, and North America.

Its maintenance division is accredited by the US Federal Aviation Administration (FAA). It has a recognized pilot training school, which was started in 1964, for its own benefit and that of other countries. In 1986, EAL started Agro-Aircraft assembly to support agricultural sectors. EAL is a national airline and has remained a success story not only in Ethiopia but internationally as well.

Four years after the current government assumed power in 1991, it tried to restructure the EAL and merge it with a non-existent Eritrean Airlines and with the marginal Djibouti Airlines. This provoked a strong opposition on the part of EAL employees in Ethiopia, former EAL employees in the US, and their former American colleagues, in response to a report by a task force established by the Transitional Government of Ethiopia (TGE). Headed by the Association of Former Ethiopian Airlines Employees in North America (AFEAENA), Americans including Prof. John H. Spencer, Attorney Donald E. Paradis, and former American executives with the EAL were instrumental in lobbying against the move in the US and Britain.[4] According

---

1 My thanks go to Ms. Clare Shea and Mr. David Levine for the permission to quote them.

2 Dejazmach Zewde Gabre-Sellassie. 2003. "Ethio–American business relations, 1903-2003." A speech delivered to African-American business people on the centennial celebration of Ethio–US diplomatic relations, Addis Ababa, Ethiopia, P. 9. I appreciate Dejazmach Zewde for sharing with me a copy of his speech.

3 Transitional Government of Ethiopia, Report by a Task Force, January 1994, "Strategy of Ethiopian Airlines and Directive for Implementation," Addis Ababa, Ethiopia.

4 Source based on a letter dated April 24, 1994 from Donal E. Paradis to Ato Gebeyehou (last name not mentioned in the letter), and a letter by the Association of Former Ethiopian

to AFEAENA, the TGE's effort to merge the EAL with others, whose existence was in name only, was aimed at benefitting Eritrea. The recommendation to restructure EAL, according to the Association's press release, had political motives, not business ones. The EAL had registered profits in the years preceding the recommendation to restructure. Thus managerial incompetence, mechanical concerns, and financial insolvency were not issues.

Tecola W. Hagos, who served in the TGE, blames two officials who were involved in the reconstruction of the Ethiopian Airlines. The Minister of Defense, Seye Abraha, who also served as Chairman of the Board of the Airlines, was alleged to have made "destructive" statements that created "rifts between the government of Meles and a number of Ethiopians."[1] The other official was Tekest Gebremichael, who was the minister responsible for economic affairs in the office of the prime minister. According to Tecola, "Tekest is an Eritrean by birth and is perceived to be promoting Eritrean interest at the expense of Ethiopia."[2]

Earlier, the military regime had tried to replace the US-made EAL passenger airplanes with USSR-made airplanes to garner support from Moscow. That move had been resisted by EAL members and the management, especially Capt. Mohammed Ahmed, and caused the *Derg* to revise its policy. It took years and considerable resources for both the Ethiopian and US governments to build the human and institutional capacities for national development. The American government had also been involved in saving the EAL, which they perceived as a model for the management of a successful enterprise. Every effort must be made to avoid losing ground.[3]

A similar attempt to undermine a state entity established by the imperial government succeeded when forty established and respected professors who had criticized the current government were summarily expelled from the faculty of Addis Ababa University.

Another area in which the US was involved in building Ethiopia's institutions was national defense. The Ethiopian Air Force was equipped mainly by the US and was rated the best in sub-Sahara Africa, with the exception only of South Africa. During the Kennedy administration, Ethiopia received F-5 fighter planes, tanks, and other advanced weapons. The US Military Assistance Advisory Group (MAAG) coordinated the delivery of US military equipment and served as a conduit to Ethiopia during Emperor Haile Selassie's rule.[4]

In addition to building defense and educational institutions, the US also built development infrastructure projects such as highways, power stations, communications facilities, water and irrigation services; modernized coffee production and marketing; and implemented livestock improvement programs. Some of the efforts, however, failed to be fully realized because the policies of the successive governments failed to maximize the past efforts and build on some of their positive aspects.

Airlines Employees in North America for radio announcement, March 3, 1994. My appreciation goes to the current Chairman of the Association for the documents.

1 Tecola W. Hagos. 1995. *Democratization? Ethiopia (1991–1994)*, Cambridge, MA. Khepera Publishers, p. 170.

2 Ibid., p.170.

3 Abate Kassa. March 1994. "The unmaking of the great Ethiopia Airlines," *Ethiopian Register*, vol. 1, no. 2, pp. 15–18.

4 Harold G. Marcus, *Ethiopia, Great Britain and the United States 1841–1974*, ibid., p. 89.

THE UNDERMINING OF ETHIOPIAN INSTITUTIONS

In spite of the effort, time, and resources spent in building and enhancing institutions, the past two governments of Ethiopia are accused of dismantling some of these institutions. When the military regime came to power in 1974, it adopted a socialist ideology and instituted a command economy. It discredited and destroyed some of the infrastructure projects, institutions, and programs because of their Western associations. The socialist military regime took an anti-West stand and increased antagonism led to the decline of the relationship between the two nations.

After the demise of the *Derg* in 1991, the EPRDF comes to power, renounced strict communism, claimed to follow market economics, and cultivated a closer alliance with the US in order to attract US financial assistance and diplomatic support and gain legitimacy in the international community and multilateral organizations.[1] Opposition Member of Parliament Dr. Merera Gudina was quoted by a reporter of *The Nation* saying that (Prime Minister) Meles "started talking about free elections and free markets — anything that was sweet to American ears."[2] When the current leadership came to power, it promised peace and democracy. The economic policy that emerged encouraged crony capitalism, and that elections were far from being fair and free. As Stephen Buckley wrote in the Washington Post, "Ethiopia's Meles is accused of arbitrarily arresting hundreds of people and allegedly has fallen into the same cronyism that has wracked so many African regimes."[3]

Meanwhile, similar to its predecessor, the Meles regime destroyed institutions built or enhanced under the previous governments except for security networks at the local levels, such as the infamous *kebele* association of the *Derg* era, used to conduct espionage on citizens. This community-based association was not only retained but strengthened.

At the national level, the army was demobilized and the defense structure was destroyed or weakened. When the EPRDF and EPLF entered Addis Ababa, Ethiopia's massive arms and ammunition depots were ignited. According to Dima Noggo Serbo, official of the OLF at the time, and Dr. Tecola Hagos, former political advisor to the prime minister and minister of foreign affairs, the destruction of arms and ammunition was attributed to the EPLF. Both organizations also "transported as much of the military hardware and other equipment as they could to Tigray and Eritrea."[4] Ironically, it took only five years for the EPRDF to rebuild the defense that it had formerly discredited and totally destroyed. At one time Mr. Meles had boasted that Ethiopia would smelt the military hardware and turn it into tools; subsequently he oversaw the frantic restoration of that hardware when war erupted with Eritrea.

Ethiopia soon resorted to arming itself and recalling some of the military personnel that had been dismissed *en masse* when the EPRDF assumed power. The army was accused of being an army of the *Derg* regime, dominated by the Amhara ethnic group.

---

1 The current Ethiopia's Prime Minister, Meles Zenawi, was head of TPLF's ideology school and was the brain behind the organization's Marxist orthodoxy. Albanian's strong man, Enver Hoxha, who headed the Albanian Communist Party and ruled Albania for four decades, was Meles's hero.

2 Paul Wachter. February 14, 2007. "Bush's Somalia strategy enables an Ethiopian despot," *The Nation*, http://www.thenation.com/doc/20070226/wachter

3 Stephen Buckley. February 2, 1995. "Authorities change face in Africa ...enlightened leaders or savvy strongmen?" p. A13.

4 Dima Noggo Sarbo. August 2007. "The Ethiopia-Eritrea conflict: Short sighted solution and long term problems," unpublished document.

As a result of rebuilding the military, the defense budget rose from 1.8 per cent of the total government expenditure in 1997 to 12 percent in 1998 and an estimated 17–20 percent in 1999.[1] Such ill-advised policy choices in the past governments have weakened institutions and wasted the efforts of countries such as the US.

In the next chapter, we will examine the fall of the monarchy, the rise of the military socialist regime, and the emergence of a new post-Cold War government.

---

1 David Heslam. 2000/01. *Nations of the World, a Political Economy and Business Handbook.* Lakeville, CT.: Grey House Publishing, p. 432.

Chapter 8. Ethiopia–US Relations during the Military Regime

The Fall of Emperor Haile Selassie's Government (1974)

In 1974 conditions in Ethiopia were ripe for change and calls for reform remained unanswered by the monarchy. The aging Emperor Haile Selassie made his last visit to the US in 1973 and explained to the Nixon Administration, mired in the Watergate scandal, that Somalia, armed by the USSR, was planning to attack Ethiopia. He requested improved US weapons but received none. The Emperor then visited Moscow to shop for weapons.

Somalia had fifty MIG fighters including twenty-four supersonic MIG 21s, several Ilyushin bombers, and T-54 tanks. At that time, Ethiopia had 37 combat planes, all obsolete with the exceptions of 9 F-5As.[1] The International Institute for Strategic Studies (IISS) reported in 1975 that Somalia had 250 medium tanks and approximately 300 armored personnel carriers compared to Ethiopia's 12 medium and 50 light tanks, and just over 100 armored personnel carriers.[2]

The cold response of the US to Ethiopia's request disappointed the Emperor but emboldened General Siad Mohamed Barre of Somalia, who supported irredentists in the Ogaden region, secessionists Eritreans, and domestic groups such as the Oromo Liberation Front (OLF) who opposed the monarchy. Ethiopia's intellectuals, armed forces, farmers, and the emerging business sector were all alienated, the economy was stagnant, and many were desperate to see some kind of reform in Ethiopia. Radical Ethiopian students, who had been opposed to the Emperor since the first coup d'état attempt in December 1960, led the movement for revolutionary changes. The students at the various Haile Selassie I colleges also had their grievances against the government. According to Fentahun Tiruneh, who was one of the five students dismissed from the university in 1965, "Between 1952 to 1957 students at the various Haile Selassie I Colleges were confronted with oppressive feudal regime and oppres-

---

1 Tom J. Farer. 1976. *War Clouds on the Horn of Africa: A Case for Détente*, Washington, DC: Carnegie Endowment for International Peace, p. 98.

2 Ibid., pp. 98-99 as quoted from IISS, 1975, *The Military Balance, 1975–1976*. London: IISS, p. 43.

sive campus administrators."[1] According to the 1954 charter that governed the colleges and the one existing university, one of the responsibilities of the Dean of Students was to "supervise the discipline of students on and off campus."[2] In other words, the Dean of Students served as a police officer. The five students dismissed from the university were Walelign Mekonnen, Getachew Sharew, Fentahun Tiruneh, Ayalew Aklog, and Gezahegn Mekonnen.

The US Embassy under Ambassador Edward Korry was reported to have assisted in defeating the December 1960 coup attempt. That made the US a target of radical students at Haile Selassie I University who demonstrated against the US in the 1960s and built anti-American sentiment. Ambassador Korry then resorted to assiduously "cultivating contacts among young, influential bureaucrats, organizing seminars ... and maintaining an active official dialogue with the Emperor and his Prime Minister [Ato Aklilu Habtewold]" in the hope of curbing the increasing anti-American fervor in Ethiopia.[3]

Bickering between the cabinet ministers and the royal family also weakened the administration and denied it a clear national vision and coherence, thus contributing to its demise. The frailty of the 82-year-old Emperor and his increasing ineffective leadership compounded the problem. The US kept its distance and looked for a potential leader who could be groomed to be his successor. In this, the US did not succeed.

We are reminded that the US wanted to obstruct what it termed as radicals and curtail communism from hampering oil transportation through the Red Sea and affecting the US influence in the region. Haile Selassie, who had been keen to stay in power, courted US support to ward off internal dissent and the external threat from radical Arab states. Besides this security concern, Emperor Haile Selassie also needed US assistance for economic development. By and large, legitimate concerns raised by Ethiopian students and the nascent middle class, such as changing the land tenure policy and dismantling the feudal system, were taken to be evidence of Russian influence. The land tenure system was also a concern for the US and the multilateral institutions such as the World Bank as it hampered economic development, though the US did not press Haile Selassie "to institute meaningful social, economic, or political reforms."[4] The government was unable to cope up with the challenges that it faced. The condition was ripe for a revolution.

THE RISE AND RULE OF THE MILITARY REGIME (1974–1991)

Eventually everyone from taxi drivers to peasants, members of the armed forces, and religious groups demanded change. Ethiopian students articulated their demands. Reform-minded non-commissioned military officers who formed the Coordinating Committee of the Armed Forces, Police, and Territorial Army, known as the

---

1 Fentahun Tiruneh. 1990. *The Ethiopian Students: Their Struggle to Articulate the Ethiopian Revolution*, Chicago, Ill.: Nyala Type, p. 15. Also refer to Messay Kebede. 2009. *Radicalism and Cultural Dislocation in Ethiopia, 1960-1974*, Rochester, NY: University of Rochester Press.

2 Taye Assefa. 2008. *Academic Freedom in Ethiopia – Perspectives of Teaching Personnel*, Addis Ababa, Ethiopia: Forum for Social Studies, p. 26.

3 Bereket Habte Selassie, "The American Dilemma on the Horn," June 1984, *The Journal of Modern African Studies*, vol. 22, no. 2, p. 262.

4 Edmond J. Keller. 1985. "United States Foreign Policy on the Horn of Africa: Policy Making with Blinders On," Ibid., p. 184.

Derg, detained government officials and the Emperor.[1] The military, politicized and radicalized by the students, took an anti-West (anti-US) stance, although there still existed a moderate pro-US group. This group lost ground in the struggle with those who were politically left-oriented. As is often the case when revolutionary changes are promulgated, there existed no forum, no opportunity to openly discuss alternative scenarios and in a rational fashion choose the one that would best serve Ethiopia. This has led Ethiopia to the abysmal condition it finds itself in now.

After Nixon left office, the successive American administrations (early 1970s to early 1990s) were unable to recover their connection to Ethiopia because of the increasing anti-American fervor of a large number of intellectuals and later of the military regime that gradually undercut the intelligentsia and marginalized it. Besides the anti-West political rhetoric adopted by the military, there was an increase in human rights abuses and the fighting in Eritrea continued. The military head, Col. Mengistu Haile Mariam, took an uncompromising stand and remained an obstacle to the Ethio–US relationship during the Carter administration. Even in the face of the demise of tens of thousands of Ethiopians as a result of famine caused by successive droughts, the Reagan administration turned a blind eye to the human calamity and refrained from sending timely humanitarian assistance

The excuse given by the administration was that food aid would be used as a political weapon and would punish areas that did not support the military regime. In that political game, thousands of Ethiopians were condemned to perish.[2] It was reported that the famine of 1985 claimed the lives of one million Ethiopians. About 6,000 people died every day at the height of the famine. When the media exposed the situation to the US public, the response was overwhelmingly pro-Ethiopian. The Reagan Administration finally sent food but a million people had already starved to death.

During the seventeen years of military rule in Ethiopia (1974–1991), the Ethio–US relationship continued to deteriorate. The Provisional Military Government of Ethiopia (PMGE) took harsh measures. On November 24, 1974, junta officers summarily executed 62 Ethiopian officials. Dejazmach Zewde Gebre Sellassie, Ethiopia's foreign minister, resigned in protest and took asylum in the United States.

Ethiopia's ambassadors to the US, Kifle Wodajo (1972–75) and Ayalew Mandefro (1977–1978) left their posts in opposition to the military government's repressive policy. According to Foreign Minister Goshu Wolde, who also defected to the US, Ethiopia "slipped further and further into totalitarianism and absolute dictatorship, with the inevitable consequences of intolerance and repression."[3] The Ethio–US relationship had been downgraded to low-level diplomacy and was conducted at the level of the Chargés d'Affaires in both countries after ambassador Frederic L. Chapin was recalled at Ethiopia's request on July 29, 1980. It was only in 1992, after the overthrow of the military regime, that the relationship between the two countries was normalized and ambassadors were exchanged.

1 Refer to Saheed A. Adejumobi. 2007. *The History of Ethiopia*, Westport, Connecticut: Greenwood Press.

2 Steven L. Varnis. 1990. *U.S. Food Aid Policy and Ethiopian Famine Relief*, New Brunswick, NJ: Transaction Publishers.

3 *The Washington Post*. October 28, 1986, p. A19.

The US sided with Somalia, a country that supported and abated irredentist groups in Ethiopia claiming the Ogaden region populated by ethnic Somalis. The CIA also helped undermine the unity of Ethiopia by engineering the secession of Eritrea through its clandestine program dubbed "seeding project."[1] Although the secession of Eritrea became a reality through a questionable referendum in 1993, neither the security of Eritrea, broadly speaking, nor the national interest of the US in the region has been fully realized.

The US, however, was committed to toppling the military regime in Ethiopia by supporting conservative groups, such as the EDU (Ethiopian Democratic Union), and even providing tactical support to Eritrean secessionist groups. Ethiopians complained that the US had no regard for the unity and integrity of Ethiopia in the pursuit of its national interest and, in many cases, worked against the best interests of developing countries. While this may be *realpolitik* from the US point of view, the clandestine support the US provided to secessionists in Ethiopia was disappointing even for Ethiopians who had no sympathy for the military regime. The US saw Ethiopia as strategically important. Yet it failed to protect that nation's unity, geopolitical weight, and national interest.

When Somalia attacked Ethiopia (1977–1978), most Ethiopians felt that the US failed to stand by their side. The Carter administration did ban arms sales to Ethiopia, as well as to Argentina and Uruguay, because of their human rights violation, as was announced on February 25, 1977. History was repeated in a peculiar way in the 1970s. The Carter Administration, early in its administration, announced its willingness to supply arms to Somalia even though Somalia was the clear aggressor. This US policy amounted to rewarding an aggressor state, similar to the US policy during World War II when the Roosevelt Administration failed to put a total embargo on fascist Italy when it invaded Ethiopia. The US was rightly opposed to the human rights abuses by the *Derg*. The foreign policy followed by the Carter Administration did not, however, deter human rights violations in Ethiopia. Rather it led Mengistu Haile Mariam to expel US military personnel and close US agencies. The military government surprised the US on April 23, 1977, by announcing the closure of the US Information Agency (USIA), Military Advisory Group (MAAG), National Medical Research Center (NMRC), and Kagnew Station. The US Consulate in Asmara was closed and the US embassy staff in Addis Ababa was reduced. On April 27, about 300 US personnel and dependents at the Kagnew Station were given four days to leave the country. This unilateral decision and short deadline was protested by the US State Department which regretted the "downward drift in relations" between the two countries. Furthermore, Western news correspondents from Reuter's news agency, Agence France Presse (AFP), and the *Washington Post* were ordered to leave the country within 48 hours.

The US retaliated by holding about $100 million worth of various kinds of military equipment, ammunition, and spare parts for communication equipment. The United States gradually started to look elsewhere as conditions compelled it to reassess its policy towards Ethiopia.[2]

Meanwhile, the military regime became violent in silencing dissidents. Amnesty International continuously accused Ethiopia of human rights violations in the 1970s which, in part, had led to an influx of political refugees into neighboring countries,

---

1 "CIA and EPLF at Kagnew Station." 1993. *Senai*, vol. 1, no. 3.

2 Harold G. Marcus. 1983. *Ethiopia, Great Britain and the United States 1941–1974*, Berkley: University of California Press, pp. 79-114.

mainly Sudan and Djibouti. In 1977, besides the mass exodus of civilian Ethiopians, there was also a large-scale defection of government officials. Mengistu's regime continued to brutalize Ethiopians who challenged his authority and the US continued its opposition to the Mengistu's regime. Thus the relationship between the two countries reached the lowest ebb in almost seventy years except for during and immediately after the fascist occupation.

Ironically, a good number of government officials and intellectuals immigrated to the United States. Ethiopians had been given a blanket protection against deportation from the US since 1974. However, on January 26, 1982, the US Department of State announced an end to that policy except for "voluntary departure," and individuals could request political asylum. This policy could have resulted in the deportation of more than 15,000 Ethiopians residing in the United States. Five months later, on July 6, 1982, the State Department reversed its policy as a result of lobbying by Ethiopians, US citizens, non-governmental organizations (NGOs) and US officials.

The number of Ethiopians in the US tops the number of diaspora Ethiopians in any other country. As the relationship between the two countries seems to be contradictory, so also is the case with most Ethiopians in the United States. They believed that the US contributed to their predicament, as a result of the Cold War politics, yet they wished to resettle in the US because of the political freedom and the economic opportunity the US promises. The immigration of Ethiopians to the US started during the "Red Terror" between 1977 to 1978 and was for political reasons, which seem now to have shifted to economic reasons.[1] Still the political condition remains a major underlying cause of the exodus of Ethiopians. Refugees from Ethiopia in some US cities numbered over 35,000 over a decade (1983–2004).[2]

ETHIO–SOMALIA BORDER WAR: A GAME OF THE COLD WAR ERA (1977–1978)

In the 1970s Arab countries and Iran, a non-Arab state, violated Ethiopia's territory by supporting Somalia, a member of the Arab League. Egypt has continuously supported Somalia starting with the border wars in 1960 and in 1964, and later in 1977–1978. This act was against the tenets of the OAU which respects colonial boundaries and upholds peaceful settlement of disputes.

As Edmond J. Keller wrote, the US support of Somalia, during the Carter Administration, later "backfired [and] the United States attempted to distance itself from the conflict in the Horn by claiming neutrality. Public charges of human rights violations by the US became more tempered and efforts were made to reestablish normal relations"[3] This attempt to correct US policy towards Ethiopia is indicative of foreign policy operation through trial and error, the pursuit of short-term tactical, not long-term strategic calculations, and the perceived insignificance of these areas. This is also a major shortcoming of US foreign policy towards developing countries in general, resulting in feeble and failed policies and unintended consequences. As a result of Carter's flawed policy, the arms race escalated in the area known as the

1 Getachew Metaferia and Maigenet Shifferraw. 1991. *The Ethiopian Revolution of 1974 and the Exodus of Ethiopia's Trained Human Resources.* Lewiston, NY: The Edwin Mellen Press.

2 Audrey Singer and Jill H. Wilson. 2006. "From 'there' to 'here': Refugee Resettlement in Metropolitan America." Washington, D.C.: Metropolitan Policy Program, the Brookings Institute

3 Edmond J. Keller, "United States foreign policy on the Horn of Africa: Policy making with blinders on," ibid., p. 188.

Horn of Africa.[1] Both Somalia and Ethiopia were militarized, which eventually led to gross human rights violation.

The Arab support for Somalia and the superpower rivalry in the area emboldened Somalia to attack Ethiopia in 1977–1978. Ethiopia, which had the largest army in sub-Sahara Africa, failed to deter the Somali aggression. At that time, the London-based International Institution for Strategic Studies (IISS) stated that Ethiopia had 71,600 regular army and 150,000-peasant militia.[2]

By April 1977, it was reported that Soviet military equipment costing from $100 million to $200 million arrived in Ethiopia. The massive shipment was intended to enable Ethiopia to withstand Somali aggression, secessionist forces in Eritrea and Tigre provinces, and forces such as the Ethiopian Democratic Union (EDU) and Ethiopian Patriotic Democratic Alliance (EPDA), which were closely associated with the monarchy and the CIA.

On May 6, 1977, Col. Mengistu Haile Mariam signed with the USSR a Declaration of the Basic Principles of Friendly Mutual Relation and Cooperation. This declaration surprised the United States. Some in the Ethiopian military, including Mengistu Haile Mariam, were trained in the US, so the US did not expect the military to declare socialism as a national ideology, or nationalize land ownership, or abandon the long-standing alliance between the two countries. That declaration, among others, enabled Ethiopia to substitute the US-made military arsenal, on which its army was trained, for Soviet military equipment, at a time when Ethiopia's security was threatened by neighboring Somalia.

Following that treaty, on May 28, 1977, Ethiopia ordered the US to cut its embassy staff by half and close its attaché office. On June 2, it ordered the return of 81 army, air force and naval personnel from training in the United States. On October 19, 1977, Anatoly Ratanov, the USSR's ambassador to Ethiopia, affirmed his country's termination of arms supplies to Somalia and provided defensive weapons to Ethiopia, thus making Ethiopia the latest USSR satellite in Africa. To Moscow, this was a reestablishment of Ethio–Russian relations dating back to the czarist era. Eventually the US left Ethiopia as the USSR had departed from Somalia.

Soon after the US moved to Somalia, the Somali government was emboldened and attacked Ethiopia in the summer of 1977. The Somali army reached the city of Harar, 300 miles from the Somali border, by November 1977. Many Ethiopians believe that the US support encouraged Somalia to invade Ethiopia and control a large part of its territory.

Ethiopia, with the military hardware, technical and personnel support it received from the USSR, Cuba, and South Yemen, managed to halt the Somali advance and reverse the tide. During the height of the fighting, in February, 1978, the number of Cuban fighters in Ethiopia reached about 18,000 and the Soviet Union provided 1,500 advisors. This international coalition cobbled together by Moscow finally rolled back the Somali force and led to its devastating defeat. According to Ethiopia's former minister of defense, Ayalew Mandefro, despite the quantity of Somali's USSR hardware, the American hardware in Ethiopia, especially the fighter airplanes, made a decisive difference as they were fast, agile and precise in their performance. The superb performance of Ethiopian pilots also made a difference in the war against Somalia

---

1 Ibid.
2 IISS. September 4, 1979. *The Military Balance, 1979-80.*

as they dominated the skies.[1] On March 9, 1978, Siad Bare pooled his troops out of Ethiopia.

In the late 1970s Ethiopia, besides having its strength depleted by the border war with Somalia and having to deal with secessionists in Eritrea and Tigre provinces, was victimized by the infamous "Red Terror" from December 1977 to April 1978. To be educated and young made one suspect. The Red Terror resulted in the death of at least 10,000 people and the arrests of as many as 20,000 young urban dwellers suspected of being members of or associated with the Ethiopian People's Revolutionary Party (EPRP), a Marxist political organization, an ideological soul mate of the military regime that ultimately fell out of favor and fought with the military and its intellectual socialist ally, *Meison*. That period, on all accounts, was the darkest moment in the recent history of Ethiopia. Western aid to Ethiopia declined sharply because of its close alliance with the USSR and the increased instability in the country. In 1982, for example, the US Department of State estimated that war against secessionist groups in Tigre and Eritrea as well as Somalia consumed more than 27% of Ethiopia's GNP. Hence the downward spiral of the country's economy and the increased human misery. The economic assistance from Eastern European countries and Cuba's medical assistance, through its doctors, failed to reverse the condition.

Cuba, a developing Caribbean country, gave significant and tangible support to Ethiopia. Cuba's commitment to the development of Ethiopia and other Afro-Marxist regimes is reflected in the airlifts on December 4 and 10, 1979, of 4,000 Ethiopian children orphaned by war. Some of the children were as young as seven years and were part of the estimated 10,000 children airlifted from Angola, Congo, Namibia, Mozambique and Guinea-Bissau. They were housed on a small island called Isla de la Juventud. The Ethiopian children attended special schools, Kara Mara and Mengistu Haile Mariam, where Ethiopian history, language and geography were part of the curriculum that trained the youth in technical skills. They were also engaged in cutting sugar cane and their Ethiopian teachers were harsh in disciplining them. They endured loneliness and hardship. There were frictions between the students. Some were orphaned children of soldiers while others were street children.[2] I met some of the former Ethiopian students from Cuba in Kingston, Jamaica, in the summer of 2001. They complained that when they were bound to return to Ethiopia in 1991, after completing their training, the current regime cancelled their return flight to Addis Ababa and claimed that they were "Mengistu's troops." While President Fidel Castro supported the youths and denounced the government's policy, some of them were still languishing abroad. Others were still in Cuba, while those who returned to Ethiopia during the military regime participated in rural development program and worked in rural hospitals.

The Carter Administration took a middle ground despite Ethiopia's poor human rights record and the *Derg*'s pro-Soviet stances, in its early period (1977–1978), the administration de-emphasized the containment of the Soviet Union, contrary to recommendations of Zbigniew Brzezinski, the National Security Advisor known for his strong anti-Soviet stand. On the other hand, objections to human rights violations,

---

1 Interview with Ambassador Ayalew Mandefro, Minister of Defense during Ethiopia's border war with Somalia.

2 Information based on interview with former Derg official, Ambassador Kassa Kebede.

recommendations for arms reduction, and continued non-intervention became the principal guidelines of US diplomacy.[1]

Meanwhile, during the Ethio–Somalia war, the US altered its policy and withdrew its support of Somalia. Somalia had a long-standing grandiose design of creating "Greater Somalia" by annexing territories from Ethiopia and Kenya and incorporating Djibouti, where ethnic Somalis have settled. Eventually the US declared that Somalia had annexed Ethiopia's territory, the Ogaden, in July 1977, thus making Somalia the aggressor. The agenda of Greater Somalia destabilizes the region and has wide repercussions. Supporting Somalia was finally deemed to work against the US interest and went against the tenets of the OAU as well. Thus the US foreign policy towards Ethiopia during the Carter Administration was characterized by vacillation and lack of clarity.

Given the comparative advantage that Ethiopia provided to the US, and its long diplomatic relationship, the loss of Ethiopia was a significant gain for the USSR. Actually some Americans felt that Ethiopia was too important to abandon to the Soviets. There was a general belief that, given Ethiopia's importance in Africa, the Soviet Union had worked to ensure that the Ethio–US relationship would not be mended. The USSR provided Ethiopia with armaments, logistics and military experts to ward off the Somali aggression that threatened Ethiopia's security and sovereignty. By providing Ethiopia with an array of military hardware, which was paraded on May Day celebrations in Addis Ababa, the USSR won the allegiance of Ethiopia's military brass.

Ethiopia is not new to the Russians, as I have indicated. Their relations date back for centuries. Some of the ancestors of Alexander Pushkin, a great Russian poet and political activist, come from Ethiopia. The Russian Red Cross Society served during the Battle of Adwa and during the Italian occupation and trained Ethiopian medics at the Balcha Hospital in Addis Ababa.[2]

The USSR, however, failed to maximize the political gain it made in aligning with Ethiopia. It did not make Ethiopia a showcase for other African countries by developing Ethiopia's economy, which would have been more impressive than flooding the country with armaments. The USSR's inherent domestic economic constraints, bureaucracy, ideological rigidity, and manifest contradictions stood in the way. Unlike American personnel in Ethiopia, the Russians were very aloof, cold, and arrogant. That did not sit well with Ethiopians.

I was told that some merchants refused to sell goods to Russian soldiers because of their association with the military regime. The first group of high-level Russian officers seemed to be unaware of the professionalism of Ethiopians with whom they worked.[3] The Ethiopian officers were highly trained, mostly by Americans, and were sophisticated. The Russians, because of their stifling political system, were stiff and controlled compared to the extroverted and friendly Americans. Furthermore, the Russians wanted to shape or manage Ethiopia's foreign policy on specific issues. The *Derg* managed to "rebuff Soviet attempts to install a permanent advisory group in its

---

1 Olav Njolstad. 1996. *Peacekeeper and Troublemaker: the Containment Policy of Jimmy Carter, 1977–1978*, Norwegian Institute for Defense Studies, p.154.

2 Robert G. Patman, ibid., pp. 28-29.

3 Interview with Ayalew Mandefro, former Minister of Defense of Ethiopia.

Ministry of Foreign Affairs"[1] during 1976–1977. If the Soviet attempt had succeeded, it would have compromised Ethiopia's sovereignty and national pride.

Ethiopia was a face-saver to the USSR after it was unceremoniously booted out of Somalia. Once the USSR was invited to Ethiopia, the US presence in Ethiopia was virtually terminated and the US was not in a position to influence the political conditions from within. Earlier, when Emperor Haile Selassie's government was faced with Somali aggression and was to be overthrown, the Nixon administration was crippled by its own Watergate political debacle. The lesson of the Vietnam quagmire resulted in a return of the isolationist tendency. Ethiopia, therefore, was unable to count on the United States. At the time of Nixon/Kissinger initiatives of détente in 1972 and in 1973, the US was redefining its foreign policy in Africa. The Nixon administration stated that "the US wants no military allies, no sphere of influence, no big power competition in Africa," including Ethiopia.[2] The US was starting to ease tension with the USSR and no other country stepped forward. Ethiopia thus faced a predicament — closely associated with the US yet left in the lurch.

In the 1980s, President Reagan and the Chairman of the Senate Foreign Relations Committee, Senator Jessie Helms, in their strong anti-Soviet stance, altered the fear of the Vietnam syndrome and the political trend in Washington. They took a bold political stand and tried to oust the USSR from Ethiopia and other Afro-Marxist states, such as Angola and Mozambique, by providing tactical support to conservative and anti-Marxist groups. The US, especially under the Reagan Doctrine[3] of the 1980s, played a major role in Ethiopia's politics from outside by arming, funding, and providing logistics to groups such as the Ethiopian Democratic Union (EDU) who fought to overthrow the military regime. It was a good moment for conservative political parties who promised to challenge Marxist regimes. EDU, headquartered in London and with a strong presence in Washington, D.C., benefitted from the Reagan administration's foreign policy against the USSR in Africa. The leaders were associated with the pro-US monarchy and were viewed by the US officials as friendly to the US and a good choice to replace the socialist military junta. It was reported that the CIA provided about $500,000 a year to the London-based dissidents for propaganda purpose.[4] Other organizations, such as the EPDA, failed to produce dynamic leadership that could have galvanized the cross section of Ethiopia's population. Their leaders were elitists and were associated with the *ancien régime.*

The Voice of America (VOA)–Amharic program was launched in 1982 to challenge the military regime and proved to be successful. The Reagan administration used the media as one of the instruments to challenge Mengistu's regime, similar to the way in which Radio Free Europe/Radio Liberty were used to undermine the USSR in Eastern Europe. The media was also used to undermine other Marxist regimes in Angola, Mozambique, Nicaragua, and Grenada. The VOA–Amharic program was also used to counter Radio Moscow's Amharic program which aired for three

---

1 Amare Tekle. 1989. "The determination of the foreign policy of revolutionary Ethiopia," ibid., p. 487.

2 Robert G. Patman, ibid., 107.

3 The Reagan Doctrine is a reference to the foreign policy of the Reagan administration (1980–1988) which was intended to destabilize Marxist regimes that were supported by the USSR.

4 Joanne Omang. February 9, 1987. "Ex-official says Ethiopia mired in 'no-win' war," *The Washington Post*, p. A18. The reference was to Goshu Wolde's defection to the US on October 27, 1986.

decades, 1961 to 1991. The VOA–Amharic played a momentous role in the overthrow of the *Derg* regime.

As the Cold War was waning, Secretary General Mikhail Gorbachev of the USSR warned Mengistu that the Soviet Union would not continue assisting Ethiopia as it was itself undergoing radical changes in domestic policies. In its foreign policy, the USSR was also pursuing the Gorbachev Doctrine of superpower cooperation. This was practically the end of the Cold War. Gorbachev advised Mengistu to make a rapprochement with the US and also seek political solutions to its domestic problems, especially to the Eritrean issue.

That came as a shock to Mengistu, who had seen Gorbachev as a revisionist (*kelbash* in Amharic), and he complained to his entourage at the Kremlin after he met with Gorbachev. Gorbachev's reformist ideas challenged Mengistu's "tight grip over Ethiopian society."[1] Mengistu's friendly visit to Moscow ended up on an unfriendly note.

Mengistu was strictly pro-Soviet and suspected the US of undermining the unity of Ethiopia and trying to topple his government. Unlike most African leaders, Mengistu even avoided addressing the customary opening of the United Nations General Assembly when he served as the chairman of the Organization of African Unity (OAU). Mengistu avoided the US and aligned with the USSR despite his training sojourn in the US during the imperial period. Mengistu's policy towards the US was drastically opposed to that of the rulers who preceded him.

In a subsequent meeting with an Ethiopian official whom I interviewed, Gorbachev scoffed at the Workers Party of Ethiopia (WPE) in a country devoid of a large working class (proletariat). That sent a message to other Afro-Marxist countries who served as pawns of the superpowers during the Cold War. They paid dearly, economically and in human terms, and have not completely recovered from the malaise they inherited. Moscow was said to intimidate its client states to follow its line even when their own interests were not served. It was believed that "secret documents contain provisions that oblige Ethiopia to adopt a pro-USSR foreign policy in exchange for effective Soviet support...."[2] The USSR exploited the Cold War superpower rivalry and the insecurity of leaders such as Col. Mengistu. Ethiopians paid the sacrifice and some of the social, economic, and political problems the country faces now are the product of the Cold War politics.

The Mengistu regime alienated people from every part of the society and did not spare civilians who criticized the government. The regime's power also gradually eroded as a result of the drought and famine that claimed thousands of lives, reminiscent of the famine of the 1970s that contributed to the downfall of Emperor Haile Selassie's government. Since 1986 the USSR, which had provided the *Derg* with military and economic assistance, reduced its support to Ethiopia. Colonel Mengistu left the country but Ethiopians are still grappling with some of the consequences of his regime.

---

1 Robert G. Patman. 1990. *The Soviet Union in the Horn of Africa: The Diplomacy of Intervention and Disengagement*, New York: NY: Cambridge University Press, p. 304.
2 Amare Tekle, ibid., p. 487.

Chapter 9. Ethiopia–US Relations: The Post Military Regime (1991–2008)

With the overthrow of the military regime in 1991 and the end of the Cold War, the Ethio–US relationship was again normalized. A civilian government with gue- rilla fighting experience replaced the military. The core of the new government is the Tigre People's Liberation Front (TPLF).

After seventeen years, the military regime of Colonel Mengistu Haile Mariam, de- spite commanding the largest military power in sub-Sahara Africa (except for South Africa), collapsed in 1991. The rebel forces of the Tigre People's Liberation Front (TPLF) and Eritrean People's Liberation Front (EPLF) coordinated their efforts on the military front and skillfully undermined the government from within and with- out. The military regime also faced an economic crisis and was almost out of hard currency as it presided over a virtual war economy. The rank and file of the military lost its zeal to fight. Morale declined, corruption of the higher military hierarchy es- calated, and Mengistu's regime brutally murdered some of the most capable military leaders after an attempt to overthrow Mengistu in 1989. The situation also embold- ened the TPLF and the EPLF. Some members of the army defected and joined forces that fought against the military regime.[1]

After USSR cut its military support, Mengistu turned to Israel for weapons in exchange for the emigration of Ethiopian Jews (Bete Israel). The Israeli's nominal support failed to shore up Mengistu's power. Mengistu's government was ultimately weakened and subsequently collapsed. Mengistu had been the sole ruler of Ethio- pia since 1977, after eliminating all his contenders for power such as Colonel Atnafu Abate, the vice-president, and Generals Teferi Bante and Michael Andom, both of whom served as presidents and were part of the force that overthrew Emperor Haile Selassie in 1974. He secretly fled to Harare, Zimbabwe, on May 21, 1991, as rebels advanced on Addis Ababa. The rebel groups, a month before his departure and before

---

1 Ruth Iyob and Edmond J. Keller, "The Special Case of the Horn of Africa," in Donald Rothchild and Edmond J. Keller. 2006. *Africa–US Relations: Strategic Encounters*, Boulder, Colorado: Lynne Rienner Publishers, pp. 105-106.

their march on Addis Ababa, had demanded Mengistu's unconditional resignation as a precondition for any peace talks.

The same day that Mengistu departed for Zimbabwe, Lt. General Tesfaye Gebre-Kidan, the vice president and former defense minister, was named acting president. Tesfaye Dinka, who had served as Foreign Minister since April 26, 1991, was named prime minister. Tesfaye Gebre-Kidan then asked the US government to help arrange a cease-fire between the government forces and those of the TPLF/EPRDF and EPLF. The US played a significant role in bolstering the rebel groups and was instrumental in their entry to Addis Ababa to maintain order and in convening the London Peace Conference — which excluded some political organizations and formed the post-*Derg* Transitional Government of Ethiopia (TGE).

Let us now examine some of the important events that had their genesis under the *Derg* and the TGE had to address.

ETHIO–US RELATIONS AND THE BETE ISRAEL (ETHIOPIAN JEWS) EMIGRATION TO ISRAEL

In mid-1989, the Ethiopian government requested to upgrade diplomatic relations with the United States. The request was rejected because of Ethiopia's human rights record. Then, supposedly because of Mengistu's political moderation and support for the emigration of Ethiopian Jews (Bete Israel), relations between Ethiopia and the US improved in 1990. Ethiopia also renewed diplomatic relations with Israel in 1989.[1] Some other African countries including Cote d'Ivoire, Kenya, Liberia, Togo, and Zaire defied the OAU embargo on Israel and resumed relations with Israel. Some of these countries needed Israel to resume supplying them with weapons and development assistance.

The Bete Israel issue is censored in Israel as some people in the Knesset, religious parties, and Jewish religious hierarchies have questioned the religion of the Bete Israelis. To these groups the Bete Israeli are not clearly enough Jewish. The Chief Rabbinate insisted that Bete Israelis undergo the ritual immersion to confirm their "Jewishness" and demanded that Bete Israeli men be "re-circumcised." This is a symbolic process whereby a drop of blood is drawn from the penis. The early immigrants complied with the Israeli demand. As their number increased, young Bete Israelis have rebelled against the counsel of their religious leaders and refused to undergo conversion. It was reported that young Bete Israelis have attacked their religious leaders for accepting the conversion requirement.[2] This demand was dropped in 1984. Prime Minister Menachem Begin later announced that Bete Israelis would be considered full-fledged Jews without complying with the Chief Rabbinate's demands. Like other Israeli Jews, they do have to prove they are Jews when they wish to marry and their legitimacy had to be determined by Ethiopian Jewish leaders as well as with the Rabbinate.[3]

---

1 Ethiopia and Israel established consular relations in 1956 and began full diplomatic relations in 1961. Ethiopia broke diplomatic relations with Israel in 1973, because of the Yom Kippur War (October War), under the threat of an Arab oil embargo.

2 Steve Rodan. March 9, 1985. "Falashas rebel in Israel – ruling of conversion threatens to alienate Ethiopian Jews in adopted land."*The Washington Post*, p. B 8.

3 Report of a Congressional Study Mission to Israel, Egypt, Sudan, Ethiopia, and Somalia. August 2–20, 1985. Submitted to the Committee on Foreign Affairs, U.S. House of Representatives, US 99th Congress, 1st Session, *Israel, Egypt, Sudan, Ethiopia, and Somalia*, Washington, DC: US Government Printing Office, 1986, pp. 2_3.

The emigration of Bete Israel and overall human-rights conditions in Ethiopia remained a priority for the United States under the Reagan and George H.W. Bush administrations. In 1986, Congress formed the Congressional Caucus for Ethiopian Jews to promote the emigration of Bete Israel.[1]

The US delegation led by Congressman Howard Wolpe, Chairman, Subcommittee on Africa, during his discussion about Apartheid South Africa and Ethiopian Jewry, reported that Israeli Foreign Minister Yitzhak Shamir put forth "a strong view that Ethiopia was not lost to the west" and advised the US and Western countries to "maintain contact with Ethiopia, work with the Government, and offer it economic aid which was the 'weak point' of Soviet assistance."[2] A well-kept secret is that Israel had provided military assistance to Mengistu "almost since the day he seized power." The Israeli military advisors were "secretly invited back by Mengistu in December 1975" after they were asked to leave in 1973. Israel also sold weapons to Ethiopian army.[3]

Israel, it seemed, was concerned not only about the immigration of the Bete Israelis but also about Ethiopia's shift towards the Soviet Union because of inept US foreign policy. Israeli officials also observed that the US "made a big mistake in 1977 when it rebuffed a message from Prime Minister Begin to President Carter to help Ethiopia repeal an invasion from Somalia — forcing Mengistu to turn to the Soviet Union."[4]

Former Sen. Rudy Boschwitz, a Republican from Minnesota and a Holocaust refugee, visited Ethiopia to negotiate the emigration of the Ethiopian Jews to Israel and brokered the agreement on April 24–29, 1991. Sen. Boschwitz was accompanied by Irvin Hicks, Deputy Assistant Secretary of State for Africa, and Robert Frasure, Director of African Affairs in the National Security Council. President George H.W. Bush sent a letter to Col. Mengistu Haile Mariam through Sen. Boschwitz in which he reaffirmed US support for Ethiopia's territorial integrity.[5] This was intended to influence Mengistu to allow the emigration of the Bete Israelis. Bush also thanked Mengistu for his support of the UN Security Council during the Persian Gulf crisis. (In 1990, Ethiopia served on the UN Security Council and supported the US by voting to condemn Iraq's invasion of Kuwait. The vote also called for imposing sanctions against Iraq and authorizing the use of force to eject Iraq from Kuwait. Actually, Colonel Mengistu's government supported Kuwait because Saddam Hussein had threatened Ethiopia's national unity by supporting secessionist forces in Eritrea. This was conveyed to the government of Kuwait and it was alleged that both countries Ethiopia and Kuwait — were victims of Saddam Hussein's policy. The government of Kuwait also provided the Ethiopian government with financial assistance as the latter was short of hard currency.[6])

The emigration of Bete Israel was lobbied by influential organizations. Two American Jewish organizations — the American Association of Ethiopian Jewry (AAEJ) and the North American Conference on Ethiopian Jewry (NACEJ), pressured

---

1 Theodore S. Dagne. June 18, 1991. "Ethiopia: New Thinking in U.S. Policy," *Congressional Research Service*, 91-489 F.

2 Report of a Congressional Study Mission to Israel, Egypt, Sudan, Ethiopia, and Somalia, ibid., p. 2.

3 Jack Anderson. January 2, 1985. "Israel aiding Mengistu in Ethiopia." *The Washington Post*, p. E 19

4 Ibid.

5 Stephen Spector. 2005. *Operation Solomon: The Daring Rescue of the Ethiopian Jews*, New York: Oxford University Press, p. 113.

6 Interview with Ambassador Kassa Kebede.

the American and Israeli governments to help Ethiopian Jews settle in Israel. The Bete Israel settlement in Israel is based on Israel's Law of Return 5710–1950. The law granted settlement to every Jew who expressed his desire to settle in Israel.[1] On May 2, 1991, Mengistu also promised Sen. Boschwitz to speed the emigration of some 18,000 Bete Israelis whose status was in limbo in Ethiopia. This emigration of the Bete Israelis was justified as a family reunion. A few members of Bete Israeli were smuggled in starting in 1979.[2] Gradually, their number increased as Sudanese State Security, CIA and the Israeli Institute for Intelligence and Special Operations (or Mossad) were involved in 1984–85 when Israel airlifted 8,000 Bete Israelis in a clandestine mission named Operation Moses.[3] Sudanese officials, under President Jaffar Al-Nimery, were said to have been bribed to smuggle members of Bete Israel. At that time, President Jaffar Al-Nimery was moving closer to the US and was one of the few Arab leaders to support the Egyptian president Sadat's rapprochement with Israel.[4] Jaffar Al-Nimery, who faced a political and moral dilemma and whose mother's origin is in northwestern Ethiopia,[5] finally acquiesced to the smuggling. The cost of smuggling Bete Israelis during Operation Moses was said to have amounted to $300 million for transportation, resettlement in Israel, and bribing the Sudanese government and others.[6] The money was raised from the "American Jewry or the United States government."[7]

Organizations fighting the *Derg* along the Ethio–Sudanese borders, EPLF, TPLF, and EDU have also benefited from the smuggling of the Bete Israelis. The US embassy in Khartoum coordinated the operation as Israel had no embassy and no diplomatic relations with Sudan, an Arab nation.

President Jaffar Al-Nimery's involvement in the scheme and close association with the US and Israel led to his downfall in 1985. Sudanese Vice-President Omer el Tayeb, who condoned the smuggling of the Bete Israelis out of Sudan to Israel, was also removed from office in a 1985 coup d'état.

The second phase of the Bete Israeli emigration, dubbed Operation Solomon, took place at an important political juncture in Ethiopia, the chaotic period of the downfall of the *Derg* and the ascendance to power of the EPRDF. The US warned the 600-strong American community to leave Ethiopia as the situation remained unpredictable. The US also pressured regional countries such as Egypt, Israel, and Saudi Arabia not to assist the Mengistu regime. Instead, the US extended its support to the EPRDF and the EPLF as they were gaining the upper hand in their war with Ethiopian soldiers.

The highlight of the airlift was on May 24–25, 1991 when Israel transported 18,000 Bete Israelis who were brought from their villages in the Gondar region, in western Ethiopia, to a camp in Addis Ababa. In Operation Solomon more than 35 airplanes made a total of 40 flights. Kassa Kebede, an Ethiopian official who was educated in

---

1 A small number of Bete Israelis began to immigrate to Israel in 1955 after the Law of Return was passed in 1950.

2 Stephen Spector, ibid., p. 33.

3 Asher Naim. 2003. *Saving the Lost Tribe: The Rescue and redemption of the Ethiopian Jews*, New York: Balantine Books, pp 9-10.

4 Ahmed Karadawi, "The smuggling of the Ethiopian Falasha to Israel through Sudan, 1991," *African Affairs*, vol. 90, p. 27.

5 Teshome G. Wagaw. 1993. *For Our Soul: Ethiopian Jews in Israel*, Detroit: Wayne State University Press, p. 63.

6 Ibid., 48.

7 Ibid.

Israel and studied Hebrew education at Ulpan Akiva, played a major role in broker-ing the immigration of the Bete Israelis. As he was closely associated with the *Derg*, he felt insecure in Ethiopia's post-military regime and left *incognito* for Israel on the last flight of Operation Solomon. He is now settled in the United States.

On May 29, 1991, the Israeli government acknowledged payment to the Ethio-pian government (the *Derg*) of $35 million to support the Bete Israel emigration. In an interview, Kassa Kebede told me that he believes that the money was designated to be used as a payment to the Ethiopian airlines to cover the airfare of the Bete Israelis.[1] But as the Ethiopian Airlines did not have enough airplanes to airlift all the Bete Israelis, Israel provided forty-one military and El Al aircraft free of charge.[2] The State Department deposited $35 million in an Ethiopian government account in the Fed-eral Reserve Bank in New York.[3] The source of the fund is unknown although some believed it to have come from the US and Israeli governments and American Jew-ish groups in the United States. After the fall of the *Derg*, Ethiopia's Prime Minister Tamirat Layne initially declined the funds. Robert G. Houdek, US Chargé d'Affaires (August 1988 to June 1991), encouraged the President of the Ethiopian Transitional Government (ETG), Meles Zenawi, to accept the unclaimed money.[4] The ETG even-tually inherited the money by default. However, it was reported that the Ethiopian Airlines did not receive the funds nor was it deposited in the Ethiopian national bank. Knowledgeable sources say that the money went to the ruling party, the TPLF.

Some Ethiopians were opposed to the process in which the Bete Israelis were smuggled or airlifted, questioned the financial transaction, called it a modern form of slavery, and raised questions about the abuse of the human rights of the Ethiopian Israelis in Israel.

After the demise of both the Cold War and the military regime in Ethiopia in 1991, the US rushed not only to support the TPLF/EPRDF but also to give it all the assis-tance it needed to once again put the Ethio–US relationship on track. The US was eager to gain its lost position in Ethiopia and apparently would have supported any regime that appeared acceptable and was willing to promote the US interest.

As for the Bete Israeli settlement and their predicament in Israel, their numbers have grown to about 100,000 and there have been complaints about discrimination, under achievement in education, inadequate housing, low-paying jobs, and a rising suicide rate.[5] A high rate of domestic violence was also reported. The State Control-ler's Office in June 2008 reported that 65% of Ethiopian Jews are on some kind of wel-fare assistance, 11% of those in battered women's shelters are Ethiopian-Israelis, and that Ethiopian-Israeli youths have problems with alcohol and drug abuse. According to the report, governments at the local and national levels have failed in dealing with the social needs of the Ethiopian-Israelis.[6]

The following incident has captured Israeli national attention. Investigative journalist Ronald Fischer reported in *Maariv*, a Hebrew daily, on January 24, 1996,

1 This information was corroborated in an interview between the author and Ambassador Kassa Kebede.

2 Stephen Spector, *Operation* Solomon, ibid., p. 175.

3 Asher Naim, ibid., p. 237.

4 Stephen Spector, ibid., pp. 187–188.

5 See Teshome Wagaw. 1993. *For Our Soul: Ethiopian Jews in Israel*, Detroit, Michigan: Wayne State University Press.

6 Yaron Druckman. May 21, 2008. "State gets failing grade on Ethiopian immigration," *Israel Culture*, http://www.ynet.co.il/english/article0,7340,L-3545844,00.htm

that the blood bank administered by Magen David Adom (MDA), meaning "The Red Shield of David," an Israeli equivalent of the Red Cross and Red Crescent Societies, overseen by the Israeli Ministry of Health, had destroyed blood donated by the Ethiopian-Israelis. The reason given was that there were high rates of infection of HIV-AB, malaria, and hepatitis-B among the Bete Israelis. The accusation failed to convince the Bete Israelis, although the blood was not discarded on the spot.[1] The Bete Israelis, 10,000 strong, previously perceived as a quiet and reserved community, demonstrated against discarding their donated blood, which they saw as a racist practice that had been going on from 1984 to 1996. The demonstration turned into a violent encounter with the police and sixty-one people were injured, including forty-one police officers.[2] The Bete Israelis were joined by their compatriots, the Ethiopian Orthodox monks in Jerusalem, who came "bearing an Ethiopian flag in an effort to make common cause."[3] Palestinian-Israelis and other Israelis also sympathized with the Ethiopian-Israelis and joined them in the demonstration.

The incident led Prime Minister Shimon Peres to establish a commission, named after former president of Israel Yitzhak Navon, to investigate the spilling of blood donated by the Bete Israelis. The commission consisted of several prominent Israelis and two members of the Bete Israel. The commission found many flaws in the decision-making process in the Ministry of Health and the Blood Bank.[4]

The assimilation of Bete Israel into Israeli society has been uneasy. Both the Israelis and the Ethiopian-Israelis faced something unexpected. The Israeli community had never been exposed to a large influx of Africans and there has been an underlying factor of racism. For most of the Ethiopian-Israelis, this was their first encounter with a predominantly white community and racism. The parties involved in transplanting the Bete Israel to their new home, the US and the Israeli governments, did not concern themselves with studying issues of acculturation or the Ethiopian identity living side by side with the Israeli identity, a multilayered, multicultural, and multiethnic Israel. Their main concern was the transfer of the Bete Israel to a new home, primarily to increase the Jewish population of Israel in response to a high Arab birth rate. The birth rates for Israeli Arabs is estimated to be among the highest in the world --- four or five children per family as compared to two or three children per Israeli Jewish families. Besides the concern with demographics, Israeli officials were trying to demonstrate to the world, especially to African countries, that it is not a racist state. For the Bete Israel as well as some Jews in other countries, the immigration of the Ethiopian Jews is a fulfillment of the biblical prophecy of the return of all Jews to Zion. Whatever the reason for the immigration of Bete Israelis to Israel might be, both Israel and its new citizens must work together to resolve their conflicts. The Israeli government has trained Bete Israelis for military service and its law enforcement units. Fewer than half a dozen Bete Israelis are posted in Israeli consulates in Africa, including Ethiopia and the United States. Bete Israelis are encouraged to give up their Ethiopian and adopt Jewish names.

---

1 Don Seeman. June 1999. "One People, One Blood": Public Health, Political Violence, and HIV in an Ethiopian-Israeli Setting," *Culture, Medicine and Psychiatry*, vol. 23, no 2, p. 159.

2 Ibid., pp. 159-162.

3 Ibid., p. 163.

4 Israel Ministry of Foreign Affairs. July 29, 1996. "Summary of Navon commission report on blood donations by Ethiopian immigrants," in www.mfa.gov.il/MFA/Archive/Communiques/1996/SUMMARY+O...AVON+COMMISSION+REPORT+ON+BLOOD+DONATI.htm?

THE RISE OF THE EPRDF AND THE US ROLE

The TPLF was established in February 1975. It was a small guerrilla band that operated in the Tigray province.[1] Currently it controls the government of Ethiopia. TPLF is the core of EPRDF, which was formed by merging the Ethiopian People's Democratic Movement (EPDM) with the TPLF at the latter's third congress in Tigre, March 10–13, 1989.[2] In order to widen its base and improve its image from that of a secessionist force to a national one, the TPLF created an alliance of ethnic-based groups from government troops captured in the fight against them and against the EPLF. It then created the Ethiopian People's Democratic Revolutionary Force (EPRDF). Though the TPLF grew up on a secessionist, anti-imperialist, and Marxist ideology, it went in a different direction, supported by the US, and came to power after a protracted war with the military regime. A "peace conference" that was held in London gave diplomatic legitimacy to the TPLF/EPRDF and the EPLF as they assumed power in Ethiopia and Eritrea.

Let us examine how the TPLF/EPRDF finally assumed power and legitimized its authority through a US-backed "peace conference."

THE LONDON PEACE CONFERENCE (MAY 26–28, 1991) AND THE US ROLE

The armed rebels with their secessionist agenda, the Eritrean People's Liberation Front (EPLF), Tigre People's Liberation Front (TPLF), a core of the EPRDF, and Oromo Liberation Front (OLF), met in London on May 27, 1991. General Tesfaye Gebre-Kidan, who replaced the exiled Col. Mengistu, had expressed his willingness to negotiate with the rebels through the United States. The Ethiopian government was represented by Prime Minister Tesfaye Dinka at the London conference. The US proposed a plan of action to facilitate the conference. That plan of action includes the following:

1. A transitional government would be composed of all political groups, including exiles;
2. Free elections would be held within one year;
3. A general cease-fire would prevail;
4. All parties would support emergency relief activates;
5. All existing administrative controls, whether government or insurgent, would remain in place; and
6. The Eritrea issue would be postponed.[3]

Officially, the EPLF indicated that it would cooperate only with an Ethiopian government that agreed to grant the independence of the province of Eritrea after a referendum process. Some delegates who were at the conference revealed later that the EPLF leader, Issayas Afewerki, agonized over secession as he believed it would be to Eritrea's interest to remain with Ethiopia in a federal relationship. It is said that for fear of creating dissention within the EPLF and the Eritrean diaspora, on whose fi-

---

1 Aregawi Berhe. 2004. "The origins of the Tigray People's Liberation Front." *African Affairs*, vol 103 no 413, Royal African Society, p. 569. The author of this article, Aregawi Berhe, was one of the individuals who started the TPLF.

2 Tigre People's Liberation Front (TPLF) was formed in 1975 by transforming Tigre National Organization (TNO) which was established in 1972 to wage a struggle for "self-determination and liberation." Refer to an earlier publication, TPLF Foreign Relations Bureau, "The general situation in Tigray," November 1982.

3 Herman J. Cohen, ibid., *Intervening in Africa- Superpower Peacemaking in a Troubled Continent*, p. 46.

---

nancial contribution the EPLF depended, the idea of giving up the secession of Eritrea was dropped. According to Dima Noggo Sarbo, one who participated at the London conference under US auspices, "whether by design or carelessness, the Eritrean question was never even raised as an important political issue." I believe US officials fully understood the gravity of the situation to both the US and Ethiopia and the Eritrean case should have not been kept on the backburner. On the other hand, according to Dima, the TPLF, EPLF, and OLF met in Massawa and Meles Zenawi told him that Issayas had been told by the US to join the transitional government. It was with that understanding that the OLF joined the TGE.[1] But Issayas reneged and remained out of the TGE. Nevertheless, some believed that the TPLF, under Meles Zenawi, was not willing to agree to a competing organization, the EPLF, gaining leadership within Ethiopia's framework and assiduously worked for the secession of Eritrea.

Later, after Eritrea gained its independence, the border war between the two countries that claimed 100,000 lives in 1998 was caused in part by the personality clash between the two leaders. Nevertheless, the secession of Eritrea was already a foregone conclusion as, according to the majority of Ethiopians, the three secessionist organizations had reached an agreement to that end. Both TPLF and OLF, secessionist organizations, were supported and abetted by the EPLF and were committed to Eritrea's secession. Hence the cooperation of the three secessionist rebel groups with whom the US had been closely associated. Other multi-ethnic political groups that espoused a united and democratic Ethiopia were excluded from the London conference.

The US Assistant Secretary for African Affairs, Herman J. Cohen, chaired the 1991 London conference. Tecola W. Hagos, who advised the EPRDF on the London peace conference to set the Transitional Government of Ethiopia, in his response to my written questions, stated that the "US played the role of facilitator, taskmaster, patron, boss — all in one." According to Tecola, the US provided funding for expenses and allowed TPLF (EPRDF) participants to travel freely to the United States. "Most importantly it was instrumental in easing all restrictions imposed on Ethiopians for travel within the European Union or NATO Member nations."

Tecola stated that the London Conference was a farce. At the very best, the government of the United States was taken for a ride by the leaders of the EPRDF. Some criticized Herman J. Cohen for his ineptness and unwise decision and believed that the whole problem was far too complex for him. Tecola even commented that "the EPRDF and EPLF leaders were far too sophisticated post-modern thinkers for Herman Cohen's traditional rustic diplomacy." The US was eager to see the fall of the Mengistu regime but seems not to have a vision for the long-term destiny of Ethiopia. Such short sightedness has contributed to the death of thousands and to the general instability in the region.

The US then resumed the active role that it had dropped during 17 years of military government in Ethiopia. At that conference, the destiny of Ethiopia fell to the US to determine. Because of Cohen's active role in the London conference, his ties to the new government, and his disparaging statements about those opposed to the ethnic-based government and the secession of Eritrea, some Ethiopians called the London conference "Cohen's Coup." Herman Cohen convinced the Ethiopian delegation to sign a cease-fire and allow the rebels to enter Addis Ababa in order to help "stabilize

---

1 Dima Noggo Serbo. 2007. "The Ethiopia-Eritrea conflict: Short sighted solutions and long-term problems." The University of Tenneesse, Knoxville. Unpublished article. I appreciate Dima for sharing the article wit me.

the situation." President Tesfaye Gebre-Kidan assented to Cohen's plan and ordered all government troops to lay down their arms. In his book, Herman J. Cohen stated that he recognized the enmity he earned from many Ethiopians who accused him of "handing over the city of Addis to the TPLF's dictatorial rule."[1]

Prime Minister Tesfaye Dinka, who led the government delegation and attended the London conference, strongly opposed this new arrangement. He also asked for guarantees of safety for the *Derg*'s officials. As an experienced and highly educated official, he was respected by the United States. When the rebels entered Addis Ababa, he found his team marginalized and ineffective and pulled the Ethiopian delegation from the London conference. The delegation immigrated to the United States. While this measure comes as a surprise to some of Tesfaye Dinka's delegation, a few delegates had already brought out their families in the anticipation of the possibility of the failure of the London conference to protect Ethiopia's long-term strategic interest.

Dima Noggo Serbo of the OLF suggested in an interview that the US should have convened the London Conference earlier, before the Ethiopian troops were in disarray. That could have given the Ethiopian government some leverage for negotiation. Dima also faults Prime Minister Tesfaye Dinka's delegation for refusing to talk to the OLF when it was contacted by the OLF to discuss issues of mutual interest. According to Dima, the *Derg* government had a simplistic view, labeling OLF a separatist organization funded by the EPLF which was also denigrated by the EPLF and the TPLF.

According to my communication with Dr. Beyene Petros, Member of the Ethiopian Parliament and university professor, it was not possible for the guerrilla forces and the government to reach an accord at the London Peace Conference as the EPRDF and the EPLF "out-maneuvered the US facilitators." According to another opposition leader and member of the Ethiopian Parliament, Dr. Merera Gudina, who is also university professor, the US role at the London Conference was that of a peace broker. The US should be blamed for its "eagerness to preside over the death of Mengistu's regime. Much of the blame for the failure of the London Peace Conference should go to the two cousins, Meles and Issayas, who [had] sealed their deal long before the London meeting." [2] Indications are that the US wanted to preserve the unity of Ethiopia and see that the "Eritrean issue is postponed," which is a vague statement. The head of the US delegation, Herman Cohen, was hoodwinked by the guerrilla fighters. Another person who chose to remain anonymous said that the TPLF/EPRDF was intent on seeing a separate Eritrea.

Thus, the TPLF/EPRDF and the EPLF were not forthright in dealing with the US delegates at the London Peace Conference. Herman Cohen followed a conventional method of peace conference in unconventional environment and where the two rebel groups only know a zero-sum game. The Ethiopian delegation had no leverage as the government in Ethiopia was collapsing. The Ethiopian opposition in the diaspora, The Coalition of Ethiopian Democratic Forces (COEDEF), was also purposely marginalized and was not allowed to attend the conference. After the Transitional Government of Ethiopia (TGE) was established in 1991, a peace conference was called in Ethiopia in 1993 by opposition organizations. Members of the COEDEF delegations were arrested on their arrival at the airport. The other opposition groups, such as the

---

1 Ibid., p. 49.

2 I appreciate Members of Parliament (MPS) Beyene Petros and Merera Gudina for responding to my queries.

Ethiopian Democratic Union (EDU) and the Ethiopian People's Democratic Alliance (EPDA), became "useless in the political equation" according to Merera Gudina. The US supported these two conservative organizations against the *Derg*, but they failed to live up to the US expectation. The US was compelled to stick with the TPLF/EPRDF. It was the only organization that promised to advance and protect the US interest. Ethiopia's national interest seemed to be secondary.

Ethiopia's veteran human rights activist, currently a member of a political party, Professor Mesfin Wolde Mariam, who attended the London Peace Conference as a private observer, stated during a Congressional hearing: "[t]he expectation of all Ethiopians was that the London Negotiation, under the chairmanship of the Assistant Secretary for African Affairs, Mr. Herman Cohen, would be able to negotiate a peace plan for a new, democratic and unified Ethiopia. There were no negotiations in London. The process broke down during the preliminary meetings, before all parties met together even once. The government delegation's press release called it 'back-door deals' and the Oromo Liberation Front (OLF) declared that the negotiations had died before they even started."[1] Commenting on this, Tecola Hagos declared that there was no meeting whatsoever between the Ethiopian government representatives, the EPRDF, and the EPLF leaders. No meeting anywhere, not even in some hidden grotto. Herman Cohen was talking to each group separately trying to work out some parameters of understanding to start the negotiation.

New Powers in Addis Ababa and in Asmara

On May 24, 1991, the EPLF had entered Asmara, four days later the TPLF/EPRDF entered Addis Ababa. Before entering Addis Ababa, TPLF/EPRDF leader, Meles Zenawi, pledged to set up a new democratic government comprising all political factions, and declared that his organization would govern Ethiopia until a "broad-based" government was formed later in the year. Herman Cohen stated that the US aid to Ethiopia was contingent upon the state of human rights, and said no democracy meant no foreign assistance. Such statements by government officials are mere rhetoric unless backed by executive order or congressional legislation. As will eventually be witnessed, foreign assistance increased despite the sorry state of democracy in Ethiopia. Meles promised that the two other rebel organizations, EPLF and OLF, and other organizations that had no armies, would be invited to a conference. The conference was scheduled to take place no later than July 1, 1991, and would devise a transitional coalition government.

Once it entered Addis Ababa, the TPLF/EPRDF rejected a cease-fire and reneged on its promise to work with the *Derg* members. The TPLF/EPRDF leadership dismissed the government of President Tesfaye Gebre-Kidan as being part and parcel of Mengistu's regime. The TPLF/EPRDF's pronouncement was despite the good-gesture release of 180 political prisoners by Tesfaye's government. TPLF/EPRDF also stormed the presidential palace to assert its power and reign over the palace guards who were opposed to surrendering the palace to rebels they considered illegitimate. Meanwhile, Tesfaye Gebre-Kidan slipped out of the palace on May 31 and took refuge in the Italian embassy. Other high-ranking *Derg* officials who took refuge in the Italian embassy were General Addis Tedla, Chief of Staff of the Armed Forces, Ato Hailu Yemenu, Deputy Prime Minister, and Colonel Berhanu Baye, Vice President of Council of States. While the demise of the *Derg* comes as welcome to most Ethiopi-

---

1 Mesfin Wolde Mariam. June 18, 1991. Congressional Hearing, "The political crisis in Ethiopia and the role of the US," p. 31.

ans, there were mixed feelings towards the TPLF and EPLF leadership. Some were not convinced that the TPLF would give up its Marxist ideology and were opposed to the idea of Eritrean secession. Others were open to the idea of a free and fair vote on a referendum in which all parties would be included in a democratic process. Still others felt that any government that succeeded the *Derg* would be better than the military regime.

In order to appease the public and the international community, especially the US, on whom Meles relied for legitimacy, he reversed some of Mengistu's policies and legacies. For example, he declared that TPLF had abandoned its Marxist principles and invited back relief workers to the Tigre region where their activities had been hampered by the war. Furthermore, Meles promised a free press, demobilized the army, and drastically reduced the defense budget. In order to prove its pro-West stance and show that it is not a follower of Marxism, the TPLF/EPRDF tore down the 33-foot bronze statue of Lenin, a gift from North Korea. Meles also readily declared his support for the independence of Eritrea, without any input from the Ethiopian people or from Eritreans who have a differing opinion about the secession of Eritrea. On May 29, 1991, Issayas Afewerki of EPLF announced that he would form a separate provisional government for Eritrea, as he would not be part of Ethiopia's transitional government but would cooperate with it.

Issayas, however, reneged on his statement of the previous day that he would join a transitional government in Addis Ababa and said that the EPLF had not fought for a mere cabinet position. This statement provoked a demonstration in Addis Ababa by those opposed to what they saw as the possible dismemberment of Ethiopia. The US was also targeted for its support of that dismemberment. The Egyptian UN secretary general, Butros Butros Gali, also supported Eritrea's secession.

Addis Ababa University students demonstrated against what TPLF and EPLF had concocted. Both organizations thus faced their first bloody encounter with the demonstrators, fired live ammunition that killed students, and banned any demonstration. This measure was against the background of an earlier statement by Meles that Ethiopia would be a democratic and united country where force has no room, but only the expressed will of the various peoples would prevail. Furthermore, Meles stated that the country would be involved in building wealth for everybody, rather than making endless wars. As time tells, his government soon proved to be undemocratic, curtailing civil liberties and free speech, and Meles is called an enemy of the free press. Within a few years the honeymoon between TPLF, OLF and EPLF ended. They began to disagree and fought among themselves. The OLF, which joined the Transitional Government of Ethiopia (TGE) as a junior member, pulled out, complaining that the general elections (1992) had been rigged.

In such a contentious "peace conference" and absence of democracy and transparency, the EPRDF presided over the dismantling of Ethiopia, thus resulting in the secession of Eritrea from Ethiopia. The EPRDF, along with the US government, is blamed by Ethiopians for being a party to the scheme that allowed the secession of Eritrea through a questionable and one-sided referendum that denied Ethiopia an outlet to the sea. The first UN-sponsored referendum on Eritrea in the 1952, wherein the US supported the unity of Ethiopia and Eritrea, led to a federal relationship with Ethiopia. Various groups had the opportunity to express their stands and garner public support. Among the different groups, the unionists — who wanted unity with

Ethiopia — carried the day.[1] The second UN-sponsored referendum in 1993 was completely different. Eritreans voted on "independence" or "slavery" only, thus denying them other choices as had been accorded to them during the previous referendum.

In Ethiopia, the new government claims to be democratic, to subscribe to a market economy, to be pro-US, to help fight terrorism and to serve as a strong US ally in an increasingly volatile region. Similar to what went on during the imperial period until 1974, the post-military regime tries to prove that it is loyal to the United States. It has joined the US financed and sponsored African Crisis Response Initiative (ACRI), which is a peacekeeping alliance for African countries. It has also readily adopted World Bank and IMF-sponsored Structural Adjustment Programs (SAP), though they are believed to implement harsh economic measures that have increasingly become oppressive to the poor while benefiting the ruling oligarchy and its foreign partners.

After the September 11, 2001, terrorist attack on the US, the interests of Ethiopia and the US increasingly converged in the fight against Islamists in Somalia, namely Al-Ittihad al-Islami (Islamic Union). Al-Ittihad, established in the 1980s, alleged to be closely associated with the al-Qaeda of Osama bin Laden, had previously attacked Ethiopia and the government claims that it is responsible for bombings in Addis Ababa. The EPRDF also believed that the National Islamic Front (NIF) of Hassan Abdullah al-Turabi of Sudan supported Islamic fundamentalists against Ethiopia in the 1990s.[2] This stand of anti-terrorism, the claimed adoption of a neo-liberal economic policy, and the subscription to globalization by Ethiopia's government perfectly fit the post-Cold War paradigm shift and purports to protect US interests in an increasingly unstable region.

The US support for the post-Mengistu regime remains a contentious issue as the US continues to support a regime that has failed to marshal the support of the majority of the people. Prime Minister Meles Zenawi, for example, is hardly seen in public and lives in virtual seclusion from the people that he claims to represent. Ethiopians see him as arrogant, showing no respect for them but successful in charming foreigners. He also provides westerners with conflicting information in which his words fail to match his actions. Similar to what went on in the Cold War era, the US is actively supporting unpopular regimes: leaders who alienate their citizens and outsmart foreign powers who are interested in quick fix and a short-term agenda. In the name of democracy and privatization, the US has continued aligning with leaders who work against the interests of the majority of their people and aggrandize themselves through corruption and the embezzlement of government funds.[3] Such conditions are bound to erupt in crisis. Democracy and stability remain elusive.

---

1 Shumet Sishagne. 2007. *Unionists and Separatists*, Hollywood, CA: Tesahi Publishers, pp. 51-80. Also refer to Zewde Reta. 2000. *Ye Eritrea Gudie, 1941–1963, (The Eritrean Case)*, Addis Ababa, Ethiopia: Central Printing Press, pp. 334-343.

2 Robert I. Rotberg, ed. 2005. *Battling Terrorism in the Horn of Africa*, Washington, DC: Brookings Institution press and Cambridge, Mass.: World Peace Foundation, p. 101.

3 Refer to Theodore M. Vestal. 1999. *Ethiopia: A Post-Cold War African State*, Westport, Connecticut: Praeger Publishers, pp. 173-182. Also refer to Assefa Negash. 1996. *The Pillage of Ethiopia by Eritreans and their Tigrean Surrogates*, Los Angeles, CA: Adey Publishing. In addition, refer to Bogale Assefaw. 2004. *Ye Hizbawe Woyane Harenet Tegrai ina ye Ihadeg ye negd empire* (The TPLF's and the EPRDF's Business Monopolies), Addis Ababa, Ethiopia: Commercial Printing Press.

CHAPTER 10. THE SECESSION OF ERITREA (1993) AND US INVOLVEMENT

In the 1970s, besides the Somali aggression against Ethiopia, another concern of the US was the secessionist movement in Ethiopia's province of Eritrea. According to the Carter Doctrine, the US policy was to refrain from military involvement in the internal affairs of another country. Military involvement, however, was justified if US security was at stake. The interpretation of this policy seems to be open-ended, as defining US security remains at the discretion of the president and the US Congress. In the 1970s, when the Eritrean secessionists received support from Arab countries and the military regime in Ethiopia received Soviet military equipment and advisors, the White House opted not to become directly involved in Ethiopia's internal affairs.

US officials had repeatedly stated that the US policy in Ethiopia, in the 1970s, was to respect the territorial integrity of Ethiopia and to support the goal of a negotiated settlement in Eritrea — leading to a federal arrangement similar to what had been implemented earlier by the UN in 1952. Conservative regional powers such as Saudi Arabia and Iran, during the reign of Shah Palavi, also believed in Ethiopia as a viable nation-state and wished to see a united Ethiopia that would contribute to regional stability. It was in the interest of conservative Saudi Arabia to have a neighbor that radical Arab countries could not control.

Eritrea's secessionist organization, the Eritrean People's Liberation Front (EPLF) under the leadership of Issayas Afewerki, reached dominance after routing the predominantly Muslim-dominated Eritrean Liberation Front (ELF). The ELF was supported by radical Arab states such as Iraq and this concerned the conservative leaders of Saudi Arabia and some Ethiopians. Later, the governor of the province of Eritrea, Ras Assrate Kassa, allegedly supported Issayas Afewerki, a Christian highland Eritrean who has a strong pro-Ethiopia family background. Both his parents come from the Ethiopian province of Tigre. Issayas Afewerki's uncle, Dejazmach Solomon Abraham, was the governor of Wollo province and Issayas had stayed with his uncle and attended high school in Dessie, the capital of Wollo, prior to attending engineering college in Addis Ababa.

Most Eritreans, especially highlanders, backed Issayas. They also had strong lineage in Ethiopia and saw him as a forceful leader who would counter the lowland Muslim Eritreans who were opposed to unity with Ethiopia in the 1960s and were supported by Arab states. The ELF, supported by radical Arab states, eliminated Christians from its own ranks and sought to convert the Red Sea into an "Arab lake." Issayas left the ELF and organized the predominantly Christian EPLF with a moderate Muslim, Usman Salah Sabe. Issayas exploited the historical suspicion between lowland Muslims and highland Christians who were pro-Ethiopia and seemed to have worked for the unity of the two countries.[1] The Ethiopian government also saw EPLF as moderate, compared to the extremist ELF, and felt that it served as a counterbalance to the latter. Ras Assrate Kassa, the governor of Eritrea, also wanted Christian Eritreans to play an active role within EPLF.[2] The ELF was eventually decimated by EPLF with indirect support from the Ethiopian government.[3] The TPLF also supported the EPLF in its effort to annihilate ELF.

The CIA is also alleged to have recruited Issayas Afewerki, who was considered to be a moderate with an ambition for leadership. According to Tesfa Michael Giorgio, the governor of the Dekemahre district in Eritrea during Emperor Haile Selassie's rule, CIA operatives at Kagnew Station managed to have Issayas work for them to protect American interests. In exchange, Issayas was given, according to Tesfa Michael, American armaments and clandestine support.[4]

The US felt that the Muslim-dominated ELF worked against the American and Israeli interests as it was close to radical Arab states. The CIA also concluded that Haile Selassie's government was shaky and could be replaced by a military regime (as there were no viable civilian organized groups) whose pro-US stance might be doubtful. The Arab supported-and-backed ELF threatened Issayas when he started his own organization, namely *Selfi Netsanit*. *Selfi Netsanit* needed support and US weapons, and Issayas was said to have presented himself to the CIA operatives as a pro-West and moderate force. Later, encouraged by the CIA operative, and because of his own ambition, Issayas dropped his pro-Ethiopia stance, and availed his service to furthering American interests and countering the predominantly Muslim ELF.

During the military regime, in a symposium in Massawa, Tesfa Michael Georgio stated that he had first-hand knowledge of the relationship between Issayas and the CIA, as he was involved in their rendezvous. At that time the US was concerned about the security of American citizens and its interests in Ethiopia, in the Red Sea region and the eastern coast of Eritrea, such as the Kagnew military communication station in Asmara. US concern was heightened after the Palestinian Black September Organization (BSO) threatened US interests in the region. On March 1, 1973, the group attacked the Saudi embassy in Khartoum and assassinated US diplomats at a reception. At the same time, the government of Emperor Haile Selassie was becoming unstable. Issayas was fighting for the independence of Eritrea from Ethiopia and had connections with anti-American circles in the region; meanwhile Issayas needed US

---

1 Tekeste Negash. 1997. *Eritrea and Ethiopia: The Federal Experience*, New Brunswick, NJ: Transaction Publishers, p. 156.

2 Haggai Erlich. 1983. *The Struggle Over Eritrea, 1962-78. War and Revolution in the Horn of Africa*, Stanford, CA: Stanford University Press, pp. 38-39.

3 For some of the allegations, refer to Dawit Wolde Giorgis. 2006. *Kehidet Bedem Meret*, Fredericksburg, VA: Aesop Publishers, pp. 302-305.

4 Tesfa Michael Giorgio revealed the EPLF connections to the CIA. This revelation originally appeared as an article, "CIA and EPLF at Kagnew Station," *Senai*, 1993.

military, economic, and diplomatic support. Hence, they collaborated to protect and further each other's interests.[1]

Issayas had also established a clandestine liaison with Ras Assrate Kassa, the governor of Eritrea from 1963 to 1973. Ras Assrate was an ambitious governor and a claimant to the throne of Ethiopia. He saw Issayas as a counter force to the predominantly Muslim ELF, launched in 1961 with the support of Egypt and other radical Arab countries such as Syria and Iraq. Issayas was seen as a moderate force. Ras Assrate's scheme and his tactical strategy were also shared by the CIA operatives and counterinsurgency experts in Asmara.[2]

This plan took place despite Ethiopia's close relationship with the US and its initial support for the unity of Ethiopia and Eritrea. The contention that the CIA supported EPLF clandestinely is plausible as the agency has its own institutional mindset and operation that at times undermines the diplomatic efforts of the State Department. The head of Ethiopia's secret service's foreign operations section, General Daniel Mengistu, reported that Issayas had worked clandestinely with Ethiopia's governor in Eritrea, Ras Assrate Kassa, and with Ethiopia's secret service.[3]

Tesfa Michael Giorgio, who had facilitated the meeting between CIA operatives and Issayas, revealed the CIA's covert action in supporting secessionist groups in Ethiopia. After the fall of the military regime in 1991, Issayas controlled Eritrea and also had a free hand in Ethiopia, Tesfa Michael Giorgio paid the ultimate price. He was assassinated in Addis Ababa. Kidnapping and assassination of vocal pro-Ethiopian Eritreans and members of the Eritrean opposition, and defectors residing in Ethiopia, was an open secret until the fallout between EPLF and TPLF in 1998. It was also reported that the EPLF run its own prison cell in Addis Ababa.

During the Marxist military regime Issayas opposed Ethiopia and the USSR alliance. He believed that Ethiopia would use military assistance from the USSR to squash the struggle for the secession of Eritrea. The stand of Issayas against the USSR further aligned him with the United States. "The enemy of my enemy is my friend." By continuously condemning the USSR and alleging not to be a Marxist, Issayas worked to prove to the US that he was pro-West and in this case pro-United States.[4] Issayas thus exploited the situation by appearing to be a pro-US ally who posed no threat to the conservative regional Arab states such as Saudi Arabia. Such were the geopolitics of the region in the 1970s.[5]

In the early years of the Carter administration, Ambassador Andrew Young, the US representative to the UN, argued that Africans were nationalists and would not easily ally with the USSR. Later on, however, the opinion of National Security Advisor Zbigniew Brzezinski dominated the thinking of the Carter administration, especially after Ethiopia got much closer to the USSR, started receiving military supplies, and signed the USSR Declaration of Basic Principles.[6]

---

1 Tesfa Michael Georgio. 1974. "Ye tegentayochna ye CIA genugenet" or "The Relationship between separatists and the CIA" in *Massawa Symposium*, Government printing press, Asmara.

2 Ibid.

3 This was an account given by Ethiopia's head of intelligence, General Daniel Mengistu, "Issayas Afewerki was our agent," *Menelik*, March 2001, p. 4.

4 Tesfatsion Medhanie. 1986. *Eritrea: Dynamics of a National Question*, Amsterdam, Holland: B.R. Gruner Publishing, Co., p. 90.

5 Tesfatsion Medhanie. Ibid., p. 41.

6 Ibid., p. 86.

Research based on declassified documents of Zbigniew Brzezinski at the Carter Presidential Library in Atlanta, Georgia, on the other hand, indicates that the Carter Administration had originally taken a pro-Ethiopian stand on Eritrea. The Eritrean case indicates that the US Executive Branch, the Department of Defense (DoD), the State Department and the CIA at times promote contradictory policies.

Accordingly, Zbigniew Brzezinski's memorandum to President Carter on March 27, 1978, provided the President with three alternatives for policy considerations regarding the US policy on Eritrea.

1. Keep a distance from the whole problem — essentially a continuation of what had been done for a long time;

2. Work actively for a negotiated solution, encouraging the Saudis, Sudanese and others to reduce their support for the insurgents;

3. Encourage greater support for the insurgents so as to make the Ethiopian–Soviet–Cuban fight more costly and increase tension between the Ethiopians and the Soviets and Cubans.[1]

The Secretaries of Defense and State favored the first option but with more active encouragement for a negotiated solution or at least a strong declaration on their part that would signal their favoring it. The CIA's view was that a military solution in Eritrea would not be easy for the Ethiopians, even with Soviet support. That meant that there would be an impasse in the war and that would not benefit the United States. Brzezinski indicated in his memo that he would like to see that Soviets and Cubans, if they did join in, paid a high price for their support of a military solution in Eritrea. The Soviets and Cubans, however, continuously stated that they were not interested in sending troops to Eritrea. Unlike the case of the Somali aggression, the conflict with Eritrea was seen as a domestic one. The logical solution in Eritrea, according to Brzezinski, was a negotiated one, though he questioned the possibility in the face of Mengistu's intransigence.

President Carter added a fourth choice, to "support a negotiated solution more strongly, and [provide] repeated public statements deploring violence and foreign military involvement. Let any foreign assistance to insurgents continue without our involvement."[2] In general, the official US policy towards Eritrea in the 1970s was as follows:

a) Maintain a hands-off policy towards the conflict in Eritrea;

b) Turn a blind eye to Sudanese and Arab support of Eritreans;

c) Continue to avoid contact with Eritrean secessionists and, while deploring the loss of life, make it clear that the US favored whatever solution could be worked out between the Ethiopian Provisional Military Government (EPMG) and Eritreans.

For a while, the US indirectly supported Eritrean secessionists by way of pro-US Arab states and also extended covert support to conservative Ethiopian forces, such as the EDU, against the military regime. That was intended to encourage, according to US officials, the military government to pressure the USSR and Cuba for more active involvement in Eritrea. That would be too costly for the latter two and give legitimacy to any official support the US might extend to moderate Eritrean forces. Brzezinski believed that the US had to increase the costs to the Soviet Union of its engagement in Ethiopia. The US was, all along, deeply concerned about the Soviet

---

1 From Zbigniew Brzezinski collections, the Carter Presidential Library, Meeting of SCC 50:1/9/78 through meetings SCC 100:8/10/78, box #28.

2 Policy choice written by President Carter in response to a memo by Zbigniew Brzezinski. April 7, 1978. Carter Presidential Library, box # 28.

airlift of military equipment to Ethiopia. The US thus instructed its ambassadors in most countries "to make a high-level approach to their host governments to express the gravity of US concern about the sharp increase in the Soviet presence in Ethiopia."[1] The use of a third source of pressure, the pro-US Arab states' support for the Eritreans, was a tactical measure Brzezinski preferred. It was aimed at the Soviet Union and Cuba in order to weaken them and especially to increase the costs to the Soviet Union for its involvement in Ethiopia.

The Arab countries' support for Eritrea heightened Mengistu's suspicion of those countries. Most Ethiopians, rightly or wrongly, believe some Muslim and Arab countries hold a historical animosity towards Ethiopia dating back to 1541 when a Muslim Somali leader, Ahmed ibn Ibrahim (Gragn Mohammad), supported by Turkey, attacked Christians and burned churches, monasteries, religious icons and manuscripts. In the 1950s, President Gamal Abdul Nasser of Egypt assiduously tried to undermine the unity of Ethiopia in his drive to create a pan-Arab and a pan-Muslim politico-religious force. He was instrumental in the birth of the Eritrean Liberation Front (ELF).

During World War II, fascist Italy also tried to enlist the support of Ethiopia's Muslims to fight against the Amhara-controlled and predominantly Christian central government. Italy tried to introduce both ethnic and religious-based conflicts between Ethiopians. Only a few found it convenient to convert to Islam to avoid the suspicion of the fascist forces, and tried to distance themselves from the central government. Muslim Ethiopians, however, are mostly nationalists, similar to their Christian Ethiopian counterparts. Among them is a noted Ethiopian Somali, Dejazmach Omar Samatar, an Ethiopian nationalist who fought against the Italian aggression during World War II. A school in Addis Ababa is named after him.

Currently, the ascendance of a fundamentalist Islamic faction, *Wahhabism*, spearheaded by Saudi Arabia and Ethiopian graduates of Islamic *madrasas* in Pakistan, have become a concern for both Christians and the largely moderate Sunni Muslims of Ethiopia. Such a fundamentalist religious group could be a destabilizing force and could threaten the unity, tolerance, co-existence and harmony enjoyed by the followers of both faiths.

These states of affairs had brought about historical insecurity of the Ethiopian leaders. They are also part of the geopolitical reality, surrounded as Ethiopia is by Muslim states, some unfriendly. Indicative of this insecurity, Col. Mengistu Haile Mariam felt that the Arabs who were against Ethiopia were deceiving the United States.[2] The government-run Radio Ethiopia English program commented on May 24, 1979, that the US had escalated subversive activities in the Horn of Africa. It also said that revolutionary Ethiopia remained the main target of the United States. According to the radio program, the CIA Chief, Admiral Stansfield Turner, had approved a plan that called on Somali and Eritrean separatists to join efforts and intensify anti-Ethiopian activities. The government-controlled radio also accused the head of the NSC, Zbigniew Brzezinski, of involvement in destabilizing the situation in Ethiopia and attempting to "undermine the mass-based revolution."[3]

---

1 Zbigniew Brzezinski Collections, Carter Presidential Library, SCC meeting 16: 6/14/77 through 47: 12/22/77, box # 27.

2 Carter Presidential Library, from the White House Situation room, February, 22, 1978, Box #11.

3 A note, "Ethiopia Radio comment on Turner and You," from Paul B. Henze to Zbigniew Brzezinski. June 1, 1979. From declassified paper, the Carter Presidential Library.

Most Ethiopians felt that this was a betrayal — but the US was merely following its perceived permanent interest. The fact is that Ethiopian leaders put the nation on a dangerous and extremist course that alienated the majority of Ethiopians. The military government sought to solve political problems with the use of force and its extremism placed the country in crisis.

Ethiopians were surprised when the country was exposed again to famine and human devastation of the 1980s and had to appeal for international assistance to help alleviate the crisis. This comes in light of Col. Mengistu's boast that he could place even nature under his control. His human rights abuses and dictatorial rule remained stifling and heart breaking to most Ethiopians. When the military regime failed to compromise or manage conflict, and failed to be realistic about the grave situation in which the country found itself, it encouraged aggrieved groups to resort to extreme positions.

To most Ethiopians during the war with Somalia, the US proved to be an untrustworthy ally. Had the Carter administration worked with the *Derg* amicably, some believe that the *Derg* would not have gone to the Soviets and turned socialist.

The State Department saw the EPLF, which opened its Washington office in 1985, as a marginal, left-wing secessionist movement. There was a change of heart in 1990 when Herman J. Cohen, US Assistant Secretary of State for African Affairs, hosted a luncheon for Issayas Afewerki at the prestigious Foreign Service Club when Issayas attended a US-sponsored talk between the EPLF and the *Derg* representative Ashagre Yigletu. During the same visit, Issayas met Sen. Edward Kennedy and Rep. Howard Wolpe, Chairman, House Foreign Subcommittee on Africa. In the same year, at a Congressional hearing (Feb. 28, 1990), Herman Cohen testified that Eritrea had a right to self-determination within the Ethiopian framework.

In October 1990, the US offered to the *Derg* and the EPLF a proposal as a means to settle their differences, featuring:

1. The overarching concept of self-government for Eritrea.
2. A negotiated structure spelling out the relationship (federal or confederal) between Eritrea and Ethiopia.
3. An eventual act of choice for the Eritreans on the longer-term viability of the structure agreed upon
4. Enforcement guarantee mechanisms, and
5. Confidence-building measures[1]

However, the *Derg* and the EPLF were not willing to compromise and solve the Eritrean case.

The previously castigated EPLF was suddenly seen as a pro-democracy organization. Issayas, a Christian, was no longer seen as an extremist. To appease the Americans, Issayas claimed to have abandoned Marxism and embraced multi-party democracy. Nonetheless, after the establishment of the independence of Eritrea, Issayas became a totalitarian ruler. He had once been heralded as one of the leaders of the African renaissance, expected to introduce democracy and uphold human rights. Even a semblance of multi-party democracy and freedom of speech and the press is non-existent in Eritrea. True democracy is indeed still lacking in Ethiopia, but Eritrea is today in a worse situation than when it was a province of Ethiopia.

Most Ethiopians felt that the US also vacillated on the Eritrean case and was not in Ethiopia's corner in time of need. The US is similarly accused of failing to sup-

---

1 Herman J. Cohen. 2000. *Intervening in Africa – Superpower Peacemaking in a Troubled Continent*, New York: St. Martin's Press, p. 40.

port Ethiopia against Somalia's aggression. Most Ethiopians hold US foreign policy responsible for the personal and national predicament during and after the military regime.

As a background note, Cuba's support for Ethiopia's territorial integrity, regarding Eritrea and the Ogaden, came after the downfall of the pro-US Emperor Haile Selassie's government. Cuba referred to Eritrea as a "territory arbitrarily annexed by Ethiopia since 1962," supported Eritrea's independence, and trained the different Eritrean guerrillas in Cuba and abroad. After the mid-1970s Cuba changed its position and referred to Eritrea as an integral part of Ethiopia and said that the problem had been aggravated by the meddling of the CIA.[1] Cuba's support for Greater Somalia was also altered after the fall of Emperor Haile Selassie and Cuba criticized Somalia for "the mad idea of greater Somalia" that led Somalia "into the arms of the imperialist camp."[2] That was a reference to the alliance between the US and Somalia in the 1970s.

In May 1991, the EPLF established the Provisional Government of Eritrea (PGE) and became a *de facto* independent country. As a result of a referendum on April 23–25, 1993, Eritrea declared independence on May 24, 1993 after a 30 years' war. The EPRDF facilitated the secession of Eritrea by providing diplomatic support at the UN and borrowing money on behalf of Eritrea at Ethiopia's expense. This must be the first time in the history of nations that a country has fully supported and facilitated its own dismemberment.

---

1 William E. Ratliff. 1986. *Follow the Leader in the Horn: The Soviet-Cuban Presence in East Africa*, Washington, DC: The Cuban American National Foundation, p. 9.

2 Ibid., p. 10, quoting Radio Havana, Havana, Cuba, April 27, 1978.

CHAPTER 11. ETHIOPIA AS A REGIONAL GATEKEEPER

THE US AND AFRICAN RENAISSANCE LEADERS: ALLIES IN THE WAR ON TERROR

The president of Eritrea, Issayas Afewerki, and Ethiopia's Prime Minister Meles Zenawi were both flattered by the Clinton Administration, which touted them as examples of the new leaders of the African Renaissance who adopted Western-style democracy and market economy. The Clinton Administration said it hoped that these young leaders would herald the dawning of a new age in their respective countries. Bill Clinton, himself a young leader, hoped that by partnering with young African leaders to mobilize African resources, helping to solve their myriad problems, and witnessing the rebirth of a continent, he could spearhead an alliance that could stand up against what the US called Islamic fundamentalism — Islamic movements whose interests were in conflict with US interests in the area.

In the fight against Islamic fundamentalism, Sudan, a country that borders both Ethiopia and Eritrea, had been labeled by the US as a harbor for terrorists. On June 26, 1995, Egypt's President Hosni Mubarak escaped an assassination attempt in Addis Ababa on his way to attend an OAU summit meeting. Mubarak alleged that Sudan had had a hand in the assassination attempt. The US also linked the assassination attempt to Sudan.

The next day, Egyptian and Sudanese troops clashed (June 27–28, 1995) in a disputed area along their common border near the Red Sea city of Halaib. Mubarak called on the Sudanese to overthrow their government. Egypt, backed by Tunisia and Algeria, tried to convince the Gulf Arab states that Sudan, under the National Islamic Front (NIF), was an "enemy of Islam rather than a friend ... and a threat to their own Islamic-based dynasties."[1] There have been efforts subsequently to isolate Sudan from both the West and the Arab world. Egypt claimed that Sudan works closely with the Shiah-dominated Iran and works to undermine the Sunni-dominated Islamic coun-

---

1 *Africa Confidential.* October 22, 1993. Vol. 34, no. 21, p.2.

tries and that Iran trains Sudanese troops.[1] The OAU foreign ministers meeting in Addis Ababa on September 11, 1995, condemned Sudan for supporting, helping, and sheltering those who tried to assassinate President Mubarak.

The Ethiopian government, for its part, accused Sudan of harboring three men involved in the attempt to assassinate President Mubarak in Addis Ababa, the head-quarters of the OAU. Ethiopia told Sudan to reduce its diplomats from fifteen to four, Sudan Airways was banned from flying to Ethiopia, and the Sudanese consulate in Gambella, a city bordering Sudan in Western Ethiopia, was closed.

Amidst the rancor between Egypt and Sudan, Ethiopia reported it had no Suda-nese nationals in its custody who were connected with the assassination attempt. They were indeed all Egyptians. An Egyptian Islamic group claimed responsibility for the assassination attempt against Mubarak in Ethiopia, saying it had targeted Mubarak "to end the bloodshed he is causing and to rescue the Egyptian people from their poverty, distress and ignorance."[2]

At the UN Security Council on April 3, 1996, US ambassador to the UN Mad-eleine K. Albright accused Sudan, which had a predominantly Muslim population, of being "a viper's nest of terrorists."[3]

Such a provocative statement could destabilize Ethiopia's complex foreign rela-tions. Ethiopia is currently seen by the US as a bulwark against religious extremists in the region. Sudan and Ethiopia are sometimes congenial neighbors, sometimes an-tagonists. Close to half of Ethiopia's population is Muslim and for centuries they have lived harmoniously side by side with those of other faiths.

When war broke out between Ethiopia and Eritrea in 1998, Hassan Abdullah al-Turabi, President of Sudan and leader of the NIF (that came to power in the 1989 coup d'état), commented that the two countries have cultural, ethnic, historical, and geopolitical ties. However, he added that while the two countries were of one family, nonetheless they were meant by God to turn on each other the weapons the US had sent to destroy Sudan.[4]

Ethiopia's and Eritrea's leaders, very close to Sudan when they comes to power, soon started complaining that President Turabi's NIF supported Islamist groups in their countries. Both leaders, aligned with the US, tried to undermine the govern-ment in Khartoum by supporting Sudanese opposition groups. In 1996, Ethiopia, Eri-trea, and Uganda received nearly $20 million in surplus US military equipment to overthrow the government of Sudan under Hassan Abdullah al-Turabi, head of the ruling National Congress (NC) or the ideologue of the NIF.[5] The military equipment, especially in Ethiopia and Eritrea, was used to repress their own people, albeit the leaders of the two countries gave the US the impression that they were committed to democracy and to serving the US interests in the region.

After the rancor between Sudan, Ethiopia and Egypt, in 2000, the latter two dropped their accusation that the NIF was harboring terrorists and announced that Sudan had given up terrorism. Soon the political equation changed.

This association of Ethiopia with the US as an ally in the fight against Islamic fundamentalism is a dangerous trend. Some Muslim countries, which are not too friendly with Ethiopia, can use this as an excuse to undermine Ethiopia's unity and

---

1 Ibid., p. 3.
2 *Facts on File News Service.* December 7, 1995. Vol. 55, no. 2871, p. 907.
3 *Facts on File News Service.* April 11, 1996. Vol. 56, no. 2888, p. 254.
4 *Africa Confidential.* May 28, 1998. Vol. 39, no. 11, p.1.
5 *The Washington Post.* November 10, 1992.

the harmony that formerly prevailed between Christianity and Islam. Some Muslim countries, such as Egypt, Pakistan, Syria, and Saddam Hussein's Iraq, already undermined Ethiopia's unity by supporting and abetting the Eritrean secession and by alleging Ethiopia to be an exclusively Christian country.

When the media labels Ethiopian troops as Christians fighting Muslims in Somalia, it is sending another dangerous message. Such labeling will increase the suspicion some Muslim and Arab countries harbor against Ethiopia. Ethiopian troops in Somalia include Christians, Muslims and Somali-speakers of Ethiopia.

During the Clinton administration, interest in Ethiopia increased as did attention in Africa over all, mainly; it seems, with the goal of opening up Africa to American trade. The USAID has supported democracy and what it categorizes as good governance since 1991 when the *Derg* regime was overthrown.[1] The US says that Ethiopia is about as free as is the average USAID-assisted country. The USAID report, however, has admitted that Ethiopia's civil liberties score, related to the rule of law and human rights issues, trails that of other USAID-assisted countries.

Nevertheless, the US builds its hopes and expectations on personalities, i.e., on current leaders, rather than encouraging the establishment of a broad-based institution that is close to the people, that goes beyond a semblance of democracy and personal rule. Prime Minister Meles Zenawi is assumed to be an important ally of the West, especially that of the United States. He has recruited the service of individuals who were US officials, such as Paul Henze, and who are Washington insiders. Meles has also recruited the lobbying services of political luminaries such as Mr. Richard Armey and Mr. Richard Gephardt to improve his government's image in the US Congress, where some members have become critical of Meles and the human rights conditions in Ethiopia.

Mr. Meles's apparent attempt to address the historical contradiction in Ethiopia through ethnic federalism was a bold undertaking, according to NSC officials. The US does not challenge this risky and unpredictable policy which has little support in Ethiopia. There are a few corrupt ethnic elites who benefit from the divide-and-rule political system and feel empowered. Meles's paternalism has bestowed upon this new elite a form of power it can enjoy as long as it remains loyal to the government. This group has an insecure basis as, once it loses its position, it will also lose all its privileges and perks.

The Meles regime seems to welcome the role of US proxy in order to gain US support for its own security. Since December 1995, Ethiopia has been engaged against the fundamentalist Muslim group *al-Ittihad al-Islami* in Somali that seeks the independence of the Ogaden region of Ethiopia. The US also claims that the al-Qaeda organization supports Islamic fundamentalism in the Ogaden region and has training camp in neighboring Somalia. The 9/11 attacks on the US lent urgency to the fight against international terrorism, including in Ethiopia, just as the campaign to counteract communist expansion made Ethiopia a player during the Cold War. Because of Ethiopia's alliance with the US against global terrorism, Ethiopia is showered with military and economic assistance. While the military assistance has created a police state, the sustainability of some of the economic assistance and its utility in uplifting the situation of the poor remains questionable.

---

1 USAID. 2001. *Bureau for Africa Program, Activity, and Reference Information*, vol.1.

ETHIOPIA AND ERITREA: COMPLICATED RELATIONS

In a bizarre occurrence, Sebhat Nega, founding member of TPLF and its chairman from 1979 to 1989, was interviewed by TPLF radio, Woyane Voice, in 2007. Sebhat boasted that the TPLF leadership had fought for the independence of Eritrea more than Issayas Afewerki of EPLF, the president of Eritrea, had done. Prime Minister Meles also gave an interview to Woyane Voice. According to the two (Ato Sebhat and Ato Meles), Issayas vacillated on the independence of Eritrea and negotiated with the *Derg* to compromise the independence of Eritreans. The two argued that the Eritrean case is a colonial issue that must culminate in independence similar to that of other colonial states. The TPLF leadership ignored the fact that Eritrea was part of Ethiopia before it was annexed by Italy, and the two had strong cultural, economic, familial and geopolitical ties.

Judging from the interviews, an attempt to reverse the current separation of Eritrea and Ethiopia would be fiercely opposed. The situation defies logic. The Prime Minister of Ethiopia, Meles Zenawi, is also known for his strong support for the independence of Eritrea.

One can only speculate why these individuals have worked against the national interest of Ethiopia. As the TPLF was initially a secessionist organization, it will always have a safe haven in Eritrea if it is disgraced and loses its dominance in Ethiopia. It may also resort to its initial conspiracy over the secession of the Tigre region and join Eritrea. The secession of Tigre would depend on the existence of an independent Eritrea and a friendly government that supports the idea. Perhaps one would be compelled by these interviews to assume that such a scenario exists.

Prime Minister Meles also said in his interview that Ethiopia does not need an outlet to the sea and that Ethiopia is faring well as a landlocked country.

Those closer to the government have revealed that, had the May 2005 elections resulted in the defeat and ouster of Prime Minister Meles and his ruling party, the different ethnic groups would have been warned that the Amharas would make a comeback and reverse the "gains" achieved under the Meles regime. The EPRDF would then ask ethnic-based political parties under the EPRDF to evoke their right, as stipulated in the Constitution's Article 39, and seek the independence of their *kilil*. The Tigre region, which is highly militarized, would ensure the achievement of that goal by employing its full military force. It was unclear how the Tigre people and others who consider themselves Ethiopian nationalists would have responded to this scenario. According to Tecola, the military could have intervened to maintain the status quo. At the moment, ethnic politics has lost followers as it has not met the basic needs of Ethiopians. The government, however, has continued to play the ethnic card, its only means for staying in power. The ethnic-based conflicts that flare up in the different regions of the country are blamed on the government. The colonial stratagem of divide and rule seems to be alive in Ethiopia's polity hindering the establishment of a strong, democratic, and united Ethiopia striving to improve the quality of life for its citizens and face the challenges of the 21st century.

Along this line, Professor Theodore M. Vestal, a long-time friend of Ethiopia, has this to say regarding ethnic-based politics and Ethiopian nationalism: "Ethiopia ... must liberate itself from the stifling past and enter into a new era with an interweaving of separate ethnic strands into a new national design. To secure the public good and private rights against the danger of ethnic factions, and at the same time to create a truly democratic government, is the great object to which freedom-loving

Ethiopians should direct their thoughts and their individual actions. Until democratic principles, norms, values, and procedures are constantly applied in Ethiopia, human rights will not be protected." He further stated that "[T]he record of the EPRDF demonstrates that these standards are not being met and that human rights suffer accordingly."[1]

There is also a bizarre situation in Eritrea. President Issayas Afewerki has claimed to stand for the unity of Ethiopia. While the leaders of Ethiopia defend the sovereignty of Eritrea, even to the detriment of Ethiopia, the leader of Eritrea, President Issayas Afewerki, seems to stand for the unity of Ethiopia. In an interview given by Issayas to Eritrean media and published by Eritrean's Ministry of Information, "The people and government of Eritrea always stand alongside with the Ethiopian people" and that "it's our persistent stance to strive for a United Ethiopia."[2] It is unclear if the unity of Ethiopia will eventually include Eritrea. This is the nature of the propaganda war that is being waged by the leaders of both Ethiopia and Eritrea, baffling Ethiopians and US officials alike.

An Eritrean scholar, Tesfatsion Medhanie, published a book in 2007 that calls for an initial confederation between Ethiopia and Eritrea that would gradually lead to federation.[3] Tesfatsion has stated to me that the idea is accepted by most all Eritreans, not only the highland Eritreans who earlier fought for the unity of Eritrea with Ethiopia but also lowlander Muslim Eritreans. On the Ethiopian side, there is a mixed response. Some say good riddance to Eritrea and feel that Ethiopia has sacrificed enough, economically and in human terms, striving for unity and harmony between the fraternal people of the two countries. Others argue that any suggestion less than federation or total unity between the two countries is a ploy to once again exploit Ethiopia. In order to bring the two countries closer, democracy must first set roots in both countries and territorial integrity be ensured.[4] Unity of the two is natural and desirable because of their shared culture, their long shared history, and economic and geopolitical realities. It seems that the so-called Eritrean issue remains unsolved at present, but the eventual convergence of both countries, under visionary leadership and democratic political environment, is inevitable. Such unity would contribute to stability in the region, economic development, and the reuniting of separated families.

To further complicate the situation, both entities are engaged in a proxy war in Somalia, each supporting domestic forces that challenge the legitimacy of the other. The condition calls for citizens and especially intellectuals of both Ethiopia and Eritrea to start a dialogue with each other to provide a democratic vision where human rights will be observed and economic development will flourish for all involved.

Other forces or countries may seek to undermine such unity. Egypt, which worked for the dismemberment of Ethiopia, most likely would be one of them. Egypt will not tolerate a strong Ethiopia at the source of Egypt's lifeline, the Blue Nile. If the US is to support unity, it will have to gain the confidence of both countries, serve as a true partner in economic development and human rights observance, reassess its role, and see the situation in a new light. The US must move away from the conventional

---

1 Theodore M. Vestal. 2005. "Human rights abuses in democratic' Ethiopia: Government-sponsored ethnic hatred." www.unb.br/ics/dan/geri/Textos/vestal.htm

2 Eritrean Ministry of Information, June 10, 2007, "One Ethiopia," Asmara, Eritrea.

3 Tesfatsion Medhanie. 2007. *Towards Confederation in the Horn of Africa: Focus on Ethiopia and Eritrea*, Germany: IKO varlag, pp. 40-41.

4 Ibid., pp. 42-46.

---

way of conducting its foreign policy, avoid unilateralism, and be creative in order to regain its respect in the region and worldwide.

The solution of the problem lies in the will and determination of both Ethiopians and Eritreans.

Meanwhile, EPRDF officials are mired in corruption and the embezzlement of government funds.[1] Families and close associates of officials are not spared from the accusation of trying to get rich quickly and shield themselves from a future that remains unpredictable. An article in *The Nation* stated that "Meles *is* corrupt." According to the article, "He has turned the state and its resources into a trough for the ruling party." For example: Ethiopia's auditor general, Lema Aregaw, reported about $600 million in state funds were unaccounted for. Meles fired the auditor general and defended regional administrations' "right to burn money."[2] According to a Transparency International Corruption Perception Index report of 2006, Ethiopia ranks 133 out of 163 countries and received 2.4 out of 10 maximum points. The government's ethnic-based politics cater to the Tigre region, which claims to be most affected by war and neglect by the previous governments. Such regional favoritism comes at the expense of other equally needy regions.

In a speech at the University of Nairobi, then Senator Barack Obama stated that corruption robs an honest people of the opportunities they have fought for — the opportunity they deserve. "Ethnic-based tribal politics is rooted in the bankrupt idea that the goal of politics or business is to funnel as much of the pie as possible to one's family, tribe, or circle with little regard for the public good." He called for an accountable, transparent government to break the cycle.[3] Senator Obama also reminded his audience about political corruption in his own state of Illinois. Illinois and the city of Chicago are known for their machine politics. However, in the US branches and different levels of governments, there are requirements for accountability and transparency in the activities of officials and mechanisms for holding them answerable for their performance in office. During his Inaugural Address on January 20, 2009, President Barack Obama reiterated his concerns about corruption. He said "[T]hose who cling to power through corruption and deceit and the silencing of dissent, know that [they] are on the wrong side of history." In the case of African countries, such as Ethiopia, corruption is a public secret and the public has no mechanism for holding officials accountable. Such a condition encourages government officials to use public property and funds as their own. It is hard to imagine development taking root, and alleviating poverty in Africa remains a futile exercise. The US has to examine its assistance and also refrain from aiding corrupt and capricious government officials simply because they promise to further the US interest.

Prime Minister Meles has meanwhile increasingly become intolerant of any critical voices. For most Ethiopians, the EPRDF is not much different from the military regime. Some say the distinction is that the military regime instantly and physically eliminated its disputants while the TPLF regime administers a slow death through psychological terror by neglecting to fight poverty and disease and by pitching one ethnic group against the other — a divide-and-rule tactic. Some still blame the US for

---

1 Refer to the different works of Theodore M. Vestal, Assefa Negash, and Bogale Assefa in ibid.

2 Paul Wachter. February 14, 2007. "Bush's Somalia strategy enables an Ethiopian despot," *The Nation*, http://www.thenation.com/doc/20070226/wachter

3 Barack Obama, "An honest government, a hopeful future." August 28, 2006. Speech at the University of Nairobi, Kenya. http://obama.senate.gov/speech/060828-an_honest_gover

supporting and shoring up the TPLF-controlled regime and an arrogant leader who has escalated human suffering and social alienation.

The London Conference, authored by the United States, is partially held responsible for not helping to bring about democracy, stability, and economic viability in Ethiopia. Ethiopia is still not free from war; the literacy rate is declining, standing at 43% in 2003; and the country is still beset with disease, malnutrition, unemployment, and abject poverty. Active US support of the regime did not bring about a meaningful change in the lives of Ethiopians, sustainable development, and true democracy; this would lead one to question US aims with regard to Ethiopia. This century-long involvement has failed to bring about the development of the country. This begs for a critical analysis of US assistance and Ethiopia's efforts to establish sustainable development.

The war between Ethiopia and Eritrea has complicated the situation, and their involvement in Somalia has further complicated the situation in the HOA.

The US and some of the post-Cold War leaders had great hope for the success of cooperation in Africa. Along with Uweri Museveni of Uganda and Paul Kagame of Rwanda, Ethio-Eritrean leaders joined a US-sponsored Rapid Military Deployment Force. The alliance of the Clinton administration and the so-called African Renaissance leaders soon proved to be a fiasco. First, critics such as Stephen Buckley, saw these leaders as a "more sophisticated, smoother-talking brand of their authoritarian predecessors" and said that "[T]hey have close relations with their major donors, drawing hundreds of millions of dollars in aid annually.... and that they woo the Western media, using grace and charm to spin reporters relentlessly."[1]

Second, two of the "renaissance" leaders led their countries to a devastating war. On May 6, 1998, a border dispute between Ethiopia and Eritrea erupted as Eritrea claimed 150 square miles of barren land, the Bademe region. The leaders of Eritrea and Ethiopia drove their peoples to deadly bloodshed that claimed 100,000 lives and displaced and maimed more people than had been lost in the entire history of these fraternal peoples. The US, therefore, has to be prudent in its evaluation of governments and refrain from supporting authoritarian regimes for its short-term interest.

---

1 Stephen Buckley. February 2, 1998. "Authority's changing face in Africa: Enlightened leaders, or savvy strongmen?" *The Washington Post*, p. A13.

CHAPTER 12. QUESTIONING THE US ROLE IN CURRENT ECONOMIC AND POLITICAL DEVELOPMENTS

Ethiopia, like other African countries, has not been a priority for America's political leaders. During the Cold War, US presidents and top foreign policy advisors, such as the NSC, looked at the Horn of Africa only through the lens of US–Soviet maneuvering. During the Carter Administration, when the Soviet involvement in the HOA was at its highest, President Carter and his NSC advisors were setting policies and providing directives in an unsuccessful attempt to avert the Soviet involvement in Ethiopia.

US foreign policy makers, at least in the case of Ethiopia and other third world countries that are not unfriendly, base their policies partly on the information they receive from standing governments. They usually avoid being too critical of some of the host country's policies unless something drastic attracts the media and the US public. The US and its diplomatic officials in Ethiopia associate with government officials and with the inner circle of the ruling elite and the sympathizers who promote ethnic-based discrimination. They in turn embrace and promote the government. This is how knowledgeable Ethiopians and leaders of different organizations view the method of operation of US policy makers. Political officers in the US embassy in Addis Ababa may contact and confer with opposition groups, human rights activists, professional and civic organizations. But their critical reports may not receive due attention by higher US government officials. Needless to say, that there are Foreign Service officers who are selfless, love the country they serve in, and maintain professional demeanor. They have passed the rigorous civil service exam and the stringent annual review for promotion. I was honored to serve as a public member on the USAID and US Department of State Foreign Service Selection Board and am impressed by the performance of most officers. The caveat is that they mostly deal with the immediate issues at hand during their tenure and have no time to develop a long-term plan to serve their assigned country or consider the wider ramifications of their policies.

For some US officials posted in Ethiopia, as in other countries, the primary concern is securing their jobs and livelihoods and staying out of controversy. Opposition to the government of Ethiopia or any constructive criticism thereof is labeled as the voice of disgruntled individuals: Amhara ethnic groups, OLF or WSLF sympathizers, remnants of *Derg* officials, anti-Tigre ethnic groups, or worst of all, anti-American factions. What used to be demonized as radical Marxist positions during the Cold War are now subject to a new labeling, usually taking ethnic and religious overtones. The Ethiopian government labels its opponents as belonging to a once-ruling Amhara ethnic group or as supporters of the military regime.

Some US officials find it easy to subscribe to such labeling. Recent US diplomats in Ethiopia have gone out of their ways to support vehemently the government of Ethiopia whose records on human rights, good governance, and respect for the rule of law have remained questionable. Perhaps they discretely criticize Ethiopian government officials when they meet with them directly; such interactions are not publicized for fear that they might offend the host country.

Several major issues illustrate the long-term interest of the US in Ethiopia.

ECONOMIC LIBERALIZATION AND DEMOCRACY

In its drive to promote economic globalization, the US is supporting countries such as Ethiopia that have embraced a market economy and opened up to foreign investors regardless of those countries' dismal records on human rights and multiparty democracy, the values that are seemingly upheld by the United States. In the post-Cold War era, the US has continued to follow a double standard and contradictory foreign policies. Besides Ethiopia and other African countries, China could be a good example. China claims it has dropped the command economy and has embraced economic liberalism or free market principles. The US has normalized trade with China and has supported China's membership in the World Trade Organization (WTO). Critics argue that the trade deal is an "abandonment of democratic principles in the name of corporate profits."[1] This is in reference to China's dismal human rights records; the same could be said of Ethiopia as well, although the latter is not as vibrant and powerful as the former.[2]

In its effort to expand market access, the US sponsored the creation of African Growth and Opportunity Act (AGOA), signed into law on May 18, 2000. The program intends to liberalize trade and investment activities between the US and sub-Sahara African countries including Ethiopia. AGOA is credited with spurring African exports by dropping American tariffs and allowing Africa to earn hard currency. AGOA was adopted as the result of sixty thousand African-Americans who sent letters to their congressional representatives supporting it.[3] This program is criticized as being narrowly limited to trade, despite its claimed commitment to supporting sustainable development, to fighting poverty, disease, and environmental degradation, and to promoting democracy. That commitment to broad-based development is questioned.

The US Embassy in Ethiopia reported that Ethiopia's exports to the US, under the AGOA, doubled in the first six months of 2008. The export included textile and

---

1 Refer to an article by Matthew Vita. September 20, 2000. "Senate approves normalized trade with China," *The Washington Post.*

2 See Getachew Metaferia. Fall, 2005. "China: Ethnic politics, nation building and its global role," *Journal of South Asian and Middle Eastern Studies,* vol. 29, no. 1.

3 Paul Collier. 2007. *The Bottom Billion: Why the Poorest Countries are Failing and What Can be Done About It.* New York, NY: Oxford University Press, p. 169.

garments, foliage/bouquet filler, live plants and fruits/nuts.[1] Farmers generally complain that foliage and bouquet filler grow on irrigated land that uses water they could use to produce sustainable and profitable food for continuing human consumptions. Growing flowers for export has, in some cases, contributed to pollution of the environment and created a health hazard because of the use of pesticides. Labor mismanagement has also remained an issue.

There is another concern as well. Ethiopia has not encouraged agrarian reform and land is not privatized. Ethiopians have no land ownership; this restriction is intended to control the population in the rural areas where 80% live. Ethiopians are struggling with high food prices and food insecurity has remained the norm. Expanding food production, emphasizing small-scale farming and integrated rural development, must be a priority. In the existing conditions, it would be hard to ensure sustainable development and fight poverty, hunger and malnutrition. External efforts to foster development and fight poverty must take these into consideration.

The export of flowers may seem to help the individual grower in the short run and gain a comparative advantage. It may seem to help the country earn hard currency. When seen from a broader perspective, it will not help Ethiopia to compete with other countries. Ethiopia will remain marginalized if it is encouraged to produce primary commodities and highly perishable items whose prices fluctuate. Export also depends on the economic health of the importing countries and the desire of the consumers to purchase luxury items.

In addition to fundamental issues of poor agricultural policy and poverty, the demise of Mengistu's regime, the exodus of Ethiopian Jews to Israel, Ethiopia's involvement in Somalia, and the resumption of the Ethiopia–US relation at a level similar to what it was before the end of Emperor Haile Selassie's reign are widely discussed among Ethiopians. The Ethio–US relationship is historically based on personalities. When these personalities leave the political scene unceremoniously and in disrepute, relations with the US become precarious. The US now has the best of diplomatic relations with the current regime, though the regime remains unpopular and divisive. Since the US is associated with this unpopular government, it is not seen favorably by the people and its public diplomacy has failed to take roots.

US support for the post-Marxist regime in Ethiopia, then, is based on the latter's claimed adoption of a market-oriented economy, the pursuit of multi-party democracy, and the upholding of human rights and freedom of the press. Elections were held in 1995, 2000, and in 2005, but the outcomes were alleged to be rigged and unfair. The opposition boycotted the 1995 elections despite efforts by a task force set up in Washington, D.C. by former Congressman Harry Johnston of Florida to try to mediate between the EPRDF and the opposition.

The economic and political practices of the government lack any semblance of good governance and transparency. According to some writers, corruption is rampant as the ruling party subsidizes its own business enterprises using public funds.[2] That does not allow small businesses to compete fairly. Yet the US seems to accept any semblance of democracy as long as the regime claims to be an ally in the fight against terrorism.

Changes in administration and in power relationships in Washington, D.C., new definitions of national interest, changes in political actors, the global condition, and

---

1 "Ethiopia: AGOA exports double in first half of '08," *The Daily Monitor* (Addis Ababa), August 22, 2008.
2 Refer to Marina Ottaway, ibid. Also refer to Theodore M. Vestal, ibid.

a general paradigm shift within the US polity will influence foreign policy after every presidential election. While changes in foreign policy tend to be incremental unless something drastic happens, such as the attack on the US on September 11, 2001, for poor African countries such as Ethiopia any change in US foreign policy tends to be drastic. Also these reactive changes tend to be tactical, quick *quid pro quo* responses that fail to take into account the long-term interest of countries in question.

One should not expect Ethiopia, a poor country, to be treated like NATO member countries or China. Beginning with the Marshall Plan, when the US spent about $14 billion in rebuilding the infrastructure of Europe which was utterly destroyed during World War II, the US has had high stakes in the politics of the region. Since that war, Europe was at the front line in the struggle against the USSR. Racial affinity and recognized cultural and historical ties with western European countries (especially Britain) continue to play a role in the positive US policy towards Europe, which is absent in the foreign policy considerations of other regions. In the case of Asia, the overarching reason for US involvement was to counter the active involvement of the USSR in that continent during the Cold War.

Africa, in the post-Cold War era, remained marginal in the US foreign policy considerations, except for Egypt, South Africa, Kenya, Ethiopia, and oil-producing countries such as Nigeria. In general, post-Cold War involvement in Africa take the form of humanitarian interventions that deal with famine and HIV/AIDS which are said to have security implication for the United States. Out of the 20 nations that receive the most US aid, half are in Africa. During George W. Bush's Administration, development and humanitarian assistance for Africa increased from $1.4 billion in 2001 to more than $4 billion in 2006. The largest recipients of US assistance, excluding military assistance, are Sudan ($771 million); Ethiopia ($625 million); Egypt ($397 million); and Uganda ($242 million).[1]

While the military interest has declined, except in Ethiopia, US economic interest in Africa has gained prominence. Terrorist attacks on the US and its properties in Kenya and Tanzania influenced US foreign policy mightily towards Ethiopia and the rest in the Horn of Africa. US troops are training their Ethiopian counterparts to "fight terrorists" and to share intelligence information. Ethio–US relations, as before, are based on furthering short-term US interests instead of being motivated by an interest to develop a well-planned, deliberate, and proactive foreign policy.

After 9/11, Ethiopia has been categorized as an ally in the fight against terrorism, especially in neighboring Somalia which has been controlled by warlords since 1991 and is referred to as a failed state. The Horn of Africa has become, according to a book by Robert I. Rothberg, a "battleground for terrorism."[2] The Ethiopian leadership is also exploiting the situation to cover up its shortcomings on human rights and good governance and to divert serious censure.

American troops, close to 2,000 of them, are stationed in Camp Lemonier, Djibouti, and monitor a region that is strategically important. American troops are also stationed in Hurso military camp in the Harar region of Ethiopia to provide training to Ethiopian troops. Mr. Meles has a free hand in sending troops into Somalia, with US approval, to hunt groups that he calls terrorists and those with alleged al-Qaeda connections.

---

1 Refer to Michael A. Fletcher. December 32, 2006. "Bush has quietly tripled aid to Africa," *The Washington Post*, A4.

2 Robert I. Rothberg, ed. 2005. *Battling Terrorism in the Horn of Africa*, Cambridge, Massachusetts: World Peace Foundation and Washington, DC: Brookings Institution Press, pp. 8-22.

Ethiopia is also accused of providing the US with prison cells for interrogating suspected terrorists from other countries. It was reported that "Hundreds of prisoners, who include women and children, have been transferred secretly and illegally — to Ethiopia, where they are kept without charge or access to lawyers and families."[1] The Human Rights Watch, in its 2008 report, stated that "agents of both the Central Intelligence Agency and the Federal Bureau of Investigation questioned detainees in Addis Ababa in early 2007." According to the report, "The Ethiopian government serves as the detaining authority for foreign nationals of interest to US and possibly other foreign intelligence officers."[2] The Ethiopian government eventually acknowledged its role in detaining terrorism suspects. This acknowledgement prompted US officials to "speak more candidly about American interrogations of the captives."[3] The collaboration of the two countries in human rights abuses have been questioned by the citizens of both countries.

In December 2006, Prime Minister Meles unleashed his troops in support of Somalia's corrupt and weak transitional government and dislodged the Islamic Courts Union leadership from Mogadishu, the Somali capital. This, again, is with the sanction of the United States. The US provided military, intelligence, and air reconnaissance support to Ethiopia. Somalia claims the Ogaden area of Ethiopia, populated by ethnic Somalis, and supports irredentism, and the two countries have fought three wars against each other (1960, 1964 and 1977–78). This part of the Horn of Africa invited superpower rivalries during the Cold War. A new development is that Eritrea is supporting the Islamic Court Union and both Eritrea and Ethiopia are waging proxy war in Somalia. The current situation will not encourage peace and economic development but rather human rights abuses and police states in the region.

Somalia may not be in a position to claim the Ogaden region by force. Somalia, a failed state, divided and weak, is not a beacon of hope to Ethiopian Somalis at the moment. However, Ethiopia must become more democratic and the rule of law and the respect for human rights must prevail to comfort Ethiopian Somalis. The current government is short of these democratic values.

THE STATE OF THE FREE PRESS

Some of the so-called African renaissance leaders go to great lengths to try to influence US foreign policy towards their countries. They spend their meager national resources to hire lobbyists to convince US officials. One such example is the following.

The Voice of America–Amharic program faced another US policy towards Ethiopia that took into account the short- but not the long-term interests of the two countries. As indicated earlier, the Voice of America–Amharic program, as an arm of the US government, played a vital role in the overthrow of the military regime in Ethiopia. The VOA's news reports, analyses, interviews, and featured guests exposed the military regime's human rights abuses and other serious shortcomings, and earned the program popularity and listeners. The program received the highest ratings for several consecutive years. The military government's attempt to jam the radio did not suc-

---

1 Anthony Mitchell. April 3, 2007. "Secret American Prison in Ethiopia," *The New York Sun*.
2 Refer to Human Rights Watch, 2008, "Arrest, detention, rendition, and torture," http://hrw. org/reports/2008/eastafrica1008/5.htm#_TOC210201068.
3 Jeffrey Gettleman and Mark Mazzetti. April 11, 2007. "Ethiopia holding 41 suspects who fought with Somali Islamists, officials confirm," *The New York Times*, p. A11.

ceed. The VOA–Amharic service also rendered laudable humanitarian service. Under the leadership of one of its staff, Negusse Mengesha, the Amharic service "sponsored a fund-raising drive in Washington in the mid-1980s to provide more than $40,000 for famine relief in Ethiopia, much of it for refugees."[1] The fund raising event was co-ordinated by the VOA–Amharic service, the Ethiopian Hunger Relief Coordinating Committee, and the Ethiopian Community Center in Washington, DC. The event took place on November 30, 1984 at the Washington Capitol Holiday Inn. Speakers at the fundraising occasion were Congressman Howard Wolpe, Tim Knight from the US Department of State, Payne Lucas, Director of Africare and Dr. Aklilu Habte of the World Bank.[2]

But after the overthrow of the military government, the future of the VOA–Amharic program did not look promising. Challenges came from both the Ethiopian government and some of its US supporters.

The current Ethiopian government was opposed to the VOA–Amharic even before its leaders came to Addis Ababa from guerrilla war against the military regime in Ethiopia. The government claimed that the VOA–Amharic program was run by Ethiopian-Americans of Amhara ethnic origin and supported the now defunct military regime or sympathizers or previous members of EPRP, which the TPLF sees it as its erstwhile enemy. Yet the VOA–Amharic program was still popular in Ethiopia.

At a US congressional hearing, Professor Mesfin Wolde Mariam aired the concerns of Ethiopians about "the diminishing role of the Voice of America's Amharic program." He stated that "[t]he contribution of this program, from 1988 to 1991, in raising level of awareness of the Ethiopian people was fostering the values of freedom of the press, in providing accurate information and a forum for all groups, had been immense." Mesfin said that he was "shocked to learn from Addis Ababa that the program was on the verge of losing its priority" and as a human rights activist, he noticed two problems. He said that if "the Voice of America's Amharic program was stifled or even appeared to be stifled for expediency, we in Ethiopia do not only lose a radio program. We lose the best thing that we can ever learn from the United States — the practice of freedom. The other problem is that it sends the wrong signal to the new powers in Addis Ababa and Asmara."[3]

VOA has also been criticized by the Ethiopian government for raising human rights issues — views that are shared by Ethiopia's opposition groups, the Ethiopian public, Ethiopian Human Rights Council (EHRCO), and international human rights watch groups. The EPRDF argued that Amharic is the language of the "oppressor" and that it must not be accorded importance. The pro-US government of Ethiopia lobbied for the termination of the program by soliciting the US embassy in Ethiopia and some members of US Congress. It was reported that in 1994, the US embassy in Addis Ababa recommended that VOA–Amharic be closed as it had outlived its usefulness.[4] According to the US embassy, VOA–Amharic was a relic of the Cold War era.

Assistant Secretary of African Affairs George Moose, through a memorandum to the Board of Governors, argued that VOA should not be supporting a single ethnic

---

1 Alan L. Heil, Jr. 2003. *Voice of America: A History*, New York: Columbia University Press, p. 262.
2 Ethiopian Community Center, Inc., Newsletter. Winter 1985, "Major fundraising for Ethiopian famine victims launched," vol. iv, no 1.
3 Mesfin Wolde Mariam. June 18, 1991. US Congressional hearing, p. 32.
4 Ibid., 265.

group in Ethiopia.[1] The National Security Council (NSC) and US Information Agency (USIA) officials, lobbied by the current Ethiopian government, attended a governors' meeting of the International Broadcasting Bureau on February 2, 1996, and suggested closing the VOA–Amharic Service.

The Chair of the Board of Governors, David Burke, stood up against the pressure to close VOA–Amharic. His instinct as a journalist — once president of CBS as well as executive vice president of ABC — helped save the VOA–Amharic program. At the hearing, Chairman Burke questioned the current regime and pointed out the benefits the US gains by reaching the Ethiopian people. Negusse Mengesha was said to be "smooth and diplomatically persuasive" at the hearing while the US Ambassador in Ethiopia "simply didn't want any broadcast to Ethiopia."[2] This was at a time when the New York-based Committee to Protect Journalists (CPJ) reported that the Ethiopian government had jailed hundreds of journalists between 1993 and 1995 and urged the retention of VOA–Amharic.[3]

After a six-month study of the program and hearings, the VOA Broadcasting Board of Governors decided not to close the VOA–Amharic program. As a compromise, VOA–Amharic was reduced to 30 minutes from an hour, and 15 minutes each was allotted to two more languages — Afan-Orom and Tigrigna — in 1996. The fact that VOA–Amharic program was not totally terminated displeased the Ethiopian government and its supporters. The program has proved useful to the US and a morning VOA–Amharic program was added in March 2008.

The attempt to close the VOA–Amharic program divided the Ethiopian diaspora. Countering the Ethiopian government's lobby to close the program, which amounts to intervention in US policy, they appealed to the US Broadcasting Board of Governors. Organizations such as CPJ accused the Ethiopia government of being anti-free press and muzzling freedom of expression. Private newspapers that had flourished when the EPRDF came to power were closed and independent journalists silenced, imprisoned or exiled. In the aftermath of the May 2005 elections in Ethiopia, five Ethiopian-American reporters from VOA–Amharic, along with several other Ethiopian-Americans, were charged with inciting genocide and treason. [Because of US government pressure, the charge against VOA–Amharic reporters was dropped.]In November 2007, the government of Ethiopia started jamming VOA's Amharic and Afan-Oromo programs and Germany's Deutsche Welle (DW) Amharic program.

Aided by technology from China, the government also filters some e-mails, popular blogs, and websites that are critical of the government. Such activity, especially the expensive jamming of radio airwaves, is reminiscent of the tactics of the Cold War era. This activity is currently tolerated by the US government, but during the military regime the US objected to jamming.

A lesson that one can learn from the predicament of the VOA–Amharic is that the current Ethiopian government has influenced the opinion of US officials, especially those at the embassy in Addis Ababa. This could undermine the long-standing US interest in reaching people. The closure of the popular VOA–Amharic service would have not only robbed Ethiopians of an alternative source of information but also made it once again obvious that the US endorses an undemocratic government.[4]

---

1 See *Africa Confidential.* March 1, 199.,Vvol. 37, no. 5, p.8.
2 Alan L. Heil, Jr., pp. 266-267.
3 Ibid., p. 268.
4 Refer to Alan L. Heil, Jr., *The Struggle for Credibility Back at America's Voice,"* Ibid., pp. 265-268.

The value of the VOA–Amharic in furthering US public diplomacy efforts is obvi-ous. Currently the program offers news and information to millions of VOA–Amharic listeners throughout Ethiopia. It also reaches Ethiopians in the diaspora through the Internet. The program covers US and world news, cultural highlights, and an in-depth coverage of social, political, and economic issues. It was reported that listener-ship in Ethiopia's rural areas has increased. More than 11 percent of Ethiopians tune to VOA–Amharic every week.[1] The need is still there.

Ethiopia is accused of being an enemy of the free press. Yet some in the US have supported Ethiopian government's effort to muzzle the VOA. Ethiopians living abroad were divided on the issue and have lobbied both for and against terminating the broadcasts.

The Ethiopian diaspora is a power to be reckoned with. It holds both economic and political power. In the following chapter, I will discuss the Ethiopian diaspora.

---

1 VOA Press Release, http://voanews.com/english/about/2008-03-03-amharic-morning-show.
   cfm

Chapter 13. The Ethiopian Diaspora in the US

Most Ethiopians in the US are recent immigrants who left their homes after the infamous Red Terror in 1977–1978 during the military regime. They settled in the US after receiving political asylum or resettled as refugees from countries neighboring Ethiopia. Despite the dearth of information regarding the population of Ethiopians in the US, one estimate puts them around half a million out of an estimated two million worldwide. Ethiopians have migrated to different parts of the world since the overthrow of Emperor Haile Selassie's government in 1974. There are more Ethiopians in the US than anywhere else outside of Ethiopia. The majority reside in metropolitan Washington, D.C., including in the suburbs of Maryland and Virginia. Ethiopians are gradually gaining political and economic visibility in the capital area.

The involvement of Ethiopians in the politics of the US — gaining citizenship, registering to vote, and casting votes in elections — has increased. Research that I conducted with Maigenet Shifferraw in the late 1980s indicated that most hoped that the political conditions that had pushed them out of Ethiopia would change and enable them to return to their country. That hope never materialized.[1]

After the overthrow of the military regime, the emigration of Ethiopians continued because of both the political and economic situations and a new US immigration policy, the Diversity Visa (DV) lottery. The Ethiopian quota of DV-lottery winners in 2007 was 6,871. A few also immigrated through the Special Occupation Workers H-1B visa which was created in 1990. Most of that population is now in the US to stay.

In order to make any political impact in the US and influence its policy towards their country of origin, Ethiopians have formed nascent organizations. It is only an organized group that makes a difference in the American pluralist polity. One such organization is the Ethiopian-American Constituency Foundation (EACF). EACF is "dedicated to being a conduit for the collective voice of Ethiopia, Ethiopians and

---

1 Getachew Metaferia and Maigenet Shifferraw, ibid.

Ethiopian-Americans."[1] The EACF pressures the US government to help bring about prosperity and enhance democratic institutions in Ethiopia.

The Ethio-American Lobby Group, a wing of the Ethiopian-American Constituency, has been established in Washington, D.C., and is becoming involved in promoting Ethiopia's interests. The first political measure it took was supporting the presidential candidacy of Vice President Albert Gore in 2000 by raising funds for his campaign. The group also supported Hillary Rodham Clinton for the US senate in New York. In the 2008 presidential election, Ethiopian-Americans organized to support the candidacy of Barack Obama, as did a number of civil rights organizations and labor unions throughout the United States.

Ethiopians also organized to help Hillary Clinton's bid for the US presidency. Both Senators Barack Obama and Hillary Clinton have employed Ethiopian-Americans in their campaign offices. In local elections where their number is significant, Ethiopians have come together to support selected political leaders. Cities such as Washington, D.C., Atlanta, Chicago, New York, Los Angeles, and Seattle have such groups. This evolving coalition is composed of formerly prominent Ethiopian officials and young Ethiopian-Americans.

Another visible organization is the Congressional Ethiopian-American Caucus. The Caucus was founded and is chaired by Congressman Mike Honda (D). Congressman Honda represents the 15th District in California and has a strong support from his Ethiopian constituency there. Ethiopian-Americans have also pressured their congressional representatives to support and join the Congressional Ethiopian-American Caucus. To date, seventeen members of Congress are members of the Caucus, which. The Caucus supports the Ethiopian community's interests both in the US and in Ethiopia.[2]

Ethiopian diaspora civic organizations in several US states work to influence local or national political leaders and institutions. Some of these civic organizations render support to the groups in Ethiopia, such as the support group for the Ethiopian Human Rights Council (EHRCO). Other not affiliated organizations include the Ethiopian Women for Peace and Development, established in 1991 in Washington, D.C. Its role, among others, is to make US government officials and the American public aware of the human rights conditions in Ethiopia and to pressure US officials to take the necessary measures to help ameliorate those conditions and promote peace and development in Ethiopia.

The Ethiopian diaspora has tried to influence US policy towards Ethiopia during wars and natural catastrophes such as drought and hunger. It also puts pressure on governments to act on issues of democracy and human rights, through public demonstrations, candlelight vigils, letter writing, emailing, telephone calls, and faxing to government officials, especially to congressional representatives and prominent US citizens. Public demonstrations and rallies against the successive Ethiopian governments have become a common sight since the last days of Emperor Haile Selassie's government. These activities have escalated as the human rights conditions in Ethiopia continue to deteriorate and the state of affairs remains unaltered.

Out of the several issues that are voiced by diaspora Ethiopians one, in particular, has marshaled the resources of Ethiopians recently to pressure the US government and impact policy. This is the Ethiopian Human Rights Bill (H.R.5680), also known

1 ‹http://www.ethiopianamerican.org
2 ‹htto://Honda.house.gov/ethiopia_about.shtml›

as the Ethiopian Freedom, Democracy and Accountability Act of 2006, authored by Rep. Chris Smith, a Republican from New Jersey.

Despite support from members of the US Congress, the bill failed to appear on the House floor because of the lobby against the bill financed by the current government of Ethiopia, the EPRDF. Because of the continued pressure by Ethiopians and the support they garnered from Congressman Donald Payne (Democrat from New Jersey), Chairman of the Subcommittee on Africa and Global Health, another version of the bill, the Ethiopia Democracy and Accountability Act, also known as H.R. 2003, was introduced in July 2007.[1] The bill requires the government of Ethiopia to observe human rights and be accountable for the way it treats its citizens. The bill has provisions aimed to help the people of Ethiopia, such as a demand for government accountability, strengthening human rights and civic society organizations, monitoring human rights, a reporting process, and training in election monitoring. The bill has infuriated the Ethiopian government as it requires travel restrictions on any government officials implicated in human rights abuses. Ethiopian-Americans have lobbied members of the US congress to support the bill. Eighty-three members of the House, including all members of the Black Caucus, have supported the bill.

Similar lobbying of local officials is also taking place throughout the United States. For example, Ethiopians residing in the City of Takoma Park, Maryland, lobbied the City Council to support H.R. 5680 and later H.R. 2003. The council passed resolutions in support of the bills. The mayor of the city, Kathy Porter, wrote the House Speaker, Nancy Pelosi, urging her to help move H.R. 2003 forward. The Prime Minister of Ethiopia responded to the proposed legislation by stating that Ethiopia is not willing to be a banana republic.

The Ethiopian government has enlisted the service of DLA Piper, a Washington, D.C.-based lobbying firm, at $50,000 a month, to block the bill from mark-up. The firm has political heavyweight lobbyists such as the former House Majority Leaders Richard Armey, a Republican from Texas, and Richard Gephardt, a Democrat from Missouri. *Harper's* magazine columnist Ken Silverstein pointed out that that money is being used against Ethiopia to protect the interests of the ruling party.[2] In addition to the lobby group, the government of Ethiopia has been supported by the Bush administration. Senator Patrick Leahy, Chairman of the Judiciary Committee, accused the Bush administration of supporting just about anyone who claims to be against terrorism, no matter how undemocratic or corrupt they may be. Such support, according to Sen. Leahy, will tarnish the image of the US and likely backfire, costing it dearly in the long term.[3]

Despite the support the bill received from Ethiopian diaspora and members of the US Congress, it failed the mark-up for discussion on the house floor. Diaspora Ethiopians were geared up for another showdown with the government of Ethiopia and they succeeded on October 2, 2007, as the US House of Representatives passed Ethiopia Democracy and Accountability Act of 2007 (H.R. 2003) — unanimously. Congressman Donald Payne forcefully accused the Ethiopian government, on the House floor, for its human rights abuses. Congressman Chris Smith, Jr. decried Meles

---

1 Scott A. Morgan. July 3, 2006. "Ethiopia human rights bill advances through the House," *Los Angeles Chronicle.*

2 Ken Silverstein. July 27, 2007. "Lobbying firms blocked action against Ethiopia's tyrant," *Harper's Magazine.*

3 Refer to "Statement of Sen. Patrick Leahy, Assistance for Ethiopia," August 3, 2007, http:// leahy.senate.gov/press/200708/08307d..htm. Also reported in *Ethiomedia*, August 8, 2007.

Zenawi's arrogance while other congressmen used terms such as "ruthless dictators" and "thugs in power" in characterizing the Ethiopian leadership. (Refer to Appendix VII for a copy of H.R. 2003.)

Both Donald Payne and Chris Smith, Jr. were supportive of the current Ethiopian government, optimistic that despite the shortcomings of Prime Minister Meles it was an improvement over the military government. In a discussion with the author in December 1993 on a flight from Boston to Washington, DC, Congressman Donald Payne was optimistic about the Transitional Government of Ethiopia, saying that the government had even brought the OLF to the fold. Birhanu Nega, opposition leader and Mayor-elect of Addis Ababa (2005), reports that when Congressman Chris Smith, Jr. visited Ethiopia on a fact-finding mission in July 2005 as chair of the House Africa Subcommittee, Mr. Smith was, "like the Bush administration, very friendly to the government of Meles Zenawi."[1] When the opposition met with Smith and asked him to communicate with Prime Minister Meles Zenawi about the need for an independent investigation of election fraud, he gave them a long lecture urging them to stand up for life and against abortion, thus expressing his socially fundamentalist views of American politics. Mr. Smith also told the opposition that he knew Meles and that he believed "that he is a polished person who would not allow [election fraud] to happen."[2] Birhanu reminded Congressman Smith that he knew his dictator very well, "including how he manipulates the *ferenjis* [foreigners]." Mr. Meles had told Mr. Smith that the allegation "was a complete lie." To the credit of Mr. Smith, he did discover that the Ethiopian leader had all along had been deceiving US officials. He and Congressmen Donald Paine are now at the forefront in condemning human rights violations in Ethiopia and they sponsored H.R. 2003.

The bill, which as of the beginning of 2009 had yet to be sent to the Senate for a vote, has angered Ethiopian leaders. Although it would be hard to overturn it, as individual senators have the power to place the bill on hold, this may be as far as the bill goes. If it is supported by the US Senate, the bill could be signed by President Obama, who says his foreign policy is different from that of President Bush.[3]

Senator Russ Feingold, Chairman of the Subcommittee on African Affairs, introduced a bill in the Senate titled "Support for Democracy and Human Rights in Ethiopia Act of 2008" in September. The bill, among its other requirements, requires the US President to take steps to support the implementation of democracy and governance institutions and organizations in Ethiopia. The bill would also limit security assistance and restrict travel by government officials allegedly involved in human rights violations. The Ethiopian diaspora, organized as the Coalition for H.R. 2003, has played a major role in promoting this bill, unprecedented in the relations between the two countries.

When the diaspora Ethiopians rallied for the H.R. 2003 Bill in the US Congress, the government of Ethiopia ironically accused them of allying with a foreign power and encouraging foreign domination and intervention. This conception was intended to create a wedge between Ethiopians in Ethiopia and those in the diaspora, another

---

1 Berhanu Nega's speech in February 2008, at Bucknell University, Pennsylvania.

2 Ibid.

3 For some of the reports on the bill, refer to C. Bryson Hull. 2007. As reported in http://www. ethimedia.com/ace/zenawi_faces_sanction.html>. Retrieved on October 4, 2007. Also refer to "US targets Ethiopia for sanctions" BBC news, 2007, http://newsvote.bbc.co.uk/mpapps/ pagetools/print/news.bbc.co.uk/1/> Retrieved on October 4, 2007. Also refer to a report by Barney Jopson and Daniel Dombey. October 4, 2007. *Financial Times*, p.4.

of the current government's divide-and-rule ploys. It is also indicative of the government's desperation and its fear. This bill, among others, will deny visas to Ethiopian government officials who are implicated in the murder of peaceful demonstrators after the trumped-up election results of May 5, 2005. The bill has infuriated the Ethiopian government, which is employing its propaganda machine, including churches, to discredit diaspora Ethiopians.

Opposition to the bill also comes from former US officials in Ethiopia. In an unconvincing op-ed that appeared in *The New York Times* of November 15, 2007, Vicky Huddleston and Tibor Nagy, former Acting US Ambassador and Ambassador (1999–2002) to Ethiopia respectively, opined that the passage of the bill was destructive because "it threatens to cut off technical assistance to Ethiopia, one of our closest allies."[1] The bill requires the government to release political prisoners, ensure that the judiciary operates independently, and permit the news media to operate freely. The bill is not opposed to the fundamental American values of due process of law, separation power, and freedom of speech. Such pronouncements by former and current US government officials could undermine efforts to build good governance and establish laws and institutions that promote and safeguard the supremacy of law. For former US officials to state that the government of Ethiopia is building democracy while it is "besieged from within and without by enemies of democracy," and to call for Congress to "put aside its bill and instead use creative diplomacy to deal with the combined threat of insurgency and war,"[2] raises questions as to their intentions or their understanding.

The role that the Ethiopian diaspora plays in pressuring the US government and influencing its policy towards Ethiopia has changed significantly from the 1980s. Ethiopian-Americans have not been politically visible until recently and have not participated in American politics through their vote.

One reason for the absence of a focused political agenda among the diaspora Ethiopians is political difference and personal rivalry. There is also a lack of ideological coherence. As a result, both political and non-political organizations have failed to work for a higher national goal and vision. An official in Ethiopia, who requested anonymity, dismissed the role of the diaspora by stating that "Democracy cannot be promoted from the vantage point of the diaspora; it must be lived through and practically exercised on the ground in Ethiopia." The role the diaspora plays, according to my source, is "a tiny contribution to a grand task." On the other hand, opposition leaders such as Merera Gudina, Chairman of the Oromo National Congress and Chairman of the Political Science Department, Addis Ababa University, are appreciative of the diaspora's efforts both in lobbying and financially supporting the struggle at home. The opposition also appreciates the support it receives from the diaspora, "especially when (weighed) against the background of a determined repressive regime that frustrates financial support to the opposition inside the country."[3] Merera questioned how much of the opposition would have survived as a political force in Ethiopia without support from the diaspora.

Recognizing that the opposition and Ethiopian NGOs get their strength from the financial support they receive from diaspora Ethiopians and international NGOs, the government is taking measures to curb that support. The government has a bill

---

1 Vicki Huddleston and Tibor Nagy, November 15, 2007, "Don't turn on Ethiopia," *The New York Times*, Op-ed.

2 Ibid.

3 I am appreciative of Dr. Merera Gudina for his comment.

passed in parliament "designed to prevent foreign interference in the country's political affairs."[1] The government is accused of violating the rights of children and disabled persons and of hindering the reform of criminal justice. The bill would stifle reports on human rights abuses in Ethiopia, reports that are currently provided by the Ethiopian Human Rights Council (EHRCO). The Council receives 90% of its financial support from abroad. This will be seen as "foreign intervention in the country's political affairs." International NGOs will be unable to continue their work for human rights, development programs, and conflict resolution. Challenging the government will be seen as subversion. Such judgment will deny the outside world any information on human rights abuses in the country and partners for development.

The government's action has "provoked a visit to Ethiopia by the US Assistant Secretary of State for Democracy and Human Rights, David Kramer, who said he feared the new law would close down a number of projects currently funded by the American government."[2] Such is the precarious state of democracy in Ethiopia.

Merera's misgivings about the diaspora were based on the discriminatory support given to some groups by disfavoring others, and "the over-militancy of some" which generally leads to the misreading of the Ethiopian reality. In this he was referring to the support some gave to EDP-Medhin, which some claim to be co-opted by the government, and the creation of two opposition camps in the US, the CUD and the UEDF. This division has virtually polarized the diaspora. Leaders and individuals both in Ethiopia and in the diaspora need to focus on bringing the different groups together, building consensus, and composing sound alternative policies to replace those of the current government. They have confused US officials by providing competing voices, undermining each other, and not providing a clear and well-articulated alternative vision for the country. Merera sees the diaspora's pressure towards militancy as having denied the opposition inside the country the opportunity to work together — and either ending in prison together or in Parliament together. They could have honestly calculated their preparation and capacity to face the regime determined to crush the opposition. The result, according to Professor Merera, could have been avoidance of both the existing "political disorientation as well as the lingering division within the opposition."

Poor political calculation by the opposition has allowed the US embassy in Addis Ababa to intervene in the domestic politics of Ethiopia. Such intervention, according to a former minister of Ethiopia under Emperor Haile Selassie, could have not been imagined during the imperial rule.

In general, resources were squandered, precious time lost, and opportunity created for political shenanigans to exploit conditions to advance personal interests. Diaspora politics in the absence of vision, a viable institution, accountability, and committed leadership can be dangerous. TPLF/EPRDF, on the other hand, has a total monopoly on the resources and institutions of Ethiopia.

The ruling party regrets that it slightly opened up the electoral process because of pressure from foreign countries and funding institutions; this revealed its own poor performance in election outcomes. Government officials have hinted they will not repeat the same mistake in the 2010 election. Does this mean the death of democracy in Ethiopia before it was born?

---

1 Elizabeth Blunt, BBC News in Addis Ababa, "Ethiopia fears over aid clampdown," http//news-vote.bbc.co.uk/mpapps/pagetools/print/news.bbc.co.uk/2hi/

2 Elizabeth Blunt, ibid.

Once-promising renaissance leaders have turned out to be Africa's big men who amass wealth and power; replacing them through elections remains a challenge, yet one that is surmountable. The fragmentation of political parties also provided excuses for US officials to continue supporting the EPRDF, despite its undemocratic nature. Opposition political parties have also continued undermining each other rather than working together and providing a viable alternative force to the EPRDF.

IMPLICATIONS FOR ETHIOPIA

Because of the nature of the international system, and the conditions in Ethiopia, the exodus of Ethiopians will continue. They will be dispersed worldwide but most are attracted to the United States. Once they arrive in the US, they can still assist Ethiopia through their education, expertise, and financial assets. Remittances sent by diaspora Ethiopians to families and relatives in Ethiopia have helped bolster the economy of the country. On October 2, 2008, Elias Loha, manager of Reserve Management and Foreign Exchange Market of National Bank of Ethiopia, reported that remittances from diaspora Ethiopians, largely from the US, accounted for $1.2 billion annually, the second largest source of income after exports. There is concern that the remittances will decline as a result of the economic crisis in the United States.[1]

There may be two sides even to this. An Ethiopian scholar and human rights activist in the US, Alemayehu Gebre Mariam, asked if "our remittances provide economic buoyancy to help keep afloat the doomed ship of a ruthless dictatorship?" Alemayehu bemoaned the lack of empirical data to find answers to this and other questions.[2] Ethiopia needs its diaspora nationals who, especially in the first generation, are not completely disconnected from Ethiopia. Second generation Ethiopians will also continue to look towards Ethiopia for their identity, culture, and history. They too will play a significant role in influencing US foreign policy towards Ethiopia. Diaspora Ethiopians will work to improve the political environment there and pressure the US government to that end.

The relationship between diaspora Ethiopians and the current and future governments in Ethiopia will not likely be cordial and harmonious all the time. Diaspora Ethiopians will work to improve the political, economic, and social conditions of their country of origin and will remain critical of governments in Ethiopia that fail to address that goal. Ethiopian governments may paint that work as interference in Ethiopia's domestic and foreign policies.

But governments in Ethiopia can draw support and inspiration from diaspora Ethiopians. Their investment, expertise, and experience in the US will be much needed in Ethiopia. There may be a love–hate relationship between the diaspora and the governments of Ethiopia. Diaspora Ethiopians may in the future demand direct representation in the body politics, such as in the parliament, as they wish to be partners in nation building and development. Increased globalization will create borderless Ethiopians and a seamless life whether in their country of origin or country of residence. The current and future leaders of Ethiopia have to brace for such happenings. They have to take advantage of all that the diaspora offers, including political discourse. Ethiopian governments, current and future, must not categorize diaspora

---

1 Tsegaye Tadesse. October 2, 2008. "Ethiopia fears U.S. crisis may cut remittances," *Reuters News Service*, http://africa.reuters.com/country/ET/news/usnL2660925.html

2 Alemayehu G. Mariam. October 13, 2008. "The political economy of remittances in Ethiopia," *Ethiopian Review*, http://www.ethiopianreview.com/content/5297/print

Ethiopians as "they" and "them" and their in-country followers as "we" and "us" — implying that they are the bane, and we the blessed.

IMPLICATIONS FOR THE US

US policy makers towards Ethiopia can benefit from diaspora Ethiopians. Their voices must not be heard as coming from disgruntled ethnic groups, reactionary supporters of previous regimes, or disenfranchised outcasts. Diaspora Ethiopians are not merely a mix of discontents nor are they a monolithic bloc. They are diverse and may have personal biases and goals. They might have different visions for Ethiopia. Some may not even want to associate with Ethiopia. Nevertheless they could collectively provide alternative information about what actually is taking place in Ethiopia.

Ethiopian-Americans have learned about democracy by living in the United States. They are involved in US politics and they campaign for American political candidates. They have first-hand knowledge of democracy in action and wish to see true democracy take roots in their country of origin.

Ethiopian-Americans could be ambassadors of goodwill for the US, thereby obviating the question, "Why do they hate us?" Ethiopians in the US come from all parts of Ethiopia, are closely connected to people living there, and have legitimate concerns about the wellbeing of their country. Most seek to build a durable friendship and alliance between Ethiopia and the US where Ethiopians in general could be the beneficiaries of US assistance and the development of programs to alleviate poverty. Ethiopian-Americans resent US foreign policies that fails to benefit their country of origin but aggrandize the positions of the ruling elite. When US policy fails to achieve stated goals like protecting human rights in Ethiopia, ensuring true democracy, and helping in economic development they, like any citizens, question the motives behind the policy.

Some US government officials believe the future would be much better if Ethiopia would harness its human capital and overcome its political problems. The current US policy of benign neglect towards Africa, however, is not helping this to happen. The George W. Bush administration, when it came to office, showed little interest in Africa.[1] After September 11, 2001, the focus shifted to fighting terrorism in Afghanistan, the Middle East, and the Horn of Africa. Under George W. Bush, Secretary of State Colin Powell's interest in Africa and the Caribbean countries seemingly placed the two regions on the radar of the Bush administration. Nevertheless, the Bush-43 administration did not put tangible plans on the table and it never got past the quagmire in Iraq. The exception is the Bush administration's commitment of $5 million to fight HIV/AIDs in Africa. This commitment surpasses the commitment to Africa by the Bushes' predecessors, Presidents Jimmy Carter and Bill Clinton, but is a token sum these days.

Given the past neglect, and the current preoccupation with other regions, one could not expect much to happen in the Ethio–US relationship. It is left to visionary Ethiopians, both at home and in the diaspora, to come to grips with reality and try to solve their nation's problems. Despite the fact that Ethio–US diplomatic relationship is more than a century old and that the US has spent significant resources there, Ethiopia's development has been unimpressive. This calls for a reevaluation of US

---

1 Getachew Metaferia. 2006. "Africa and the making of U.S. foreign policy in the era of globalization," Alice M. Jackson, ed., *Political Issues in America: A Multidimensional Perspective*, Boston, MA: Pearson Publishing.

policy. Ethiopia has to be committed to national development and its leaders must refrain from squandering national resources, including its human capital.

CHAPTER 14. ETHIOPIA, THE US, AND THE HOA: A TRIANGULAR RELATIONSHIP

The Horn of Africa comprises Ethiopia, Djibouti, Somalia, Kenya, Uganda, Eritrea, and Sudan. They belong to the Intergovernmental Agency on Development (IGAD), an interregional organization for development and the promotion of security and trade among member countries, created in 1986. Upon becoming independent in 1993, Eritrea joined IGAD, but declared its suspension of membership in 2007.

Djibouti, Eritrea, and Somalia control the northeastern gate of Africa and the important sea lane of the Red Sea. Hence, the strategic importance of the HOA to both the US and the West is high. The Horn of Africa countries have diverse populations, resources, and historical and geographic background. They also share certain similarities; are interdependent, and face the same destiny. In general, the Horn of Africa (HOA) is neither cohesive nor homogeneous. The region has earned a name for political instability, food insecurity, and proliferation of illegal firearms, an interwoven movement of refugees, internally displaced people, environmental degradation and war. Given a capable leadership, regional cooperation, and positive international attention, these unfortunate faces of the HOA can be altered and the problems are surmountable.

Donor government and agencies generally do not accord Africa adequate attention or resource allocation in spite of its mounting problems. Whenever there are budgetary cuts in donor countries such as the US, the continent will be most affected and resource allocation will sharply decline. The Horn of Africa received undue attention by the superpowers during the Cold War period. It did not benefit economically but remained a dumping ground for military hardware which has contributed to the sorry conditions currently unfolding in Somalia. Now, once again, the region is receiving US attention. The US is concerned about destabilizing forces of religious extremism and international terrorism assumed to train and operate in Somalia.

After the end of the Cold War, there emerged new regimes in Ethiopia and Somalia. A new nation, Eritrea, was born. The civil war between the North and South Sudan came to an end. These mostly positive situations in the region did not last long. After what was perceived to be political normalcy, economic development, and stability, most countries of the region seem to have entered a downward spiral. The much-expected peace, the introduction and establishment of democracy, and stability did not materialize. The US is still involved in the region and the relationship between Ethiopia and the US has been closer — similar to what it was during the reign of Emperor Haile Selassie. Ethiopian Prime Minister Meles Zenawi has represented himself to the US as the antithesis of Col. Mengistu Haile Mariam. Nevertheless, the region experiences economic, political, and social crisis. Citizens have increasingly become powerless. Poverty, ill health, and environmental degradation have remained the hallmarks of most of the countries of the region. Internal and external forces share the blame. We will examine the conditions in the countries of the HOA and the roles of Ethiopia and the US in these countries.

DEMOCRACY IN ETHIOPIA: THE MAY 2005 ELECTION AND US INVOLVEMENT

In Ethiopia, in the May 2005 election, the United Ethiopian Democratic Forces (UDEF) and the newly established Coalition for Unity and Democracy (CUD) were on the ballot. UDEF is a coalition of different political parties. Members who are from Ethiopia and in the diaspora were represented by Dr. Beyene Petros and Dr. Merera Gudina. In the short time of its establishment and despite its lack of a strong institution, CUD galvanized Ethiopians in the country and in the diaspora. Diaspora Ethiopians who supported CUD in its goal to replace the current regime through elections raised funds for CUD's campaign. CUD did indeed win election in Addis Ababa and in some other regions.

However, the incumbent invalidated the election and CUD leaders were jailed for two years on flimsy charges. The support of Ethiopians in the diaspora and in Ethiopia failed because they lacked a clear agenda, an effective institution and inspiring, organizing, and galvanizing leadership. The focus was shifted to getting the imprisoned CUD leaders, supporters, and journalists freed and exposing to the world the undemocratic government of Ethiopia.

The government passed stringent laws to curb parliamentary rights and made it practically impossible to execute legislative responsibilities. If the CUD members had joined the Parliament, perhaps they could have provided a forum to expose the government's shortcomings while educating their constituencies.

Some Ethio-Americans also share the blame for confusing the situation and influencing some CUD leaders. The diaspora may have contacts and wealth, but it lacks political knowledge and skills. It lacks wide vision, the drive for consensus building, and conviction regarding inclusive politics. The diaspora has also contributed to the fragmentation of the opposition.

Ethiopia, the most pro-US country in the region and the recipient of the most US assistance, remains politically unstable especially since the 2005 elections. The public has lost confidence more and more in the government and in the opposition, especially the CUD. The incumbent government of the EPRDF, especially the dominant TPLF, has pursued the policy of staying in power by any means necessary. After losing the election to opposition parties, they deployed a special force, the *Agazi*, and killed some 193 peaceful demonstrators and arrested 30,000 people.

Judge Wolde Michael Meshesha, who was appointed by the government to investigate election-related unrest, accused the government of trying to suppress the results of the probe and questioned "Prime Minister Meles Zenawi's commitment to democratic reform." In addition, according to the chairperson of the inquiry, Judge Frehiwot Samuel, "many people were killed arbitrarily [and] old men were killed while in their homes and children were also victims of the attack while playing in the garden."[1] The two judges fled Ethiopia fearing for their safety. Six government troops were reported killed. US-supplied humvees were also used against peaceful civilian demonstrators. Opposition leaders were thrown behind bars for two years on what most people claim to be false accusations. People and regions accused of supporting opposition groups are harshly treated by the government and its cadres under the pretext of preserving internal security.

In a meeting with European Members of Parliament (MPS), Mr. Meles accused opposition groups of trying to "change the constitution by unconstitutional means ... [that] the objective of the election campaign is to carry out what they call a rose revolution, ... use the electoral campaign to mobilize support for their agenda, discredit the electoral process and carry out the rose revolution."[2] The Ethiopian Foreign Minister, Seyoum Mesfin, even challenged some in the US for raising these issues. He asked, "Why should countries like Ethiopia be taken to task? There is no country that has established perfect institutions of democracy or human rights, even countries like the United States."[3]

The role of the US embassy in dealing with the jailed opposition leaders must be mentioned here. Dr. Birhanu Nega was a member of the Coalition for Unity and Democracy (CUD) and won the election for the Mayor of Addis Ababa. He was jailed at Kaliti prison. Dr. Birhanu shared with me a copy of a speech in which he told his audience at Bucknell University, Pennsylvania (where he once taught), that the US Chargé d'Affaires Ms. Vicky Huddleston and the French Ambassador to Ethiopia visited him in the prison. The two diplomats told him that they were worried about the instability in the country in the aftermath of the election and that "some important small towns in Oromia were being rocked by demonstration." Ms. Huddleston told Birhanu that the US and EU governments "have no way to force the government to abide by its own laws" that ostensibly uphold democracy. To avoid instability the US diplomat, according to Birhanu, suggested he "abrogate [his] Mayorship and tell the public to accept as Mayor the person chosen by the government."[4] According to Birhanu Nega, Huddleston told him that since the public listened to him, they would accept that outcome and peace and stability would return to the country and the "government would be stable again."[5] Otherwise, he was warned that he was "going to be in prison for a very long time." Ironically, Huddleston invited families of the political prisoners to the embassy to "ask them to pressure [the prisoners] to accept the government demands."

According to Merera Gudina, Chairman of the Oromo National Congress, Ambassador Vicky Huddleston "consciously participated in the weakening and division of the opposition" by sending wrong signals to the international community. Accord-

---

1 Anthony Mitchell, Associated Press writer, September 18, 2006, "Judge says Ethiopian forces killed 193," http://www.ethiomedia.com/addfile/police_kill_193.html

2 "Notes taken during meeting between Meles Zenawi and European MPs" on May 13, 2005. Reported by Binyam Kedir Abdu, former First Secretary at Ethiopian Embassy in Kuwait, February 22, 2007. Quote taken from http://www.ethiomedia.com/articles/meles_zenawi_and_european_mps...

3 Nora Boustany. May 14, 2005. "Ethiopia defends record on rights," *The Washington Post*, p. A12.

4 This information is based on a copy of the speech Birhanu Nega shared with me. He gave the speech at Bucknell University, Pennsylvania, February 2008.

5 Ibid.

ing to Merera, in the run-up to the election, during the election, and after the election, "the heart of the American leaders was with the EPRDF regime and they systematically worked to salvage the friendly Meles regime." Merera, in response to my written queries, said that "democracy is not a commodity to be imported and exported" as the US tried to do in Ethiopia. He advises "America to stop dining and wining with dictators under the guise of directing a war against terror." Dictators who terrorize millions of their own citizens cannot be dependable allies in the war against terrorists. Merera believes Zimbabwe is more democratic than Ethiopia. The US, he feels, could use its leverage as a sole superpower to support the cause of democracy as it says it is doing in Zimbabwe.

Birhanu also said that the US Ambassador, Aurelia Brazil, in a private conversation forewarned him that "the US was not prepared for such a drastic change [a defeat of the government] and that she suspected the government would not accept defeat." The Ambassador, an African-American, told him that "it took African-Americans hundreds of years to get their rights" by working through the system peacefully.

This statement compels one to examine three points: One, the Ethiopian opposition is being told diplomatically to wait years for democracy to be realized. Second, the Ethiopian opposition has categorically pronounced that it wants to change government through peaceful and democratic processes based on the law of the land. Third, from all indications and from Dr. Birhanu's speech, the government has broken its own rules and taken undemocratic measures to silence the people's voice. Such, therefore, is the US double standard as far as democracy in Ethiopia goes. It seems that Ethiopians are "not yet ready" for democracy. Throwing funds at building institutions, as if that were the only means necessary to achieve the goal of realizing democracy, will not be sufficient. The US must throw its weight and resources into saving democracy from totalitarian leaders. Long-term national interests must be considered and not the short-term interests of ruling parties.

It is partly because of such policy and the idiosyncrasy of rulers that Ethiopians are suffering abject poverty. The US, especially the Ronald Reagan administration, was known for its support of the apartheid regime in South Africa; they accused Nelson Mandela's African National Congress (ANC) of being a notorious terrorist organization. At the same time, the anti-apartheid movement efforts of American citizens helped in the dismantling of the regime. Members of the Congressional Black Caucus (CBC) such as Congressman C. Diggs, Jr., Donald V. Dellums, William Gray, and Walter E. Fauntroy also helped in the dismantling of the regime.[1] Some members of Congress have started expressing their concerns about the situation in Ethiopia and are challenging US diplomats.

One has also to reflect on the method and demeanor of some diplomats in their interactions. A US diplomat who visited the elected mayor of Addis Ababa, Birhanu Nega, in Kaliti prison, gave Birhanu copies of the *New Yorker* and told him to read them in his spare time. The offer was no doubt meant to be a friendly gesture but could be seen as patronizing and not to the point. Prisoners may have a lot of time free for reading. But they also may occasionally have to consult with their lawyers, meet visitors, appear in court, or be subjected to psychological or physical torture.

The authoritarian rule of the government is not necessarily a response to the opposition it faced by the people, such as during the May 2005 elections, but is the ingrained technique it uses to deal with dissent even within its own rank and file, as

---

1 For anti-apartheid movement in the US Congress, refer to *Voice — African American Voices in Congress*, www.avoiceonline.org/aam/history.html

do undemocratic forces worldwide. Dima Noggo Sarbo, who used to be a member of the OLF and well knew both the TPLF and EPLF said in an unpublished article that he shared with me, the two organizations "never tolerated any rivals, or internal criticism and dissent." Commanded by authoritarian leaders who have disregard for human rights, Ethiopian troops have been accused of extra-judicial killings, torture, rape, and burning of villages in Gambella and the Ogaden regions. Local government cadres are also accused of harassing and jailing citizens who are alleged to be sympathizers and supporters of opposition groups in all regions of the country. As a reporter from *Financial Times* commented, similar to the situation in Pakistan and Egypt, the US is supporting an "awkward bedfellow ... for security goals but one that pursues its own, sometimes brutal, agenda regardless of American pressure."[1] As the BBC World Affairs correspondent, Peter Biles, stated in a report, "The Ethiopian government may point to the fact that there was no freedom of expression whatsoever during Mengistu's rule, but a heavy-handed reaction from Mr. Meles' security forces to public demonstration in Addis Ababa is certain to be viewed as another blow to Africa's so-called "renaissance."[2] The Ethiopian government and its foreign supporters have set the Mengistu regime as a yardstick for comparison. Comparing one undemocratic regime with Meles' government will not show either in a better light and is a mockery of democracy.

At times US officials, knowingly or unknowingly, collaborate with governments that commit crimes against their own people. As a result of the May 2005 elections in Ethiopia and as indicated earlier, opposition leaders were put behind bars. One of them was Birtukan Mideksa, a young leader of the Coalition for Unity and Democracy (CUD) or *kinijit*. In an "Open Letter to Ambassador Vicki Huddleston" from Kaliti prison, she reminded the ambassador that she was trusted by CUD leadership and was invited to attend CUD's Urgent Executive Meeting, before the CUD leaders were imprisoned, so that she could witness first-hand how democratic and transparent the organization was. In her open letter, Birtukan wished that the Ambassador had "remained ... an honest and trustworthy broker." The young lawyer accused the ambassador of "efforts ... directed to a fervent championship for the creation of another *kinijit* to continue the political process; a process which would leave the people alienated.... [S]uch a distinguished American diplomat as you are shouldn't facilitate the politics of alienation which has been the scourge of this ancient country." The US embassy was accused of undermining the CUD by organizing a duplicate political party that would discredit the existing and legitimate party whose leaders were imprisoned. The government accused the party of inciting violence, an accusation denied by the party. The actual crime of the party was winning elections and discrediting the government. In spite of what the American embassy did to her party, Birtukan Mideksa stated that she had not "yet lost hope in [the Ambassador's] capacity to invest [her] country's political capital and help solve the political problem of Ethiopia." Such expectations of Ethiopians are often not fulfilled by US diplomats.

As Birtukan Mideksa's letter shows, Ethiopians have trusted the US government too much and ultimately have been let down; US officials are mesmerized by the manipulations of the Ethiopian leaders; the US is interested in fighting purported in-

---

1 Barney Jopson. October 11, 2007. "A dismissive Ethiopia tests the limits of US indulgence," *Financial Times*, p. 11.

2 Peter Biles, "Profile: Ethiopia's leader Meles Zenawi," httop://newsvote.bbc.co.uk/mpnpps/pagetools/print/news.bbc.co.uk/2/hi/

ternational terrorism and can accommodate leaders who terrorize their own people; a token democracy and symbolism is good enough for Ethiopia and other African countries; and finally, whatever is the US interest, justice and democracy can be delayed until such time that the US regards its own agenda is not threatened.

The opposition has also remained fragmented, rampant with personal rivalry. It has not established strong institutions nor sound policy alternatives. The government's power is a result of the weakness of the opposition political parties who operate from within and outside of the country. According to a report by *Africa Confidential*, the government of Ethiopia is "blessed with an internal opposition which is even more inchoate than its own political institutions and the opposition in exile is becoming more irrelevant by the day to most Ethiopians."[1]

Ethiopia appeared in the media once again, in 2008, as famine again took its toll on innocent victims: children, women, and the elderly. The government's failed policies, poor priority choices, and the self-aggrandizement of its leaders at the expense of the citizenry, and uncritical support by foreign governments, are to blame for the economic failure and political instability in Ethiopia. Most importantly, hunger and starvation are affecting even the fertile regions of the country. Environmental degradation, unemployment, alienation, hopelessness and powerlessness have remained the characteristics of the country at the moment. Meanwhile, dissent against the government is escalating in all regions of the country. These, certainly, are not signs of stability and peace. The prevailing conditions in Ethiopia contribute to the precarious situations in the Horn of Africa. Internally, the government's intolerance for any challenge through legal and democratic means continues to stymie any movement towards change. This also has a wider regional implication. A country's foreign policy is merely an extension of its domestic policy. We will briefly examine this.

Ethiopia and Eritrea: A Challenge to US Diplomacy

The Clinton administration had proclaimed the leaders of the two countries, who had worked together to overthrow the most anti-American regime of Mengistu Haile Mariam, to be at the forefront of the new African renaissance. They were expected to bring about peace and development to their respective countries. The US also hoped the two leaders would serve as a bulwark against the forces of Islamic fundamentalism and global terrorism that used Sudan and Somalia as training grounds and as a springboard to destabilize other countries of the region.

The leaders of Ethiopia and Eritrea, Meles Zenawi and Issayas Afewerki, were interviewed just before the border war between their countries erupted. Both said that bilateral relations between the two countries were "strong and satisfactory," although differences in outlook could exist. The Eritrean Minister of Defense Sebhat Efrem and the Ethiopian Presidential Security Chief Abreha Kassa were observed socializing in Addis Ababa a week before the war.

The border war between Ethiopia and Eritrea, 1998 to 2000, has claimed the lives of 100,000 people on both sides. The proximate cause of the war was the tension over monetary questions. Both countries had been using the Ethiopian *birr*; then Eritrea introduced its own currency, the *nakfa*, and stopped using the *birr*. Eritrea wanted the exchange rate for the *nakfa* to be equivalent to that of the *birr*. Ethiopia surprised Eritrea when it introduced new *birr* notes so that Eritrea would not be able to use the older *birr* notes that it had accumulated.

---

1 *Africa Confidential*. January 21, 1994. Vol. 35, no.2, p.3.

Border skirmishes on May 6, 1998, led to a major war. This derailed US optimism regarding its regional policy. The Ethiopian leadership vowed to remove Eritrea's elements of "command and control" — which meant removing Issayas Afewerki, and assisted groups opposed to the Eritrean leadership such as the Kunama-Baria organization — The Democratic Front for the Liberation of Setit and Gash, that called to establish an autonomous region in Western Eritrea.[1] The Afar people, some of whom are now in Eritrea, also wanted to establish their own autonomous region within a democratic Ethiopia. The Afar Revolutionary Democratic Unity Front (ARDUF) fights against both governments.

The region remains tense and unpredictable. Hence, human rights violations, development, peace, and human security remain unfulfilled.

After all the sacrifice paid for the independence of Eritrea, the people of Eritrea have not enjoyed the fruits of independence and the country is worse off than it was before. The dividends of political independence remain unrealized. The country is still under a single party dictatorship and is a police state. President Issayas Afewerki and the People's Front for Democracy and Justice (PFDJ), that replaced the EPLF, remain the dominant political actors in Eritrea.

Eritrea was optimistic and hopeful when it gained its independence. Even before it gained its *de jure* independence in 1993,[2] Eritrea attempted to broker peace in the region, such as in Somalia in 1992, and was perceived as a constructive and neutral party. Issayas Afewerki was also taken to be a lightening rod and a democrat who challenged the old order and modus operandi in the UN and the OAU. In his first appearance at the OAU opening day, on June 28, 1993, Issayas Afewerki blasted the organization for its incompetence. He said, "I must stress again — that we do not find membership in this organization under the present circumstances spiritually gratifying or politically challenging."[3] Issayas soon proved to be mercurial and joined the long list of undemocratic African leaders. Some of his long-time supporters distanced themselves from him.

In addition to a total lack of internal democracy, Eritrea had antagonized its neighbors at different times. Even the once friendly states of Sudan, Yemen, Djibouti, and Ethiopia were attacked by Eritrea despite its limited resources. Eritrean leadership operated its guerilla war from Sudan and owed its political independence partially to the successive Sudanese governments. Two years after Eritrea declared independence, in 1995, Eritrea terminated relations with Sudan. Both countries massed their troops on the border and, encouraged by the US which had labeled Sudan as a terrorist state, Eritrea sheltered forces opposed to the Sudanese leadership.

Meles had assured the public, mainly the international community, that bilateral relations between Ethiopia and Eritrea remained "strong and satisfactory" despite some differences in outlook which could appear within "a family."[4] The honeymoon between the new leaders of Ethiopia and Eritrea did not last long. The worst Eritrean conflict was the border war it waged with Ethiopia from May 1998 to June 2000. Personality conflict between the leaders, among other sore points, has contributed to the demise of 100,000 from both countries. Force, not diplomacy, was given priority in resolving disputes. The two-year bitter fight between the TPLF/EPRDF and the

---

1 Refer to *Africa Confidential*. May 29, 1998. Vol. 39, no. 11.

2 Eritrea had a de facto independence since 1991 when it separated from Ethiopia. In 1993, it declared independence from Ethiopia after a referendum conducted by EPLF.

3 *Africa Confidential*. July 16, 1993. Vol. 34, no. 14, p. 2.

4 *Africa Confidential*. January. 23, 1998. Vol. 39, no.2.

EPLF became a war between states, and its political implications became wider and the human cost severe.

The close association of the TPLF and EPLF organizations and the leaders, Meles and Issayas, proved to have been a short-term tactical alliance, not a long-term strategic one. According to Dima Noggo Sarbo, the TPLF "owes its origins and growth as well as eventual conquest of state power in Ethiopia to the support it received from the Eritrean fronts at critical stages of its development."[1]

The root cause of the Ethio–Eritrean border dispute was actually economic. In 1997, after Eritrea had dropped the Ethiopian *birr*, Ethiopia demanded that all cross-border transactions more than 200 *birr* must be paid in US dollars. In the hope of destroying development infrastructures such as the pharmaceutical industry in Mekele, Eritrean planes bombed Mekele and killed 40 civilians on June 5, 1998. The war then triggered an increase in the defense budget of Ethiopia — $467 million in 1999 as compared to $140 million prior to the war. Ethiopia once again resorted to buying weapons from former Soviet states such as Bulgaria. The UN Security Council, on May 17, 2000, imposed an arms embargo on both Ethiopia and Eritrea in an effort to restart peace negotiation between the two.

As a result of the embargo, the suspicion of some Ethiopians as to the role of the US increased. About 100,000 people demonstrated in Addis Ababa against the US and the UN, opposing the weapons embargo on Ethiopia. Earlier, in response to anti-American feeling in both Eritrea and Ethiopia, on February 11, 1999, the US State Department had ordered nonessential employees at US embassies to leave both countries.

When the attack was imminent, Ethiopia frantically had to appropriate emergency funds, went on a weapon-purchasing spree, and recalled Ethiopian army and air force personnel who had been dismissed earlier. Meles has been adept at outfoxing his adversaries starting from his years during the guerilla war against the *Derg*. Once again, according to a report by *Africa Confidential*, in order to consolidate his position internally, he toughened his stance towards Eritrea and remained in the good books of his allies.[2]

On the battlefield the Eritrean army was defeated, and on May 25, 2000, it was forced to retreat from the Ethiopian area that it occupied. On May 31, Mr. Meles declared that the war with Eritrea was over and claimed that all the land had been recovered. This unilateral decision by the Prime Minister surprised some on the battlefield and added to the suspicion that he remains pro-Eritrean at the expense of Ethiopian national interests. Many who do not believe in annexing Eritrea by force still advocate nonetheless protecting the interest of Afar Ethiopians who have a legitimate claim to the Red Sea coast where the seaport of Assab is located.

Some initial allies of Prime Minister Meles such as Gebru Asrat, former President of Tigre, and Siye Abreha, former Minister of Defense, who were founding members of the TPLF, have charged Prime Minister Meles with failing to support Ethiopian nationalism and undermining the country's interest. Others accuse him of working for Eritrea's interest, if only because of his familial connections to that region and not necessarily because of ideological conviction. For example, he was warned that Eritrea intended to attack Ethiopia and that funds needed to be allocated in preparation against the expected war. Meles argued that Eritrea was not in a position to attack

---

1 Dima Noggo Sarbo. August 2007. "The Ethiopia-Eritrea Conflict: Short sighted solution and long-term problems."

2 Ibid.

Ethiopia despite what it had done to its other neighbors. During the preparation for the military confrontation with Eritrea, Meles Zenawi "was reportedly sidelined following the publication of [his] friendly letters to the Eritrean president and [he was] excluded from the military council set up to deal with the emerging border crisis in 1998."[1]

In both countries the leaders boasted of more war. Each in his own way had earlier destroyed Ethiopia's defense institutions and drained its national resources and wealth when they came to power. Each then bestowed benefits on his own ethnic group and region. Soon, however, both leaders resorted to rearmament and continued bloodshed that has exceeded even that of the thirty years civil war between the Ethiopian army and Eritrean guerrillas.

The defeat of Eritrea by the Ethiopian army exposed the vulnerability of the Eritrean army, once considered to be a formidable force, and led to the disillusionment of many of the supporters of Eritrean leader Issayas Afewerki. They were opposed not only to his authoritarian leadership but also held him responsible for the defeat of the Eritrean army. Some even manifested the ethnic chauvinism they harbored against Tigrigna-speakers of Ethiopia, currently in power, whom they saw as inferior to the Tigrigna-speaking people in Eritrea, once colonized by Italy.

Both countries then signed, on June 18, 2000, a preliminary cease-fire agreement. A peace treaty was signed by Meles and Issayas on December 12, 2000, in Algeria, brokered by OAU and the US envoy Anthony Lake. The US once again became active in Ethiopia's politics and tried to outshine the OAU.

The war shocked the Clinton administration, which dispatched its former National Security Advisor, Anthony Lake, on a whirlwind of shuttle diplomacy between Addis Ababa and Asmara. The US all along said it wanted to be an honest mediator between the two, though US officials privately held Eritrea to be the aggressor. This was before the UN officially pronounced Eritrea as an aggressor. Ethiopians nonetheless remain skeptical about the US role. It was reported by David Heslem that "fearing a potential coup" against Meles, the US and Israel supplied Ethiopia with satellite-photographs of Eritrean positions during the border war between the two countries.[2] This, if true, is similar to another US action that some believe to have taken place when the current Ethiopian and Eritrean leaders fought with the *Derg* and the US provided both forces with satellite-based information regarding the movements of Ethiopian troops.

The secession of Eritrea, despite the Clinton administration's acknowledgement of the strong bond between Ethiopia and Eritrea, was seen by some as a US device to weaken Ethiopia. This was another round in the cycle of the distrust of the US among some Ethiopians that dates back to the aggression of fascist Italy in 1936 when the US, for example, abstained from imposing an oil embargo on Italy.

As for the delineation of the border between Ethiopia and Eritrea, US officials say, in hindsight, that it should have been firmly established in 1993 when Eritrea broke away from Ethiopia. The US supported boundary demarcation between Ethiopia and Eritrea, which the UN and the OAU also supported. This boundary demarcation, which assumes colonial boundary delineation between Ethiopia and Italy as the colonial ruler of Eritrea at the time — in 1903, 1906, and 1908 — never happened. Italy violated the treaty and attacked and occupied a large part of Ethiopia for five

---

1 David Heslem. 2000/01. *Nations of the World, a Political Economy and Business Handbook*, Lakeville, Ct.: Grey House Publishing, p. 431.

2 Ibid.

---

years. Second, Italy's occupation was terminated by force when Ethiopian patriots, including some Eritreans, and the allied forces under the British leadership, ejected Italy from the region. Unlike colonial boundary demarcations in other countries, that between Ethiopia and Eritrea was not clearly chalked during the Italian presence or during the British administration subsequent to the Italian defeat during World War II.

The conflict in 1998 between Ethiopia and Eritrea, according to the officials of the Clinton administration, came as a surprise, history not withstanding. The security of the Red Sea areas that protect the uninterrupted flow of oil from the Middle East and in the containment of "rogue states" and terrorist groups continue to be the primary US interest in the area. In such a security consideration, peace between Ethiopia and Eritrea is important for the US and the region. In efforts to find a solution to the conflict, the US saw the leaders of Ethiopia and Eritrea as unyielding and strove to bring the two leaders closer.

There is a general belief that Ethiopia still has an influence on some of the regional issues such as conflicts in Sudan and Somalia, especially the latter, and on regional security development and economic programs, such as between the Nile River riparian states. During the war between Ethiopia and Eritrea, US influence in the region declined. The US geopolitical strategy of working with both countries and Uganda to attack Islamic fundamentalism in the Horn of Africa was halted. Nevertheless, Ethiopia emerged as a staunch supporter of the US strategy by attacking the Islamic Court Union in Somalia in December 2006. Uganda is a junior actor and Eritrea has become a problem for the region. In regard to fighting Islamic fundamentalism in Somalia, it is not clear if Prime Minister Meles Zenawi has inherited the Ethiopian leader's psyche and perception of Arab and hostile Muslim encirclement of Ethiopia or is serving the US interest in fighting global terrorism. When Meles came to power he was an idealist or was naïve, and believed in creating a borderless Ethiopia, open to its neighbors. For a while, the Somalis from Somalia and others were free to enter Ethiopia without visa requirements. Meles is said to have appointed some of Siad Mohamed Barre's officials who had fought against Ethiopia and tried to pay them back for the favor they had shown him during his exile in Somalia.

Despite its close identification with the US, the Ethiopian government has also complained about it. During the war with Eritrea, the Ethiopian government objected to the US failure to condemn Eritrea's aggression. Some in the US government argue that doing so will not keep the US neutral nor help in its being able to broker peace negotiation. Some also argue that condemning Eritrea will force her to be drawn more to the Arab world. That would enable Arab countries to encircle the Red Sea, a development that would not be welcomed by Israel.

At the same time, Eritrea was not impressed by the failure of the US to support it in its war with Ethiopia. The Carter Center's effort to mediate between the two countries also failed. Nevertheless, Meles Zenawi of Ethiopia and not Issayas Afewerki of Eritrea has been a staunch supporter of US efforts against Islamic expansionism. This is despite the fact that Eritrea received from the US $6 million in Foreign Military Finance (FMF) and $2 million in International Military Education and Training (IMET) — in only seven years (1994–2001).[1] Meles remains close to the US; he needs US support as his legitimacy is questionable, especially after the May 2005

---

1 Dan Connell. 2005. "Eritrea: On a slow fuse." In Robert I. Rotberg, ed. *Battling Terrorism in the Horn of Africa, ibid.,* p. 69. Quoted from Victoria Garcia, "Terrorism: Eritrea." May 19, 2004. www.cdi.org/program/document.cfm?documentid=2223&programID=73&from_page=../.

elections. Such support of an individual leader may not benefit the people and may alienate them from the United States.

When we look at the region, the political unpredictability in the Greater Lake region where the armies of Congo, Rwanda, Angola, Uganda, Namibia and Zimbabwe faced each other, we observe a cooling of US interest. This has changed As a result of the terrorist attack on the US on September 11, 2001. The US has started to reevaluate its national interest in the region and sees it as an important front in the fight against terrorism.

The overall objective of the Clinton administration in the Horn of Africa, as in the rest of the continent, was to assist countries in their economic development and advance the US interest. This objective, however, was temporarily subverted by the Ethio-Eritrean border conflict that led to the diversion of the meager resources of Ethiopia and Eritrea that could have been invested in development. Both countries spent a million dollars a day and purchased sophisticated weapons. The Eritrean diaspora also raised about $200 million a year to fight what they called the Tigre/Woyane or derogatorily, the *Agame*. This term is used because Tigrigna speakers from the Tigre region of Ethiopia used to work as laborers in Asmara, Eritrea. Their cousins, Tigrigna speakers of Eritrea, looked down on them. Some Eritreans also take pride in having been colonized by Italy, believing that that experience has elevated them to a more cosmopolitan level than that of their cousins who lived under feudal rule in Ethiopia. There is a deep-rooted antagonism between these Tigrigna speaking ethnic groups. These ethnic groups respectively control the current governments of Ethiopia and Eritrea.

On human terms, both lost 100,000 people in a World War I style trench war using modern weapons. The US interest to maintain peace in the region would best be promoted by boosting development that would directly and indirectly spur the economies of Ethiopia and Eritrea. In their effort to secure from the US Congress resources for Africa, White House officials during the Clinton Administration suggested that Africa needed a strong constituency in the United States.

Africa does have a constituency in the United States. The National Summit on Africa that met on February 20, 2000, in Washington, D.C. drew some 5,000 people. Its goal is to become a strong lobby for African issues in the United States. The group says that Africa has long been mishandled, misjudged and ignored. It has called for a Marshall Plan style of assistance for Africa, similar to the plan used to rebuild Europe after World War II.[1] The call by the group has not yet been translated into policy Many complexities make the marshalling of such an entity a daunting challenge. For example, there is no consensus among Ethiopians on how to lobby for Ethiopia, as most diaspora Ethiopians are opposed to the current government because of both its domestic and foreign policies. The potential for Ethiopia to be a viable country is there. Nevertheless, the lack of good governance, abject poverty, and other indigenous forces, such as the difficulties of harnessing its developed human resource, coupled with external negative forces, will slow Ethiopia in realizing its full potential.

The US, a strong ally of both regimes, was unable to persuade either one from taking such drastic action. The war undermined the US vision of a new Africa ruled by new leaders of an African renaissance. The situation has been drastically altered after 9/11 and the US declaration of war on terror. The region has also come under the command of DoD and the State Department was overshadowed by the Pentagon in the

---

1 See "Africa Summit 'Bold' Policy Marshal Plan Style Solutions Sought." February 21, 2000. *The Washington Post.*

time of Secretary of Defense Donald Rumsfeld. Ethiopia received $100 million from the US project, East Africa Counterterrorism Initiative (EACTI).[1] Hence, Ethiopia and the Horn of Africa in general are shown to have military implications for the US long after the end of the Cold War.

After the devastating war, a UN peacekeeping force was deployed until the boundary between the two countries is demarcated and acknowledged. The two countries signed a comprehensive peace agreement in Algiers on June 18, 2000, calling for a temporary demilitarized security zone within Eritrea. Meanwhile, a 4,200 UN peacekeeping force — UN Mission to Eritrea and Ethiopia (UNMEE), patrols the demilitarized zone between the two countries. UNMEE was established in July 2000 by UN Security Council and is commanded by a UN envoy, Legwaila Joseph Legwaila, from Ghana. The two countries are still posed for another round of bloodshed. Because of the unsettled border issue, the situation between the two countries remains unpredictable. A UN Boundary Commission to delimit and demarcate the border between the two countries decided the city of Bademe would be on the Eritrean side. Ethiopia went to war with Eritrea after the later occupied Bademe, which had never been administered by Eritrea, either during the Italian occupation nor in the post-occupation period.

The Bademe situation has created acrimony between the two countries. In April 2002, Ethiopia's Foreign Minister, Seyoum Mesfin, had prematurely announced that the UN Permanent Court of Arbitration, based in The Hague, had rewarded the border town of Bademe and other areas of Alitena and Zalambessa to Ethiopia. These were tracts of land over which both countries went to war. To the surprise of Ethiopians, it was later reported that the area was indeed rewarded to Eritrea, not Ethiopia. Some had hoped that the negotiation would include Assab and return the seaport to Ethiopia. That none of their expectations were fulfilled increased Ethiopians' mistrust in their government.

On April 15, 2003, the Ethiopian government rejected the UN decision on Bademe and accused the Boundary Commission of unfair actions in its ruling. Ethiopia is faulted for providing inadequate argument and using foreign experts, and not Ethiopians, who had no full historical knowledge of the case. Ethiopia had also committed itself to upholding the ruling of the Boundary Commission under the agreement reached in Algiers.

The general concern is that, as in the previous war, an unintended move could ignite another border war. Eritrea, because of its domestic political situation, lack of natural resources, and poor economic performance, has suffered the most. In addition to Ethiopia and Sudan, Yemen (in 1995) and Djibouti (in 2008) have been victims of Eritrean aggression where instrument of force is given priority over diplomacy. The situation in Eritrea has thus contributed to the tenuous situation in the HOA.

DJIBOUTI: NOW THE PRIMARY PORT FOR ETHIOPIA, AND THE US PRESENCE

The former French Somaliland, or Côte de Somali, Djibouti was a French colony. The French had been at the port of Obock since 1839 and in 1885 they signed a treaty with local chiefs that enabled them to occupy the key geographic area in the region.

---

1 Robert I. Rotberg, ed., ibid., p. 111.

The French controlled Bab el-Mandeb, a doorway to the Red Sea.[1] The French Foreign Legion in Djibouti, numbering 2,850, is the largest in Africa.

Djibouti is the smallest country in the region, the population less than half a million; it is a desert country without any resources. Djibouti's economy mainly depends on Ethiopia because of the railway that connects the two countries. The port of Djibouti serves about 60% of Ethiopia's foreign trade and is the primary outlet to Ethiopia, landlocked after the secession of Eritrea. Ethiopia, with a population of about 80 million, is the world's largest landlocked country.

In June 2008, Eritrea and Djibouti had a military clash at their border. Djibouti accused Eritrea of sending its troops across the border. Both France and the US accused Eritrea of violating the border.

The US, after the September 11, 2001, has posted about 2,000 forces in Djibouti — the Joint Combined Task Force Horn of Africa (CJTF-HOA). They share the base with the French Foreign Legion. The region was given importance by the Pentagon and security has dominated the thinking of officials both in the DoD and the US Department of State. The US Africa Command (AFRICOM) has been established to protect the security and military interests of the US by working in tandem with African military personnel.

Kenya: An Ally of Ethiopia and the US

Economically, Kenya is one of the strongest countries in the Horn of Africa. Kenya, Tanzania, and Uganda revived the East African Community (EAC) in 1999. EAC has launched ambitious goals of custom union, common currency, and citizenship. This has heightened investors' hopes, especially as EAC plans to expand to include Burundi, Democratic Republic of Congo, and Rwanda, accentuating Kenya's position. These countries may learn from the experience of the earlier EAC which existed from 1960 to 1977. One of the reasons for the demise of EAC then was political difference. The objectives of the Community remain cooperation in transport, communication, trade and industry, security, immigration, and the promotion of investment. The headquarters of EAC is in Arusha, Tanzania. Kenya, with its strong economy, is expected to play a major role in EAC but has to put in order its politics and settle ethnic disputes that have come to the open during the 2008 election.

Kenya has had peaceful relations with Ethiopia since Kenya's independence in 1964. The personal friendship between Emperor Haile Selassie and President Jomo Kenyatta, the first president of Kenya, goes back to the Italian occupation of Ethiopia. At that time Kenyatta, as a student in London, raised his voice with other pro-Ethiopia groups and wrote vehemently opposing the invasion of Ethiopia. Kenyatta wrote that, "Ethiopia's invasion was an insult to the Black race as it was the only remaining pride of Africa and Negros."[2] After the liberation of Ethiopia and the independence of Kenya, the leaders of the two countries built a strong foundation of amity between their two countries.

---

1 Emmanuel Gebreyesus. 1992. *Somalia in Difficulties: Country, People, Politics, Refugees in the Netherlands*, Amsterdam, The Netherlands: Federation of Refugees Organizations in the Netherlands (VON), p. 34.

2 Jomo Kenyatta, September. 1935. "Hands off Abyssinia," *Labour Monthly, London, vol.16, no 9, p. 536.1*

At times cattle raiding among the Borana people, who reside on both sides of the Ethio–Kenyan border, results in minor security issues. The idea of Greater Somalia is a greater threat to the security of Kenya. That idea includes a claim on the Northern Frontier District (NFD) of Kenya where Kenya's Somalis reside. It was because of the concern over Somali irredentism that Kenya entered into a security pact with Ethiopia. The two countries signed a mutual defense pact in 1963 and a treaty of co-operation and friendship in January, 1979.[1] During one of his state visits to Ethiopia, President Kenyatta observed an air show by the Ethiopian Air Force. After watching a demonstration of the precise air-to-ground missile attacks on a target, Kenyatta commented that any country who desired to attack Ethiopia must be blind. That was a message to the Somali leadership. In the subsequent wars with Somalia, Ethiopia's Air Force proved to be formidable and dominated the skies, thus delivering a decisive victory. President Jomo Kenyatta made a blunt statement about Kenyan Somalis in the NFD. He said that those who did not want to be Kenyans could leave.[2] Emperor Haile Selassie, on the other hand, had believed in the multi-ethnic character of Ethiopia, in the Somali Ethiopians being part of the rich tapestry of Ethiopia. In the 1980s, Somalia normalized its relationship with Kenya in an effort to isolate Ethiopia. Kenya wanted to have normal relations with both heavily armed countries.

Kenya had its worst political crisis after the election of December 30, 2007. The incumbent, President Mwai Kibaki, won a second term in a disputed election outcome. In the aftermath of the election, ethnic-based violence erupted, pitting the majority Kikuyu against the Luo and others who had felt disenfranchised and marginalized by the Kikuyu since the dawn of Kenya's independence. In the post-election conflict, quoting Kenyan Red Cross, Doctors Without Borders reported that more than 1,000 people lost their lives and some 300,000 Kenyans were internally displaced.[3] The ethnic-based violence almost took the nation to civil war. The Kikuyu ethnic group was targeted for attacks. Some who lived outside of the Kikuyu area were forced to leave their home, similar to the unfortunate waves of ethnic cleansing in Rwanda. The situation surprised the world because Kenya was said to be peaceful and to have a sound economy. But politicians and others with their own narrow agendas can exploit differences to ignite crises and bring about conflict between people who had lived together harmoniously for a long time.

Mr. Kofi Annan, the former UN Secretary General, helped negotiate between President Mwai Kibaki and his contender, Raila Odinga of the Orange Democratic Movement (ODM). After a long negotiation, an agreement was reached whereby a coalition government was formed with Mwai Kibaki as president and Raila Odinga as prime minister. They are now expected to heal a nation torn apart, which will take some time. The Kenyan situation is indicative of the delicate and as yet unsettled situation of the HOA. There is a need for the different ethnic and religious groups in the region to live in harmony, trust, and the belief in building their respective nations. The HOA is in need of visionary and selfless leaders.

---

1 Refer to Samuel Makinda. Jan./Feb. 1985. "Shifting alliances in the Horn of Africa," *SURVIVAL*, vol. 27, no. 1, p. 12.

2 Peter Woodward. June 1984. "Relations between neighboring states in north-east Africa," *The Journal of Modern African Studies*, vol. 22, no. 2, p. 275.

3 http://www.doctorswithoutborders.org/news/article.cfm?id=2502

SUDAN, ETHIOPIA, AND THE US: PRECARIOUS RELATIONS

Upon gaining independence on January 1, 1956, Sudanese leaders were eager to establish diplomatic relations with Ethiopia in order to counter the desire of President Gamal Abdul Nasser of Egypt to dominate Sudan and the Nile Valley in general.[1] President Nasser overthrew King Farouk through a coup d'état and came to power in 1952. The relations between Ethiopia and Sudan were cordial during the reign of Emperor Haile Selassie, especially during the rule of General Ibrahim Abud who came to power through a coup d'état in 1958 and ruled until 1964. During the December, 1960, coup d'état attempt against Emperor Haile Selassie, while he was on a state visit to Brazil, General Abud offered to send Sudanese troops to Ethiopia to help crush the Imperial Body Guard that had staged the coup. That indicates the close relations that the two leaders and, by extension, the two countries had. The Emperor even had good relations with rival clans and political actors who ruled Sudan successively. According to John Spencer, advisor to the Ethiopian Ministry of Foreign Affairs, Emperor Haile Selassie was close with the two major rival clans who ruled Sudan — the Khatmiyya of the Mirghani and the Ansar of the Mahdists.[2] Cultural exchanges between the two countries were common and the citizens of the two countries had fondness for one another's music. When the Emperor was overthrown by a military coup d'état in 1974, President Jaffar Al-Nimery of Sudan offered asylum to the octogenarian emperor. The Sudanese President announced that the Emperor was not only Ethiopia's leader but also that of the whole of Africa as well. It was said that Al-Nimery had Ethiopian friends and that his mother's origin is in northwestern Ethiopia.[3]

In spite of such apparent cordiality, yet some diplomatic glitches did manifest between the two countries. Certain unsettled domestic problems of one country resonated in the other, resulting in occasional diplomatic rancor between the two countries. Both countries extended or ceased supporting the other country's opposition groups or secessionist forces from time to time. According to Lemmu Baissa, the relationship between the two countries was marked by alternating periods of cordial friendship and hostility.[4] The issue of supporting groups that challenge the central governments by raising arms, such as the Southern Sudanese and the Eritreans, remained a bone of contention. Nevertheless, the two countries had not waged an outright war. Emperor Haile Selassie's as well as Col. Mengistu's efforts in pressuring Sudan to restrict the activities of Eritrean and Tigrean secessionists did not fully materialize. As Peter Woodward said, Sudan was not only unable to control its borders effectively but its strong allies such as Saudi Arabia supported the different liberation movements in Ethiopia.[5]

In response to Sudan's support for liberation movements against Ethiopia, Col. Mengistu intensified his support to the Sudan People's Liberation Army (SPLA). General Jaffar Al-Nimery accused both Ethiopia and Libya of conspiring to overthrow

1 Lemmu Baissa, "Ethiopia-Sudan relations, 1956-91: Mutual deterrence through mutual blackmail?" *Horn of Africa*, vol.13, no 3 and 4, (1990). Vole .14, no 1 and 2, (1991.), pp. 1-3.

2 John H. Spencer's statement at US Congressional Hearing, ibid. August 4, 5, and 6, 1976. P. 32.

3 Teshome G. Wagaw. 1993. *For Our Soul: Ethiopian Jews in Israel*, Detroit: Wayne State University Press, p. 63.

4 Lemmu Baissa, ibid.

5 Peter Woodward. 1990. *Sudan 1898–1989: The Unstable State*, Boulder, CO: Lynne Rienner Publishers, p. 172.

his government. Jaffar Al-Nimery accused Mengistu for aligning with Russia and creating a blood-thirsty system of oppression. Mengistu referred to Jaffar Al-Nimery as the worst enemy of Ethiopia, a tyrant, and a puppet in the service of imperialists.[1] The Russian-supported military regime in Ethiopia armed and trained Southern Sudanese fighters and also sheltered Sudanese refugees in Gambella, Western Ethiopia. The Sudanese support for the Ethiopian secessionist forces and others who were opposed to the *Derg*, such as the Ethiopian Democratic Union (EDU), intensified after the *Derg* came to power and declared Marxism as state ideology. It undertook radical actions such as nationalizing land, gross human rights abuses, and antagonizing the United States. Above all, it summarily executed government officials. The military regime was unpopular among Ethiopians, disliked by most of the conservative governments in the area, such as Saudi Arabia, and by the United States.

In domestic affairs, the conflict in Darfur started in 2003, where the government is accused of genocide, is a serious example of human rights abuses. Darfur, in the northwestern part of Sudan along the Chad border, is populated by Muslims who are farmers and herders in the African tradition and those who identify themselves as Arabs and try to dominate them. Government-sanctioned Arab militia forces, called *janjaweed*, are accused of systematically uprooting, raping, starving, and murdering Darfurian Africans. More than half a million are murdered and about two and half million are displaced. This gross human rights abuse or genocide targets an ethnic group for elimination.[2] President Omer Hassan Ahmed el Beshir was charged on July 14, 2008 with ten accounts of crimes against humanity, genocide, and war crimes.

The situation in Southern Sudan remains untenable. The first war between the north and the south took place between 1955 and 1972. A peace accord, called Addis Ababa Peace Accord, was signed under the auspices of Emperor Haile Selassie between the Sudanese government and the rebellion force (SPLA) in the south. This was a shift in the foreign policy of Ethiopia under Emperor Haile Selassie. In the 1960s, the Emperor used to support the *Anya Nya* guerrilla movement in the south. The *Anya Nya* was armed and trained by Israel. After a decade of normalcy between the Sudanese government and the SPLA, another civil war, led by John Garang, Chairman of Sudan People's Liberation Movement, was fought from 1983 to June 2005, when a Comprehensive Peace Agreement (CPA) was signed. The agreement included power sharing between the north and the south and a self-determination referendum that will be conducted after six years, i.e., in 2011.

John Garang, whose name was associated with SPLM, died in a helicopter crash on July 30, 2005. The situation between the two regions is unstable. Issues that remain unsettled include resource distribution. The south is endowed with oil, a treasure that has proven to be a bane in most African countries. The discovery of oil in the South Sudan, especially in the Abyei region that strides the border between the north and the south, has once again raised the possibility of conflict. In general, sustainable peace in Sudan has remained unrealized and this contributes to the precarious condition of peace, development, and the protection of human rights and the environment throughout the HOA.

---

1 Lemmu Baissa, ibid. Quoted from *The Times* (London), February 5, 1977, p. 1 and May 25, 1977, p. 7.

2 For the definition of genocide, refer to United Nations Convention on the Prevention and Punishment of the Crime of Genocide. 1948. Article 2. Genocide is violent crime committed against groups with the intent to destroy the existence of the group.

Unless the government of Sudan is judicious in dealing with the southern Sudan, the conflict between the north and south Sudan could become more pronounced. Oil remains to be the reason for conflict between the ruling party in the north, the National Congress Party (NCP), and SPLM in the south.

China, which pursues its economic interests despite the human rights abuses of Sudan, is involved in the exploration and exploitation of Sudanese oil. Chinese National Petroleum Corporation holds a large oil concession in Sudan. China is also supplying arms to the Sudanese army and is further complicating the instability in the region. China's involvement, especially its close relationship with totalitarian regimes such as in Sudan and Ethiopia, has been at the expense of human rights and development. US claims associating Sudan with al-Qaeda and global terrorism further complicate the situation.

SOMALIA

Historical Background

Prior to colonization, Somalia did not exist as an entity. The people of the region were nomadic, dependent on their herds of camels and goats, and they moved back and forth over wide territories with the animals that were their livelihood. Beginning in 1886, the British controlled what they called British Somaliland. The Italians also had carved out an area they dubbed Italian Somaliland in 1888. The Republic of Somalia was created in 1960 when the previous colonies gained independence and then were merged, but without any previous arrangement or discussion of power sharing and governance arrangements.

The Horn of Africa had been partitioned between three European countries: Britain, France, and Italy, in disregard for the close affinity of the associated people. Somalia is unique in the region in that it is populated by people who have long shared the same identity: they are predominantly Muslims, speak the same language, and have close ties to each other.

Britain administered the combined Somaliland after Italy was defeated during World War II. Britain was also in Ethiopia after it assisted the restoration of Emperor Haile Selassie at the end of the Italian occupation. Britain controlled the eastern part of Ethiopia, the Ogaden, adjacent to Somalia and populated by ethnic Somalis. The Ogaden is a grazing pastoral area which has always been vital to nomads and pastoralists. Close to a million herdsmen have migrated from what is now Somalia to the Ogaden each year in search of water and pasture, staying at least for six months.[1] According to a quote by John Spencer, the Ogaden, compared to the current so-called Somalia, is a paradise.[2] Successive Somali governments have focused on the annexation of Ogaden, and even have encouraged Somali irredentism, and fought over the Ogaden twice, in 1964 and in 1977–1978.

In 1955, the Ogaden, the region known as the Reserved Area, and Haud, were returned to Ethiopia by Britain as a result of the 1897 treaty. The British, however, implanted the idea of Greater Somalia that would bring together all Somalis under a single rule. The British Foreign Minister, Earnest Bevin, proposed the lumping together of British Somaliland, Italian Somaliland, Ethiopia's Ogaden region, and

---

1 Alice Bettis Hashin. 1997. *The Fallen State: Dissonance, Dictatorship, and Death in Somalia*, Lanham, MD: University Press of America, p.99.

2 This was a statement by a "prominent Somali official" and was quoted by John H. Spencer, *Ethiopia at Bay*, ibid., p. 302.

Kenya's Northern Frontier District (NFD) in the belief that they could comprise an economically viable entity. That proposal was unacceptable to Ethiopia as it meant losing the Ogaden, for which she had fought the Italians at Walwal, leading to the Ethio-Italian war and five years of Italian occupation.[1] According to Paolo Tripodi, following the defeat of fascist Italy during World War II, the British annexed the Ogaden and the Haud and brought the region under British military administration.[2]

During Somalia's independence, the Somalis felt deceived by the British because the two Somali-populated areas — the Ogaden and the NFD — were not included as part of the Republic of Somalia. As a result, the idea of Greater Somalia persisted and Somalia decided to claim the areas by force. This was against the cardinal rule of the OAU which upheld colonial boundaries as sacrosanct.

When the Republic of Somalia was established, Ethiopia could have claimed Somalia as historically part of Ethiopia but the British presence in Somalia complicated the situation. Ethiopia had opted to recognize the independence of the Republic of Somalia and hoped to establish strong economic, security and defense ties and live side by side as good neighbors.

Ethiopia and Somalia went to border wars twice, in 1964 and 1977. The situation also compelled Ethiopia and Kenya to enter into a collective security agreement to aid each other militarily against Somali aggression. Ethiopia, having the superior force, did not need military assistance from Kenya during the two border wars. The treaty between Ethiopia and Kenya was mainly to protect Kenya, as the two leaders, Haile Selassie and Jomo Kenyatta, had developed close ties. The two Ethio-Somali border wars, instigated by Somalia, were the result of economic, political, cultural, and nationalistic pressures. The Somali flag has stars to depict the five areas where Somalis have settled — in the British, Italian, and the French territories and in the Ogaden region of Ethiopia and the NFD in Kenya.

In the 1970s, Gen. Siad Bare, the President of Somalia, organized, assisted, and armed anti-Ethiopian forces such as the Western Somali Liberation Front (WSLF) and the Oromo Abo Liberation Front (OALF) that attacked Ethiopia. OLF and TPLF also had their offices in Somalia and the leaders of these organizations, including the current Prime Minister of Ethiopia, Meles Zenawi, was said to travel on a Somali passport. According to Abdul Mohammed, "During the 1970s and 80s, EPRDF leaders travelled on Somali passports and received much appreciated assistance from Somalia."[3]

As a *quid pro quo*, Mengistu responded by arming Somali insurgents against Siad Bare. Somali insurgents such as the Somali Salvation Democratic Front (SSDF), numbering about 3,000 and led by Abdullahi Yusuf Ahmed, the current president of the TFG (he resigned in January 2009), were armed and trained by Ethiopia with the intention of destabilizing Somalia and deposing Siad Barre. The Somali opposition group, among others, targeted Gen. Siad Bare's clan, the Marehan/Darod, and also used radio propaganda, aired from Ethiopia, to undermine the Somali government. General Siad Barre managed to repulse the attack by the SSDF and he vengefully attacked Northern Somaliland as the majority of the SSDF came from there. The north, especially Hargesa, the capital of Northern Somalia, was bombed, according to Alex

---

1 Ibid., pp. 37-39.

2 Paolo Tripodi. 1999. *The Colonial Legacy in Somalia*, New York: St. Martin's Press, Inc. p. 64.

3 Abdul Mohammed. February 20, 2007. Ethiopia's strategic dilemma in the Horn of Africa," http://hornofafrica.ssrc.org/Abdul_Mohammed/printable.html p.8.

de Waal, "with one of the most vicious scorched-earth policies witnessed in Africa."[1] In order to broaden and strengthen opposition to Siad Barre, the SSDF was pressured by Ethiopia, Libya, Yemen, and the Soviets to join with a leftist group and created the Democratic Front for the Liberation of Somalia (DFLS).

In the 1977 border war, Somalia had initially penetrated deeply into Ethiopia's territory. The Ethiopian army suffered setbacks because it was thinly stretched as it diverted its experienced fighting force to the north to fight the pro-west and royalist EDU as well as the Eritrean (EPLF) and the Tigrean (TPLF) secessionist forces. With support from the Soviet Union, Cuba, and Yemen, Ethiopia rebuffed Somali forces.

The defeat of the Somali force led Somalis to challenge President Siad Barre, but he responded by taking punitive measures against those who questioned his authority and his conduct of war, according to people I have interviewed. Siad Barre surrounded himself with his own clan and family members who took repressive actions against others. A wedge was created between clans and regions. Gross human rights abuses were reported in Somalia, and in January 1991, General Siad Barre was overthrown. He fled Somalia for Nigeria, where he died in 1995. There was no institution or authority, no mechanism for transfer of power when Siad Barre left, and this power vacuum in Somalia has threatened Somalia and its future as a viable nation state.

Similar to other dictators, Siad Barre failed to go beyond personal rule, failed to introduce meaningful democratic institutions and to create a culture where power is transferred peacefully and the rule of law remains the norm. Somalia slipped into chaos, and the country fell into the hands of warlords who had only one goal: to protect their parochial interests. Food shortage and famine forced Somalia to accept food assistance and the presence of international Peacekeeping forces.

In yet another unsettled case Ethiopia, with the blessings and support of the US, sent its forces into Somalia in December 2006, where it is bogged down, lacking any sound exit policy. Ethiopia claims that its national security is at risk as Islamist extremists have targeted Ethiopia and are trying to destabilize it. Al-Ittihad al-Islami (Islamic Union), an Islamic extremist group, has claimed, from Somalia, that it attempted on July 8, 1996, to assassinate Abdul Majeed Hussein in Addis Ababa. Abdul Majeed was Minister of Transport and Communications of Ethiopia and Chairman of the Ethiopian Somali Democratic League (ESDL). In the same year, bombs were detonated in Addis Ababa at the Ghion and Ras Hotels and in Dire Dawa, in the eastern part of Ethiopia. The Ethiopian government believes that radical Islamist forces, such as al-Ittihad al-Islami and Islamic Jihad, are trained in Southern Somalia and are bent on destabilizing neighboring countries such as Ethiopia.

Ethiopia, with US blessings, sent troops into Somalia to attack al-Ittihad al-Islami beginning in August 1996. When the troops left Somalia in January 1998, Ethiopia left behind the Somali National Front (SNF) to fight the Islamists. Ethiopia did not succeed in this effort, as the SNF had formed a splinter group and the two groups antagonized each other.[2]

Currently Somalia is the most unstable country in the Horn of Africa. What unfolds in Somalia has a direct impact on the region and on the US policy for the region. Ethiopia is the most directly affected by what happens in Somalia. The triangular interests and influences of Ethiopia, Somalia and the US are important.

---

1 A report by Alex de Waal, London-based human rights group Africa Watch, December 1992, "The Horn of Africa - Howitzer culture," in *New Internationalist*, issue 238, http://www.newint. org/issue238/culture.htm p.3.

2 *Africa Confidential*. April 3, 1998. Vol. 39, no 7, p. 8.

Somalia Unfolding: Conditions Post Siad Barre (1991–2008)

When a new government in Ethiopia assumed power after the fall of both Col. Mengistu Haile Mariam in Ethiopia and Gen. Siad Barre in Somalia, the relationship between the two countries seemed to be amicable. Some of the new leaders in Ethiopia, as indicated earlier, had taken refuge in Somalia when the TPLF waged guerilla war against the *Derg*. When a transitional government was established in Ethiopia, some of Siad Barre's officials were given high posts as a *quid pro quo*. However, I was unable to confirm this allegation.

A year after the overthrow of Siad Barre in 1991, the US took the lead in trying to bring peace and stability under a UN program. Accordingly, on December 3, 1992, the UN Security Council voted to authorize US-led forces to safeguard shipments of food to Somalia. Within six days, the US Marine Corps troops landed in Somalia at the head of the international humanitarian relief effort called Operation Restore Hope. The UN then took command from the US of an International Peacekeeping Force. The situation deteriorated after two dozen members of the UN Peacekeeping Force from Pakistan were killed and gun battle ensued between the troops of General Aideed, called Somali National Alliance, and US troops. There was no peace to be kept. Operation Restore Hope was terminated in May 1993.

The situation compelled President Clinton to announce the withdrawal of US troops. On October 3–4, 1993, 18 US troops and 300 Somalis were killed and more than 75 wounded. The UN withdrew its force in 1994. As of early 2009, Somalia has not pulled itself out of the quagmire it has found itself in for more than a decade and half.

After the overthrow of Siad Barre, clan-based warfare broke out in Somalia. Siad Barre has to share the blame, due to the collapse of the central authority, the division of Somalia, and foreign intervention. In Somali politics, balancing clan power and regional benefits remains crucial, and the major actors in charting the clan equation are elders who are adept at negotiating. Somalis are known for their oratory and poetry, even in politics and clan relations as they articulate issues and concerns of the people. Clan and religious leaders traditionally took the responsibility of enforcing law and order based on their own cultural guideposts of fairness. It seems that the modern situation has been overwhelming for these traditional authorities and cultures. They may still function at a lower stratum, but have proven to be ineffective at higher levels — both regional and the national.

Because of the ineffectiveness of the secular authority, a religious group, Islamic Union Court (IUC), assumed power and brought a temporary modicum of peace and stability to the country albeit there were mixed feelings about the ICU. The ICU was a force for stability in the sense that it did fill the vacuum left by the secularists. Others saw the ICU as composed of religious fundamentalists that tried to impose the *sharia* or the Islamic laws. The Sunni Muslims of Somalia are generally said to be moderate. The rise of the IUC has also invited international criticism especially from Ethiopia and the United States. Both countries accused the ICU of having ties to al-Qaeda and to "international terrorism." As allies, Ethiopia and the US accuse Somalia of providing haven to international terrorists and undermining other countries in the HOA.

It has been obvious that after Said Bare was deposed, Somalia disintegrated under warlords and rival heads of the different clans. There had not yet been any effective central government. There was a concern, especially on the part of the US, that Islamic fundamentalists groups such as al-Ittihad al-Islami operatives, suspected of having a linkage with al-Qaeda, would exploit the lawless situation in Somalia to export their ideology to other African countries. Somalia is also seen by the US as a gateway to Africa for illicit drugs and international terrorism, arms, and global crime syndicates. Somali pirates have threatened ships on the high seas. They have hijacked ships and demanded ransom. The Strait of Bab-el Mandeb, an entrance to the Red Sea from the Indian Ocean, is made unsafe by Somali pirates. Somali pirates have even blocked food from United Nations World Food Program from reaching Somalis dying of famine. Foreign aid workers in Somalia and Somalis associated with foreign organizations are also targeted. Situations of full-scale war, full-scale famine, and human misery have indeed been created in Somalia. According to Ken Menkhaus, these outlaws and pirates are locals and seem to have no trace of an international connection with terrorist groups. It would be hard for non-locals to operate even in the collapsed state of Somalia. The international terrorists, argues Menkhaus, would be susceptible to betrayal by local people.[1]

The US security concern in the area has persisted for a long time. Going back to the Cold War era, currently in post 9/11, and now with Somalia as a failed state, the US has kept its eye on the HOA. It is also concerned by the "mining of the straits of Hormuz and the Bab el-Mandeb, sabotaging of the Suez Canal, targeting of oil tankers, terminals and pipelines, and even the assassination of key technical personnel"[2] that all have economic and political implications for the United States. Furthermore, the US strategic interests in the region, according to Richard B. Remnek, are, first, the use of facilities ashore to support US military operations in the Southwest Asia–Indian Ocean area both in peacetime and wartime, and second, freedom of international navigation through the Red Sea/Bab el-Mandeb. Of the two, the military role of the HOA has received far greater attention and is of greater salience.[3]

The US has a persistent strategic military interest. It views the Bab el-Mandeb as an important gate to the Red Sea, providing free passage to all, especially to its strategic and historically, the state of Israel. During the October 1973 war, Egypt's warships tried to prevent Israel's ships from passing through the Bab el-Mandeb.[4] Ethiopia, during Emperor Haile Selassie's reign, was afraid that the Red Sea would turn into an "Arab Lake," with Ethiopia denied access by the secession of Eritrea. That concern was also shared by Israel; hence its support for the Marxist and anti-US military regime in Ethiopia. These fears were intensified when Arab countries did in fact declare such an intent at their meeting in Ta'izz, North Yemen, in March 1977.[5] Egypt undermined the unity of Ethiopia by supporting Eritrean secessionists, Israel supported Ethiopia's governments in order to counter Egypt's design.

The HOA is of great interest to China, Egypt, France, Israel, Russia, and Saudi Arabia. The HOA countries are worried by the increased threat to the region. The fact that Somalia has become a failed state and the gateway to the Red Sea is increasingly threatened by pirates is now a concern to countries of the area and beyond.

To make the situation worse, Northern Somalia seceded and declared its independence, as Republic of Somaliland, from the unstable former Italian Somaliland in 1991.

---

1 Ken Menkhaus. 2004. *Somalia: State Collapse and the Threat of Terrorism*, New York: Oxford University Press, pp 72-73.

2 Richard B. Remnek. Autumn 1990. "The strategic importance of the Bab-el-Mandeb and the Horn of Africa," *Naval War College Review*, vol. 43, no. 4, sequence 332, p. 12.

3 Ibid., p. 17.

4 Ibid., pp. 19-21.

5 Ibid., p.10.

The *de facto* independent Republic of Somaliland is not recognized by other countries, especially by the African Union (AU) and the UN. Another administrative region, Puntland, located in the Northeastern tip of Somalia, was created on July 1, 2007, as a semi-autonomous Puntland State of Somalia. Southern Somalia had been chaotic and the clan-based conflict had torn apart the state fabric. Puntlanders seem to be moving away from the chaotic Southern Somaliland. The leadership of Puntland promises to provide security and uphold the rule of law. Both the Republic of Somaliland and Puntland have distanced themselves from Southern Somaliland which is beset by clan-based conflicts and government degeneration. The president of the Transitional Federal Government (TFG), Abdullahai Yusuf Ahmed, is originally from Puntland. When he moved to Somalia, he brought with him troops, weapons, and trucks from Puntland. This has further complicated the situation.

Ethiopia will continue in its engagement with Somalia in one way or the other. The US, as long as it is engaged in fighting the so-called terrorism globally, will also continue to post its troops in neighboring Djibouti and use Ethiopia as a proxy. The voice of dissent against Ethiopia's involvement in Somalia is stifled by the government of Meles Zenawi. Prime Minister Meles needs the US for the survival of his political life. As Paul Wachter wrote, in his article titled "Bush's Somalia strategy enables an Ethiopian despot," the Bush administration is "all too happy to overlook the undemocratic excesses of a dictator who will do its bidding in the "war on terror""[1] The economic, diplomatic, and military support that the US provides Meles's regime is at the expense of democracy in Ethiopia. The Ethiopian government, for all matters, is beholden to the Bush administration for its survival. Most probably, the relationship pales Emperor Haile Selassie's government that was accused of being US puppet. Despite the fact that the Meles regime is averse to democracy and the people's voice, the Bush administration regards it as its only ally in Somalia against war on terror. Prime Minister Meles, in frustration, has recently hinted that he would pull out his troops from Somalia and the Islamists have also threatened to escalate attacks on both the Ethiopian and the TFG troops.

Reconciliation Efforts among the Somalis

A decade after the US troops left Somalia in 1993, the US returned to Somalia in support of the Transitional Federal Government (TFG). The US forces left Somalia after the Somalis downed two US Black Hawk helicopters. Eighteen US army rangers were killed and their bodies dragged through the streets of Mogadishu. Eighty-four marines were also wounded. Despite that incident, and despite Somalia's lack of strong government, the US is back in the region after the attacks on the US in 2001. In the absence of a strong central government, outlaws and terrorist groups are less restrained in Somalia, and the US is compelled to monitor Somalia from neighboring countries of Ethiopia, Djibouti, and Kenya.[2] In addition, according to Ken Menkhaus, the US seems to use uncritically exaggerated information it receives from Ethiopian military intelligence.[3]

Ethiopia and other regional countries became active in trying to bring peace between clans in Somalia. The TFG was established in Addis Ababa on March 3, 1993,

---

1 Paul Wachter. February 14, 2007. "Bush's Somalia strategy enables an Ethiopian despot," *The Nation*, http://wwwthenation.com/doc/20070226/wachter

2 Ken Menkhaus. 2004. *Somalia: State Collapse and the Threat of Terrorism*, London: The International Institute for Strategies Studies, pp. 48-76.

3 Ibid., p. 68.

as a result of an UN-sponsored conference. Participants at the conference came from fifteen clans and included intellectuals, women, and traditional leaders.[1] The TFG claimed to fight terrorism in Somalia and initially operated from Nairobi, Kenya.

A misstep by the Ethiopian officials has had longtime negative implications for the Somalis. During an attempt to broker peace between Somali factions, the Ethiopian leader Meles Zenawi sided with Mohamed Farah Aideed. This alienated the other Somali groups at the peace conference and undermined not only the peace conference but also Ethiopia's role as a neutral mediator.[2] Regional countries at the conference, such as Egypt and Eritrea, also took sides. Egypt sided with one of the Somali factions led by Ali Mahdi.[3] Eritrea sided with the Islamic Court Union.

The CIA-backed TFG has several shortcomings and its viability and effectiveness is questioned. For example it has been unable to broaden its base and recruit support outside of its clan, is accused of corruption, warlordism, and has faced hostility from the Islamists and others for its exclusiveness. Most importantly, its alliance with Ethiopia, whom some Somalis see as their adversary, has not strengthened the TFG's position. The TFG does not receive substantial external financial and material support and its friends are limited. The lack of security in the country discourages foreigners and diaspora Somalis from working in Somalia and assisting the TFG in building the country. The presence of Ethiopian troops seems to have worsened the situation and their unilateral withdrawal is demanded by most Somalis. The situation remains unpredictable as even the withdrawal of Ethiopian troops would probably not guarantee normalcy in Somalia. The Ethiopian government has stated that troop withdrawal is contingent upon the presence of AU forces in Somalia but no such presence appears likely. Thus the prospect of Ethiopian troop withdrawal seems to be postponed. (Ethiopia pulled its troops out of Somalia in January 2009. Somalia remained chaotic and the security of Ethiopia questionable.)

Somalia produces refugees and their effort to cross the Red Sea in order to land on the shores of Southern Yemen has cost many Somalis their lives. Somali refugees in the neighboring countries such as Kenya put pressure on the environment, food and water, and they remain health concerns for countries that already have their own problems.[4] In 2008, Somalia also had more than 600,000 internally displaced people.

There are victims of fighting between Ethiopian and the TFG troops on one hand and supporters of the ICU and its radical wing, Al-Shabaab, and those opposed to both the Ethiopian and the TFG on the other. Kenya is also concerned about the influence the Somali religious extremists would have on its ethnic Somali citizens, although Somalia, at the moment, does not seem to appeal to ethnic Somalis in the region. There is nothing that Somalia can offer except turmoil and the vision of greater Somalia that remains on paper only. Somalia has lost the force of invigorated and galvanized nationalism and irredentism.

---

1 Refer to Ahmed I. Samatar, "The curse of Allah: Civic disembowelment and the collapse of the state in Somalia," in Ahmed I. Samatar, ed. 1994. *The Somali Challenge: From Catastrophe to Renewal?* Boulder, CO: Lynne Rienner Publishers, p. 127.

2 Ken Menkhaus. 1997. "International peace building and the dynamics of local and national reconciliation in Somalia," Walter Clarke and Jeffrey Herbert, *Learning from Somalia: The Lessons of Armed Humanitarian Intervention*, Boulder, CO: Westview Press, p. 47.

3 Ibid.

4 Ibid., p. 50.

Ethiopia's Intervention in Somalia (2006–2008)

Ethiopia, with encouragement from the US, has been sending its troops into Somalia to fight religious extremists. Ethiopia at first denied this but soon admitted that it had a few military trainers in Somalia. Ethiopia backed the Transitional Federal Government of Somalia (TFG) and its troops entered Mogadishu, on December 28, 2006, and forced out the leaders and forces of the Union of Islamic Court (UIC) from Mogadishu and other cities such as Burhakaba, Jowhar, and Luuq. The Ethiopian government claimed self-defense for its intervention in Somalia as the UIC supported the Ogaden Liberation Front. Ethiopia also claimed that Somalia was responsible for the extremist al-Ittihad al-Islami's bombing of civilian targets in Addis Ababa in 1996. After the Ethiopian forces entered Somalia, the UIC declared a *Jihad* (holy war) against Ethiopia. Having no exit strategy, Ethiopia seems to be bogged down in Somalia as its troops are still there in 2008 and efforts to reconcile the TFG and the UIC did not succeed. Both the TFG and the Ethiopian troops are regularly ambushed and the bodies of Ethiopian troops are dragged in the streets of Mogadishu, reminiscent of the US troops in 1993. Ethiopian troops in Somalia are seen by the Somali public as an occupying force.

Ethiopia's current involvement in Somalia has renewed anti-Ethiopian sentiment. The previous Somalia governments exploited that sentiment to divert the people's attention from domestic problem and their concentration on end in the pursuit of greater Somalia which would compromise the Ogaden region of Ethiopia.

The Islamists want to install the Sharia law (or Islamic law). All Somalis may not prescribe to this law, as they tend to be moderate Sunni Muslims. They are, however, supportive of the UIC as it had brought order to Mogadishu in the six months it controlled the country, even if some of its policies, such as closing cinema houses, did not sit well with some Somalis. In retaliation to attacks on the Ethiopian and TFG troops, indiscriminate shooting had made Mogadishu residents insecure and forced them to leave the city. There are more than 600,000 internally displaced Somalis. Mogadishu's Bakara market, for example, has been practically destroyed because of bombing. As in similar cases in other parts of the world, civilians, especially children, women, and the aged are the most affected. People in Mogadishu are afflicted by malnutrition, disease, and insecurity. Aiding and assisting the displaced has not been easy because of the poor security situation. The situation in Mogadishu is also described as one of the worst humanitarian crises in Africa.

Ethiopia's initial involvement in Somalia was a miscalculation, although, according to Foreign Minister Siyoum Mesfin, it was in self-defense against Islamic extremists in Somalia who had declared war on Ethiopia. Some believe that "Ethiopia intervened not because it was a choice but because it was imposed by the United States."[1] Members of the Ethiopian Parliament, such as Drs. Beyene Petros, Merera Gudina, and Negaso Gidada (former President of Ethiopia) have challenged Ethiopia's invasion of Somalia. For example, according to Negaso Gidada, "Somalia is not a threat to Ethiopia.... The Somalis didn't attack us, so why are we fighting them?" The outspoken MP and political scientist, Merera Gudina said that for Meles, Somalia wasn't the risk. "It was the prospect of losing Washington's support, and the Somalia adventure insured that didn't happen." Merera questioned: "Do [Americans] think that

---

1 Quoted by Nora Boustany. May 14, 2005. "Ethiopia defends records on rights," *The Washington Post*, p. A12.

if Meles was gone and terrorists attacked Ethiopia, we wouldn't respond?"[1] As for Ethiopia's involvement in Somalia, in what newsman David Ignatius calls "Ethiopia's Iraq," he quoted a senior US diplomat in Addis Ababa who said Ethiopia's aim was to "Get it done quickly and get out."[2] The Ethiopian leaders seem to be shortsighted and not able to learn from the US involvement in Iraq. As Ethiopian opposition leaders say, Meles was fulfilling the American bidding. It seems that there was no clear and crisp goal to be achieved, no strategy to build confidence of the people, and no exit strategy. Although the Islamic fundamentalists in Somalia support ethnic Ethiopian Somalis in Ogaden, Prime Minister Meles exploited the situation to demonstrate that he is a US ally in the war on international terrorism.

There are other issues one can read into the situation:

1. By calling Prime Minister Meles an ally on global terrorism, the Bush administration was able to disregard his abuse of power and gross human rights violations.

2. There is financial gain to be made by supporting the US foreign policy on international terrorism. It is reported that about 70% of Ethiopia's budget comes from international flow of funds in the form of foreign assistance and grants from sources that support this policy.

3. The US claims to be involved in the conflict in Somalia indirectly. War on terrorism was the mainstay of the Bush administration, especially after September 11, 2001. US AC-130 gunships were used in January 2007 to try to kill senior Somali Islamists who were suspected to be in South Somalia, bordering Kenya.

It was reported that US officials such as General John Abizaid, commander of the US Central Command, overseeing, among other regions, the Horn of Africa, and Jendayi Frazer, Assistant Secretary of State for Africa, warned against Ethiopia deploying its forces in Somalia, but Ethiopia went ahead. This report could be seen as a public relations ploy as the US might welcome a third country conducting war against its potential enemy, Somali Islamists. That would cost the US less than having to put its own troops on the ground. It would also avoid the US being blamed for collateral damage or for things possibly going awry. The US is also preoccupied in an unpopular war in Iraq and would shun, if at all possible, overtly opening another front in Somalia.

Terrorists who simultaneously bombed US embassies in Nairobi, Kenya and Dar es Salam, Tanzania, on August 7, 1998, were said to be hiding in Somalia. The US, therefore, might be pleased to see Ethiopia sacrifice its troops, as Ethiopia does not have government checks and balances nor is transparency in government required. Prime Minister Meles Zenawi, similar to other authoritarian rulers, enjoys a free hand in Ethiopia. The parliament rubber stamps any legislation the prime minister presents. All opposition leaders in parliament, except for EPD-Medhin, questioned the rationale for Ethiopia sending troops into Somalia. According to Dr. Beyene Petros, UEDF had opposed troop deployment into Somalia and asked for protecting Ethiopia's borders with Somalia from any incursions from outside. The opposition also called for immediate troop withdrawal and proposed that Ethiopia's involvement in Somalia peacekeeping be limited within the framework of AU and the UN missions.

---

1 The quotes of MP Merera Gudina and former president Negaso Gidada were taken from an article by Paul Wachter. February 14, 2007. *The Nation*, http://www.thenation.com/doc/20070226/wachter

2 David Ignatius. May 13, 2007. "Ethiopia's Iraq," *The Washington Post*, p. B7.

I was also informed that in the opposition's meeting with the Prime Minister, he was strongly advised not to send Ethiopian troops across the border and was reminded that even the US, with all the resources it has at its disposal, including its superior technology, has not resolved its situation in Iraq. They also advised him to defend Ethiopia from its side of the border. When he felt he could not convince the opposition, he overrode their recommendations and said that expressing such ideas could be considered tantamount to treason against the nation. The government's propaganda machine moved against the opposition a day after they voted against the bill to send Ethiopia's troops into Somalia. The opposition has remained firm in its positions.

The Eritrean government supports the Islamist groups in Somalia: my enemy's enemy is my friend. As Ethiopia and Eritrea are at loggerheads, they fight each other in Somalia through their respective proxies. There is also an entangled relationship that has drawn together disparate countries. It is reported that funds from Libya and Saudi Arabia are used to buy arms from Israel, using Eritrea as a conduit to channel arms to Islamist groups.[1] In the final analysis, the situation has become detrimental to peace, stability, and development in Somalia and, by extension, to the region.

Prime Minister Meles Zenawi stated that Ethiopian troops will leave Somalia once an international peacekeeping force arrives in Somalia. Nigeria, Ghana, and Malawi promised 800 troops each and Uganda promised 1,500 troops. The total promised is 4,000 short of the minimum troops considered by the AU to be needed in Somalia for peacekeeping. The security situation in Somalia seems to deter troop deployment as well as any peace dialogue between the TFG and those opposed to it. Neither plan has yet materialized.

The Western Somali Liberation Front (WSLF) has also complicated the situation between Ethiopia and Somalia. The WSLF, which used to be supported by the governments of Somalia, fights for the independence of the Ogaden region of Ethiopia. The Ogaden region is also complicated because of the potential for oil exploitation. The Ethiopian government said that another group, the Ogaden National Liberation Front (ONLF), on April 24, 2005, killed Chinese and Ethiopian workers who were employed in oil exploration. ONLF, founded in 1984, also claimed killing 74 people, including nine Chinese in Jijiga, Ogaden. The Ethiopian government retaliated by taking punitive measures of collective punishment of Ethiopian Somalis in Ogaden. The measure included summary execution, rape, assaults on civilians, and detention of those suspected of supporting the ONLF. Human Rights Watch, in its report of June 12, 2008, titled "Collective Punishment: War Crimes and Crimes against Humanity in the Ogaden area of Ethiopia's Somali Region," stated that Ethiopia's Somali Region is experiencing serious abuses and that crisis looms. Georgette Gagnon, the Africa Director at Human Rights Watch, accused Ethiopia's major donors, including the US, of "maintaining a conspiracy of silence around the crime committed by the Ethiopian government."[2]

CONCLUDING REMARKS

Ethiopia is a key country in the Horn of Africa. It borders all countries of the Horn of Africa. Ethiopia's population of 80 million makes it the second most populated country in Africa after Nigeria. Its landmass, raw materials, and mineral deposits

---

1 *Africa Confidential.* November 3, 2006. Vol.47, no. 22, p. 9.

2 See Human Rights Watch report of June 12, 2008, www.hrw.org/english/docs/2008/06/12/ ethiopia19029.htm

are significant. Furthermore, as the water tower of the Horn of Africa, regional countries such as Somalia, Sudan, and Egypt have an interest in it. Ethiopia is a source of major rivers such as the Baro, the Blue Nile (Abay), and the Tekeze that feed the Nile; the Awash that flows into the Denkel Depression in the East; the Shebele and the Genale that flow to Somalia; and the Omo River that flows into Lake Turkana in Kenya. These major rivers deliver life.

The United States' interest in Ethiopia has persisted from 1903 well into the 21st century, and Ethiopia's importance will continue. Ethiopia is the headquarters of the AU and other UN agencies such as the ECA.

In order for the mutual benefit of Ethiopia and the US to be sustained, there must be democratic government. Unless there is human security, rule of law, and human rights protection in both countries, their alliances could be reversed, as they were after Emperor Haile Selassie's reign. Unless true democracy is allowed to prevail and as long as human-centered security desires of each nation's people remain unfulfilled, these countries could become burdensome to one another. Principled governance must be the foundation of this relationship as it must be of geopolitics worldwide.

The current crisis in Somalia that is affecting the HOA in general has its roots in the Cold War superpower rivalry. It is the proliferation of small arms and light weapons in the region, as a result of the Cold War, which has become a problem now.[1] Now civilians are armed. These arms, small arms and light weapons, do not require extensive logistical capabilities and are useful for highly mobile operations such as those in Somalia.[2] Innocent people are victimized by these weapons that have contributed not only to human insecurity but also to poor economic performance and development. The UN members, since 2001, have endorsed collective efforts against illegal arms circulation such as in Somalia.

Governments are urged to "tighten controls on manufacturing, marketing, tracing, brokering, exporting, and stockpiling small arms and to cooperate to restrict illicit flows, particularly to regions perennially in armed conflict."[3] A network of 800 civil societies in 120 countries has established a global movement against gun-related violence called the International Action Network on Small Arms (IANSA). The IANSA lobbies to stop the proliferation and misuse of small arms and light weapons (SALW) and better control on arms exports.[4] In spite of such broad-based concerns about the proliferation of deadly small arms some interest groups, such as the gun lobby in the US and arms exporting countries such as China and Russia, seem to be unsympathetic to the plight of civilians in countries such as Somalia.

Arms sales drain the economies of African countries. Conflicts in the continent since the end of the Cold War have cost £150 bn ($900 bn.) according to an Oxfam report. This is a sum equivalent to all the foreign aid Africa has received over the same period.[5] The purchases of arms intended to control and/or intensify conflicts in the continent results in the drastic reduction of funds available to provide human

---

1 Kiflemariam Gebrewold and Siobhan Byne. 2006. "Small arms and light weapons in the Horn: Reducing the demand," in Dorina, A. Bekoe, ed. *East Africa and the Horn*, Boulder, Colorado: Lynne Rienner Publishers, pp. 21-36.

2 Ibid., p. 23.

3 C.J. Chivers. July 19, 2008. "U.S. position complicates global efforts to curb illicit arms," in *New York Times*.

4 http://www.iansa.org/about.htm

5 Chris McGreal. October 11, 2007. "The devastating coast of Africa's wars: 150 billion and millions of lives," *Guardian*. Also refer to the report by UN Secretary General about small arms. UN Security Council, S/2008/258, April 17, 2008.

security: health services, prenatal care, the prevention and treatment of malaria and HIV/AIDS; education; economic growth, and the protection of the environment. The HOA countries, especially Eritrea, Ethiopia, Somalia, and Sudan receive the lion's share of the blame.

The countries of the Horn of Africa are also internally beset with conflicts based on clan, ethnic, to religious affiliation, and regional and political differences. Disagreements over sharing scarce resources and the legacy of colonialism that pits one group against the other and promotes suspicions have also contributed to the sorry situation. One can also add to the list the undemocratic leaders in all Horn of Africa countries who ignore the wellbeing of their citizens. All have exploited ethno nationalism and the paraphernalia of elections for political expediency at the expense of the people.

Some have proposed federalism for the region, as its countries have interdependent economies and certain similarities. Paul Henze, for example, predicts the "inevitability of political federalism in the Horn."[1] Although a federal arrangement between the HOA countries could be possible in theory, the prevailing situation does not promote optimism. Ethiopia and Eritrea have experience in federalism and unity and have had historical and cultural ties, but they have split apart and engaged in a catastrophic war. Federalism and close cooperation between the HOA countries could help them avoid unnecessary and expensive cost for security and armament.[2] The federalism envisaged for the region must be the integration of the different sovereign states in which they give up some of their sovereignty for the common good of the member states. Under visionary leaders and statesmen, confidence built between the peoples of the region, and a process that is amicable to all, federalism could take place in the HOA. That situation is currently nonexistent but must be encouraged in the HOA. Meanwhile, economic marginalization, environmental degradation, and the sharing of scarce resources have remained as causes of conflict in this, perhaps the poorest region of the world.[3] Unification of the countries of the HOA seems remote, yet the US and other powers must encourage such a process rather than funneling weapons to the region and promoting further destruction.

---

1 Paul B. Henze. 1994. "The economic dimensions of federalism in the Horn of Africa," Peter Woodward and Murray Forsyth. *Conflict and Peace in the Horn of Africa — Federalism and its Alternatives*, Brookfield, Vermont: Dartmouth Publishing Company, pp. 124-130.

2 Terrence Lyons. 1994. "Crisis on multiple levels: Somalia and the Horn of Africa," in Ahmed I. Samatar, ed. pp. 189-207.

3 Christopher Clapham. Sep./Oct. 1980. "The political economy of conflict in the Horn of Africa," *SURVIVAL*, vol. 32, no5, pp. 403-419.

Chapter 15. Summary and Conclusion

The diplomatic relationship between Ethiopia and the United States, dating back to 1903, was founded on twin pillars of mutual interest. After more than 100 years, we can assess whether either side has achieved its stated or unstated objectives in this relationship. We can assess whether the policies as they were set, and the policies as they were implemented, were suited to those objectives, and we can assess whether either of the two parties or both of the parties — and other nations — have benefited from the relationship.

Although the US at the end of the 19th century had not fully changed its long-standing policy of global isolationism, it wanted to establish a trade relation with an independent African state. Historically, the US had been linked only with Liberia. The rest of Africa was under the yoke of colonialism. Ethiopia had started to gain prominence, especially after the Battle of Adwa (1896), and Western countries recognized the sovereignty of Ethiopia. Ethiopia's agricultural resources, untapped resources, and potential for foreign business were attractive. Furthermore, there was no colonial power dominating Ethiopia. As an independent country, Ethiopia could sign agreements to grant the US access to products that Ethiopia could provide. The US, therefore, wanted to enter into a trade pact with Ethiopia.

Ethiopia had a keen interest in the United States based on the perception that the US, unlike the European countries, had no colonial ambition and would not threaten Ethiopia's sovereignty, while the US economic clout and technological advances could be useful to Ethiopia.

Emperor Menelik II, who was suspicious of the motives of European powers, was instrumental in establishing trade relations. He believed such a tie with a powerful independent country would help restrain the activities of those countries that did have a colonial motive.

Ethiopia and the US had good relations under the successors of Emperor Menelik II, especially with Emperor Haile Selassie I. Haile Selassie believed in the US as an ally against aggressors and a partner in economic development. The relationship collapsed when fascist Italy occupied Ethiopia and the US officially turned its eyes the other way. The US offered no political or military support to Ethiopia.

After the end of World War II and with the emergence of the Cold War, US interest in Ethiopia centered on its possible strategic contributions to America's overarching rivalry with the USSR. Ethiopia's independence, her proximity to the Middle East oil fields and to the sea lane for transporting oil, her accessible aerial link to the Middle East and beyond, all increased US interest in Ethiopia.

During the Cold War, Emperor Haile Selassie remained a staunch supporter of the US although the US failed to live up to the Emperor's expectation. The Nixon administration, embroiled in the Watergate debacle, refused to sell Ethiopia the weapons that she needed to defend herself. Instead, sensing that the Emperor was losing political ground because of his old age and the increasingly restless citizenry, the US prepared to abandon its ally the Emperor and started to look for an alternative in order to protect its own national interest.

After the Emperor was overthrown in 1974 and a military junta (called *Derg*) assumed power, Somalia attacked Ethiopia in 1977 and seriously threatened its sovereignty. The Carter administration impounded military equipment that Ethiopia had purchased earlier and used human rights violations in Ethiopia as the reason for the embargo. Despite this measure, human rights violations escalated in Ethiopia. The military regime that was in power for seventeen years was increasingly pro-Soviet Union and the relationship with the US further deteriorated.

The Ethiopia–US relationship was mended in 1991 after the overthrow of the military regime by an alliance of ethnic-based political groups, but that alliance has weakened Ethiopia by encouraging and supporting the secession of Eritrea. The EPRDF has yet to establish a democratic political system. It has had no mandate from the people and has evidenced no transparency. Contrary to the values it proclaims, the US has condoned these undemocratic actions, thereby reflecting its muddled foreign policy. As a result, the US long-term interest seems not to be well served in the region.

The US is criticized for its double standard of claiming to uphold democracy and yet supporting undemocratic regimes. The forces of economic liberalization and globalization, the World Bank/IMF Structural Adjustment Program (SAP) and other similar policies that are supported by the US alienate other countries. A more visionary foreign policy, devoid of paternalism and unilateralism, one that takes into account not only US interests but also the concerns and aspirations of other countries, needs to be formulated. It is only when we have such a foreign policy that the long-term interests of the peoples of all countries will be served.

A century of US efforts in Ethiopia have not yet resulted in meaningful development. The US has invested considerable resources in Ethiopia but Ethiopia's economic performance and its record on human rights remain wanting. The responsibility for Ethiopia's multifaceted problems fall mainly on the shoulders of its leaders, but external forces have continuously held Ethiopia back. The policy needs to be re-evaluated. One may witness new economic activities in Ethiopia (such as in the construction sector) after the demise of the *Derg*, but the sustainability of these activities, transparency concerning their execution, and their contributions to uplifting people from poverty remain questionable.

A new development in the Horn of Africa is Ethiopia's involvement in Somalia with the sanction and support of the United States. Ethiopia supports the weak and unpopular Transitional Federal Government (TFG) of Somalia. It is debatable how much of a threat Somalia may be to Ethiopia's security, although Somalia's internal situation must concern Ethiopia. Somalia's irredentism in the Ogaden region, populated by Ethiopian Somali ethnic groups, has lost currency. Somalis in the Ogaden regard the current situation in the so-called the Republic of Somalia as chaotic and want no part of it. Ethiopian Somalis, similar to other Ethiopians, want true democracy, human security, and the rule of law.

In general, the presence of Ethiopian troops in Somalia, human rights abuses, the breakdown of law and order, the indirect role of regional entities such as Eritrea have all complicated the conditions in Somalia. The US has once again become active in the strategic region of the Horn of Africa. The role of the US has also remained controversial, as it was in the Cold War period, because of its support for an unpopular regime in Ethiopia. The government has continued its abuse of human rights and contributed to Ethiopians' feeling of powerlessness.

In the US, there is an expectation or at least a hope that US foreign policy in general will be revisited in the administration of President Barack Obama, especially its Africa policy and relations with undemocratic rulers who have undermined not only human rights and democracy but also the creativity and self-actualization of their citizens. The Obama administration is urged to review US foreign policy towards Ethiopia and other African countries whose leaders seek to stay in power by using any means necessary. This time, substance must accompany accomplished rhetoric.

Ethiopia and other African countries can learn much from the 2008 US presidential election in which Barack Obama appears to have forged unity with many of those whose policy platforms were different from his; he has included many disparate voices in his administration. Serving Ethiopia also calls for visionary leaders and consensus builders; not leaders surrounded by sycophant supporters. Business as usual must not be the way to embark on the 21st century that is going to be more and more complex.

In this book I have presented historical and contemporary developments between Ethiopia and the US and provided a microcosm of international relations. May this book serve you well as you reflect on the dynamics and intricacies of any and all such relations.

Appendix I. Ethio–US Treaty 1903

Treaty between the United States and the King of Ethiopia to regulate the commercial relations between the two countries. Signed at Addis-Ababa, December 27, 1903; ratification advised by the Senate, March 12, 1904; ratified by the President, March 17, 1904; King of Ethiopia notified of ratification, August 2, 1904; proclaimed, September 30, 1904.

By THE PRESIDENT OF THE UNITED STATES OF AMERICA.

A PROCLAMATION.

Whereas a treaty of commerce between the United States of America and His Majesty Menelik II, King of Kings of Ethiopia, was concluded on the twenty-seventh day of December one thousand nine hundred and three, the original of which treaty, being in the Amharic* and French languages, is word for word as follows:

TREATY OF COMMERCE.

His Majesty Menelik II., King of Kings of Ethiopia, and the United States of America having agreed to regulate the commercial relations between the two countries and develop them, and render them more and more advantageous to the two contracting Powers:

His Majesty Menelik II, King of Kings of Ethiopia, in the name of the Empire, and Robert P. Skinner, in the name of the United States of America, have agreed and stipulated that which follows:

ARTICLE I.

The citizens of the two Powers, like the citizens of other countries, shall be able freely to travel and to transact business throughout the extent of the territories of the two contracting Powers, while respecting the usages, and submitting themselves to the tribunals of the countries in which they may be located.

ARTICLE II.

In order to facilitate commercial relations, the two Governments shall assure, throughout the extent of their respective territories, the security of those engaged in business therein, and of their property.

ARTICLE III.

The two contracting Governments shall reciprocally grant to all citizens of the United States of America and to the citizens of Ethiopia, all the advantages which they shall accord to other Powers in respect to Customs duties, imposts, and jurisdiction.

ARTICLE IV.

Throughout the extent of the Ethiopian Empire, the citizens of the United States of America shall have the use of the telegraphs, posts and all other means of transportation upon the same terms as the citizens of other Powers.

> Amharic text not printed.
> Translation furnished by Commissioner.

ARTICLE V.

In order to perpetuate and strengthen the friendly relations which exist between Ethiopia and the United States of America, the two Governments agree to receive reciprocally, representatives acceptable to the two Governments. These representatives shall not however, be maintained at their posts, unless they are agreeable to the receiving Power, in such cases, they shall be replaced.

ARTICLE VI.

The duration of the present treaty shall be ten years. It is understood that at the expiration of these ten years the two Governments shall be able to modify all or any part of this treaty. The Government which shall request at that time the modification, shall make its proposal to the other Government one year before the expiration of the treaty.

ARTICLE VII.

The present treaty shall take effect if ratified by the Government of the United States, and if this ratification shall be notified to His Majesty Menelik II, King of Kings Ethiopia, within the period of one year.

His Majesty Menelik II King of Kings of Ethiopia, in the name of his Empire; Robert P. Skinner in virtue of his full powers, in the name of the United States of America, have signed the present treaty, written in double text, Amharic and French, and in identical terms.

DONE at Addis-Ababa, this seventeenth day of December, one thousand eight hundred and ninety-six, in the year of grace (corresponding to December 27th, 1903).

> [Seal of MENELIK II]
> ROBERT P. SKINNER
> *Consul General and plenipotentiary*

And whereas it is provided by the said treaty that it shall take effect "if ratified by the Government of the United States of America and if this ratification shall be notified to His Majesty King Menelik II, King of Kings of Ethiopia, within the period of one year";

And whereas the said treaty has been duly ratified on the part of the United States of America and notification of such ratification was given to His Majesty Menelik II, King of Kings of Ethiopia, on the second day of August, one thousand nine hundred and four;

Now, therefore, be it known that I, Theodore Roosevelt, President of the United States of America, have caused the said treaty to be made public, to the end that the same and every article and clause thereof may be observed and fulfilled with good faith by the United States and the citizens thereof.

In testimony whereof, I have hereunto set my hand and caused the seal of the United States of America to be affixed.

Done at the City of Washington, this thirtieth day of September, in the year of our Lord one thousand nine hundred and four, and of the Independence of the United States of America the one hundred and twenty-ninth.

    [SEAL]   THEODORE ROOSEVELT.

By the President:

    FRANCIS B. LOOMIS,

Acting Secretary of State.

———

Source: The Statutes at Large of the United States of America from November, 1903, to March, 1905, vol. 33, part 2. Washington, DC: Government Printing Press, 1905, pp 2254–2256. Amharic text not printed; translation (from French to English) "provided by Commissioner."

Appendix II. The First American Party to Ethiopia, 1903

Commissioner.
Robert P. Skinner.
Surgeon.
Dr. A. P. L. Pease.
Secretary.
Horatio W. Wales.
Lieutenant (U.S.N.).
C. L. Hussey.
Captain (U.S.M.C.).
G.C. Thorpe.
Sergeant.
Glenn, Robert J.
Corporal.
Wood, Walter.

Privates.

Gates, Leonard L.
Flay, Hudson J.
Nelson, Charles.
Coleman, John M.
Durland, Ralph A.
Freel, John F.
Herbert, Benjamin F.
Howell, Theodore E.
Nilton, John G.

O'Connor, Patrick
Scott, Henry J.
Steele, Harry R.
Tweig, George J.
Vernon, William.
Maddock, Ritchie S.
Aldrich, Roy M.
Schultz, William.
Rossell, Joseph A.

Hospital Steward.
Fearnley, William H.
Messenger, American Consular Service.
Riviere, Hubert Vivien

Source: Robert Skinner, 1906, Abyssinia of Today: An Account of the First Mission sent by the American Government to the Court of the King of Kings (1903–1904). London: Edward Arnold Publishers to the Indian Office, p. 222.

Appendix III. Proclamations, 1910.

By THE PRESIDENT OF THE UNITED STATES OF AMERICA.

A PROCLAMATION.

WHEREAS it is provided in the Act of Congress approved August 5, 1909, entitled "An Act To provide revenue, equalize duties and encourage the industries of the United States, and for other purposes" —

That from and after the thirty-first day of March, nineteen hundred and ten, except as otherwise specially provided for in this section, there shall be levied, collected, and paid on all articles when imported from any foreign country into the United States, or into any of its possessions (except the Philippine Island and the islands of Guam and Tutuila), the rates of duty prescribed by the schedules and paragraphs of the dutiable list of section one of this Act, and in addition thereto twenty-five per centum ad valorem; which rates shall constitute the maximum tariff of the United State: *Provided*, That whenever, after the thirty-first day of March, nineteen hundred and ten, and so long thereafter as the President shall be satisfied, in view of the character of the concessions granted by the minimum tariff of the United States, that the government of any foreign country imposes no terms or restrictions, either in the way of tariff rates or provisions, trade or other regulations, charges, exactions, or in any other manner, directly or indirectly, upon the importation into or the sale in such foreign country of any agricultural, manufactured, or other product of the United States, which unduly discriminate against the United States or the products thereof, and that such foreign country pays no export bounty or imposes no export duty or prohibition upon the exportation of any article to the United States which unduly discriminates against the United States or the products thereof, and that such foreign country accords to the agricultural, manufactured, or other products of the United States treatment which is reciprocal and equivalent, thereupon and thereafter, upon proclamation to this effect by the President of the United States, all articles when imported into the United States or any of its possessions (except the Philippine Islands and the islands of Guam and Tutuila), from such foreign country shall, except as otherwise herein provided, be admitted under the terms of the minimum tariff of the United States as prescribed by section one of this Act.

AND WHEREAS satisfactory evidence has been presented to me that the Government of Abyssinia imposes no terms or restrictions, either in the way of tariff rates or provisions, trade or other regulations, charges, exactions, or in any other manner, directly or indirectly, upon the importation into or the sale in Abyssinia of any agricultural, manufactured, or other product of the United States, which unduly discriminate against the United States or the products thereof, and that the Government of Abyssinia pays no export bounty or imposes no export duty or prohibition upon the exportation of any article to the United States which unduly discriminates against the United States or the products thereof, and that the Government of Abyssinia accords to the agricultural, manufactured, or other products of the United States treatment which is reciprocal and equivalent:

Now, THEREFORE, I, WILLIAM HOWARD TAFT, President of the United States of America, by virtue of the power in me vested by the aforesaid Act of Congress, do hereby make known and proclaim that from and after March 31, 1910, and so long thereafter as the aforesaid Act of Congress is in existence and the Government of Abyssinia imposes no terms or restrictions upon the importation or sale in Abyssinia of the products of the United States which unduly discriminate against the United States, all articles when imported into the United States, or any of its possessions (except the Philippine Islands and the islands of Guam and Tutuila), from Abyssinia shall be admitted under the terms of the minimum tariff of the United States as prescribed by Section one of the Tariff Act of the United States approved August 5, 1909;

Provided, however, that this proclamation shall not take effect from and after March 31, 1910, but shall be null and void in the event that, at any time prior to the aforesaid date, satisfactory evidence shall be presented to the President that the Government of Abyssinia has made such change or changes in its present laws or regulations affecting American commerce in Abyssinia as to discriminate unduly in any way against such commerce, and in the further event that a proclamation shall have been issued.

IN WITNESS WHEREOF I have hereunto set my hand and caused the seal of the United States to be affixed.

DONE at the City of Washington, this twenty-first day of February, A.D. one thousand nine hundred and ten, and of the independence of the United States of America the one hundred and thirty-fourth.

WM H TAFT

By the President:
Huntington Wilson
Acting Secretary of State.

Source: The Statute at Large of the United States of America from March 1909 to March 1911, vol. 36, part 2. Washington, DC: Government Printing Press, 1911, pp. 2540-2541.

APPENDIX IV. TREATY — ETHIOPIAN EMPIRE. JUNE 27, 1914.

Treaty of commerce between the United States and the Ethiopian Empire. Signed at Addis Ababa, June 27, 1914; ratification advised by the Senate, September 15, 1914; ratified by the President, September 19, 1914; Prince Lidj Yassou notified of ratification, December 20, 1914; proclaimed, August 9, 1920.

BY THE PRESIDENT OF THE UNITED STATES OF AMERICA.

A PROCLAMATION.

Whereas, a treaty between the United States of America and the Ethiopian Empire, to regulate and develop the commercial relations between the two countries, was concluded by their respective plenipotentiaries at Addis-Ababa, on the twenty-seventh day of June, one thousand nine hundred and fourteen, the original of which Treaty, being in English and Amharic, is word for word as follows:

Treaty of Commerce.

His Royal Highness, Prince Lidj Yassou, successor of Menelik II, King of Kings of Ethiopia and the United States of America, having agreed to regulate the commercial relations between the two countries and develop them, and render them more and more advantageous to the two contracting Powers:

His Royal Highness, Prince Lidj Yassou in the name of the Empire and John Q. Wood, in the name of the United States of America, have agreed and stipulated that which follows:

Article I.

The citizens of the two Powers, like the citizens of other countries, shall be able freely to travel and transact business throughout the extent of the territories of the two contracting Powers.

Article II.

In order to facilitate commercial relations, the two Governments shall assure, throughout the extent of their respective territories, the security of those engaged in business therein, and of their property.

Article III.

The two contracting Governments shall reciprocally grant to all citizens of the United States of America and to the citizens of Ethiopia, all the advantages which they shall accord to the most favored Power in respect to customs duties, imposts and jurisdiction.

Article IV.

Throughout the extent of the Ethiopian Empire, the citizens of the United States of America shall have the use of the telegraphs, posts and all others means of transportation upon the same terms as the citizens of Ethiopia or of the most favored foreign Power.

Article V.

In order to perpetuate and strengthen the friendly relations which exist between Ethiopia and the United States of America, the two Governments agree to receive reciprocally, representatives acceptable to the two Governments; Diplomatic representatives appointed by either Government who are not acceptable to the Government to which they are accredited shall be replaced.

Article VI.

This treaty shall continue in force for a period of four years after the date of its ratification by the Government of the United States. If neither of the contracting parties, one year before the expiration of that period, notifies officially its determination to terminate the treaty, it shall remain in force for a further period of ten years; and so on thereafter unless notice is given officially by one of the contracting Powers, one year before the expiration of said period, of its intention to terminate said treaty.

Article VII.

The present treaty shall take effect if ratified by the Government of the United States, and if this ratification shall be notified to His Royal Highness Prince Lidj Yassou, successor of Menelik II, King of Kings of Ethiopia within the period of six months.

His Royal Highness Prince Lidj Yassou in the name of his Empire; and John Q. Wood in virtue of his full powers, in the name of the United States of America, have signed the present treaty, written in double text, Amharic and English and in identical terms.

Done at Addis-Ababa, this twenty seventh day of June, one thousand nine hundred and fourteen, in the year of our Lord.

JOHN Q. WOOD
[Seal of Prince Lidj Yassou]

[Amharic text not printed.]

And whereas, by Article VII of the said Treaty it is provided that the said Treaty shall take effect if ratified by the Government of the United States, and if this ratification shall be notified to His Royal Highness, Prince Lidj Yassou, successor of Menelik II, King of Kings of Ethiopia, within the period of six months;

And whereas the said Treaty was duly ratified by the Government of the United States, and the said ratification was notified to His Royal Highness Prince Lidj Yassou on December 20, 1914:

Now, therefore, be it known that I, Woodrow Wilson, President of the United States of America, have caused the said Treaty to be made public, to the end that the same and every article and clause thereof may be observed and fulfilled by the United States and the citizens thereof.

In testimony whereof, I have hereunto set my hand and caused the seal of the United States to be affixed.

Done in the District of Columbia, this ninth day of August in the year of our Lord one thousand nine hundred and twenty, and of the Independence of the United States of America the one hundred and forty-fifth.

[SEAL]
WOODROW WILSON

By the President:
BAINBRIDGE COLBY
Secretary of State.

Source: The Statute at Large of the United States of America from May 1919 to March 1921, vol. 41, part 2. Washington, DC: Government Printing Press, 1921, pp. 1711-1712.

Appendix V. United States Consul Generals and Ambassadors to Ethiopia

1. Frank R. Mower, Minister Resident, Consul General, December 20, 1906 to January 3, 1907
2. US interest kept by Vice Consul General, 1907–1909
3. Hoffman Philip, Consul General, July 6, 1909 to February 8, 1910
4. No US diplomat stationed in Ethiopia from 1910 to 1928. US interests were entrusted to the British legation in Addis Ababa and to the US Consul at Aden.
5. Addison E. Southard, Minister Resident, Consul General, March 1, 1928 to October 26, 1934.
6. No information available from 1934 to 1936
7. Cornelius Van H. Engert, Minister Resident, Consul General, April 30, 1936 to May 4, 1937
8. John K. Caldwell, Minister Resident, Consul General. August 31, 1943 to December 9, 1943
9. John K Caldwell, Envoy Extraordinary and Minister Plenipotentiary, December 9, 1943 to August 26, 1945
10. Felix Cole, Envoy Extraordinary and Minister Plenipotentiary, October 5, 1945 to October 8, 1947
11. George R. Merrell, Envoy Extraordinary and Minister Plenipotentiary, January 1, 1948 to May 21, 1949
12. George R. Merrell, Ambassador Extraordinary and Plenipotentiary, June 28, 1949 to March 17, 1951
13. J. Rives Childs, Ambassador Extraordinary and Plenipotentiary May 14, 1951 to January 19, 1953
14. Joseph Simonson, Ambassador Extraordinary and Plenipotentiary, October 6, 1953 to May 1, 1957
15. Don C. Bliss, Ambassador Extraordinary and Plenipotentiary, June 22, 1957 to June 4, 1960

16. Arthur L. Richards, Ambassador Extraordinary and Plenipotentiary, August 26, 1960 to November 25, 1962
17. Edward M. Korry, Ambassador Extraordinary and Plenipotentiary, April 20, 1963 to September 22, 1967
18. William O. Hall, Ambassador Extraordinary and Plenipotentiary, October 27, 1967 to May 15, 1971
19. E. Ross Adair, Ambassador Extraordinary and Plenipotentiary, July 8, 1971 to February 12, 1974
20. Arthur W. Hummel, Jr., Ambassador Extraordinary and Plenipotentiary, April 3, 1975 to July 6, 1976
21. Frederic L. Chapin, Ambassador Extraordinary and Plenipotentiary, July 21, 1978 to July 29, 1980
22. Marc Allen Bass, Ambassador Extraordinary and Plenipotentiary, June 24, 1992 to July 8, 1994
23. Irvin Hicks, Ambassador Extraordinary and Plenipotentiary, July 22, 1994 to June 26, 1996
24. David H. Shinn, Ambassador Extraordinary and Plenipotentiary, July 2, 1996 to August 14, 1999
25. Tibor P. Nagy, Jr. Ambassador Extraordinary and Plenipotentiary, October 12, 1999 to July 19, 2002
26. Aurelia E. Brazeal, Ambassador Extraordinary and Plenipotentiary, November 20, 2002 to September 2, 2005
27. Donald Yamamoto, Ambassador Extraordinary and Plenipotentiary, December 6, 2006 to present (January 2008).

Note: Because of political conditions in Ethiopia, there was no US Ambassador from 1980 to 1992. The embassy was maintained at the rank of Chargé d'affaires. The embassy was run at the same level from September 2, 2005 to December 6, 2006.

Source: Collected from http://en.wikipedia.org/wiki/United_States_Ambassador_to_Ethiopia and other sources.

Appendix VI. Ethiopian Ambassadors to the United States

1. Blatengeta Ephrem Tewelde Medhin, Ambassador Extraordinary and Plenipotentiary, November 9, 1943 to March 27, 1945
2. Ras Imiru Haile Selassie, Ambassador Extraordinary and Plenipotentiary, May 6, 1946 to September 1949
3. Lij Yilma Deressa, Ambassador Extraordinary and Plenipotentiary, September 11, 1953 to April 1957
4. Dejazmach Zewde Gabre Hiwot, Ambassador Extraordinary and Plenipotentiary, August 25, 1958 to October 8, 1960
5. Lij Michael Imiru, Ambassador Extraordinary and Plenipotentiary, May 11, 1960 to April 1, 1961
6. Ato Birhanu Dinke, Ambassador Extraordinary and Plenipotentiary, April 28, 1961 to June 15, 1965
7. Afenegus Teshome Haile Mariam, Ambassador Extraordinary and Plenipotentiary, August 25, 1965 to October 19, 1968
8. Dr. Minasse Haile, Ambassador Extraordinary and Plenipotentiary, October 18, 1969 to June 11, 1971
9. Ato Kifle Wodajo, Ambassador Extraordinary and Plenipotentiary, April 26, 1972 to April 10, 1975
10. Ato Ayalew Mandefro, Ambassador Extraordinary and Plenipotentiary, November 4, 1977 to June 1978
11. Ato Birhane Gebre-Christos, Ambassador Extraordinary and Plenipotentiary, March 16, 1992 to June 19, 2002
12. Ato Kassahune Ayele Ambassador Extraordinary and Plenipotentiary, Ambassador Extraordinary and Plenipotentiary, June, 2002 to March 2006
13. Dr. Samuel Assefa, Ambassador Extraordinary and Plenipotentiary, May 2006 to present (January 2008).

Source: Ethiopian Embassy, Washington, D.C.

110th CONGRESS
1st Session
H. R. 2003
IN THE SENATE OF THE UNITED STATES

October 3, 2007

Received; read twice and referred to the Committee on Foreign Relations

AN ACT

To encourage and facilitate the consolidation of peace and security, respect for human rights, democracy, and economic freedom in Ethiopia.

Be it enacted by the Senate and House of Representatives of the United States of America in Congress assembled,

SECTION 1. SHORT TITLE.

This Act may be cited as the 'Ethiopia Democracy and Accountability Act of 2007'.

SEC. 2. STATEMENT OF POLICY.

It is the policy of the United States to —

(1) support the advancement of human rights, democracy, independence of the judiciary, freedom of the press, peacekeeping capacity building, and economic development in the Federal Democratic Republic of Ethiopia;

(2) seek the unconditional release of all political prisoners and prisoners of conscience in Ethiopia;

(3) foster stability, democracy, and economic development in the region;

(4) support humanitarian assistance efforts, especially in the Ogaden region;

(5) collaborate with Ethiopia in the Global War on Terror; and

(6) strengthen United States–Ethiopian relations based on the policy objectives specified in paragraphs (1) through (5).

SEC. 3. SUPPORT FOR HUMAN RIGHTS IN ETHIOPIA.

The Secretary of State shall —

(1) provide financial support to local and national human rights groups and other relevant civil society organizations to help strengthen human rights monitoring and regular reporting on human rights conditions in Ethiopia;

(2) provide legal support, as needed, for political prisoners and prisoners of conscience in Ethiopia and assist local, national, and international groups that are active in monitoring the status of political prisoners and prisoners of conscience in Ethiopia;

(3) seek to promote and bolster the independence of the Ethiopian judiciary through—

(A) facilitation of joint discussions between court personnel, officials from the Ethiopian Ministry of Justice, relevant members of the legislature, and civil society representatives on international human rights standards; and

(B) encouraging exchanges between Ethiopian and United States jurists, law schools, law professors, and law students, especially in legal fields such as constitutional law, role of the judiciary, due process, political and voting rights, criminal law and procedure, and discrimination;

(4) establish a program, in consultation with Ethiopian civil society, to provide for a judicial monitoring process, consisting of indigenous organizations, international organizations, or both, to monitor judicial proceedings throughout Ethiopia, with special focus on unwarranted government intervention on matters that are strictly judicial in nature, and to report on actions needed to strengthen an independent judiciary;

(5) establish a program, in consultation with Ethiopian civil society, and provide support to other programs, to strengthen independent media in Ethiopia, including training, and technical support;

(6) expand the Voice of America's Ethiopia program;

(7) support efforts of the international community to gain full and unfettered access to the Ogaden region for —

(A) humanitarian assistance organizations; and

(B) independent human rights experts; and

(8) work with appropriate departments and agencies of the Government of the United States and appropriate officials of foreign governments—

(A) to identify members of the Mengistu Haile Mariam regime and officials of the current Government of Ethiopia who were engaged in gross human rights violations, including those individuals who may be residing in the United States; and

(B) to support and encourage the prosecution of individuals identified under subparagraph (A) in the United States or Ethiopia.

SEC. 4. SUPPORT FOR DEMOCRATIZATION IN ETHIOPIA.

(a) Strengthening Local, Regional, and National Democratic Processes —
The Secretary of State shall —

(1) provide assistance to strengthen local, regional, and national parliaments and governments in Ethiopia, as needed;

(2) establish a program focused on reconciliation efforts between the Government of Ethiopia and political parties, including in minority communities, in preparation for negotiation and for participation in the political process; and

(3) provide training for civil society groups in election monitoring in Ethiopia.

(b) Democracy Enhancement —

(1) ASSISTANCE — United States technical assistance for democracy promotion in Ethiopia should be made available to all political parties and civil society groups in Ethiopia.

(2) RESTRICTION —

(A) IN GENERAL — Nonessential United States assistance shall not be made available to the Government of Ethiopia if the Government of Ethiopia acts to obstruct United States technical assistance to advance human rights, democracy, independence of the judiciary, freedom of the press, economic development, and economic freedom in Ethiopia.

(B) DEFINITION — In this paragraph, the term ˋnonessential United States assistance' means assistance authorized under any provision of law, other than humanitarian assistance, food aid programs, assistance to combat HIV/AIDS and other health care assistance, peacekeeping assistance, and counter-terrorism assistance.

SEC. 5. ENSURING GOVERNMENT SUPPORT FOR HUMAN RIGHTS, DEMOCRACY, AND ECONOMIC DEVELOPMENT IN ETHIOPIA.

(a) Limitation on Security Assistance; Travel Restrictions —

(1) LIMITATION ON SECURITY ASSISTANCE —

(A) IN GENERAL — Except as provided in subparagraph (B), security assistance shall not be provided to Ethiopia until such time as the certification described in paragraph (3) is made in accordance with such paragraph.

(B) EXCEPTION — Subparagraph (A) shall not apply with respect to peacekeeping assistance, counter-terrorism assistance, or international military education and training for civilian personnel under section 541 of the Foreign Assistance Act of 1961 (commonly referred to as 'Expanded IMET'). Peacekeeping or counter-terrorism assistance provided to Ethiopia shall not be used for any other security-related purpose or to provide training to security personnel or units against whom there is credible evidence of gross human rights abuses or violations.

(2) TRAVEL RESTRICTIONS — Beginning on the date that is 60 days after the date of the enactment of this Act and until such time as the certification described in paragraph (3) is made in accordance with such

paragraph, the President shall deny a visa and entry into the United States to —

(A) any official of the Government of Ethiopia —

(i) who has been involved in giving orders to use lethal force against peaceful demonstrators or police officers in Ethiopia; or

(ii) against whom there is credible evidence of gross human rights abuses or violations;

(B) security personnel of the Government of Ethiopia who were in-volved in the June or November 2005 shootings of demonstrators;

(C) security personnel responsible for murdering Etenesh Yemam; and

(D) security personnel responsible for murdering prisoners at Kaliti prison in the aftermath of the election violence in 2005.

(3) CERTIFICATION — The certification described in this paragraph is a certification by the President to Congress that the Government of Ethiopia is making credible, quantifiable efforts to ensure that —

(A) all political prisoners and prisoners of conscience in Ethiopia have been released, their civil and political rights restored, and their prop-erty returned;

(B) prisoners held without charge or kept in detention without fair trial in violation of the Constitution of Ethiopia are released or re-ceive a fair and speedy trial, and prisoners whose charges have been dismissed or acquitted and are still being held are released without delay;

(C) the Ethiopian judiciary is able to function independently and al-lowed to uphold the Ethiopian Constitution and international human rights standards;

(D) security personnel involved in the unlawful killings of demonstra-tors and others, including Etenesh Yemam, and Kaliti prisoners are held accountable;

(E) family members, friends, legal counsel, medical personnel, human rights advocates, and others have access, consistent with internation-al law, to visit detainees in Ethiopian prisons;

(F) print and broadcast media in Ethiopia are able to operate free from undue interference and laws restricting media freedom, including sec-tions of the Ethiopian Federal Criminal Code, are revised;

(G) licensing of independent radio and television in Ethiopia is open and transparent;

(H) Internet access is not restricted by the government and the ability of citizens to freely send and receive electronic mail and otherwise obtain information is guaranteed;

(I) the National Election Board (NEB) includes representatives of political parties with seats in the Ethiopian Parliament and the NEB functions independently in its decision-making;

(J) representatives of international human rights organizations en-gaged in human rights monitoring work, humanitarian aid work, or investigations into human rights abuses in Ethiopia are admitted to Ethiopia and allowed to undertake their work in all regions of the country without undue restriction; and

(K) Ethiopian human rights organizations are able to operate in an environment free of harassment, intimidation, and persecution.

(4) WAIVER —

(A) IN GENERAL — The President may waive the application of paragraph (1) or (2) on a case-by-case basis if the President determines that such a waiver is in the national security interests of the United States.

(B) NOTIFICATION — Prior to granting a waiver under the authority of subparagraph (A), the President shall transmit to Congress a notification that includes the reasons for the waiver.

(b) Treatment of Political Prisoners and Prisoners of Conscience —

(1) IN GENERAL — The President, the Secretary of State, and other relevant officials of the Government of the United States shall call upon the Government of Ethiopia to immediately —

(A) release any and all remaining political prisoners and prisoners of conscience, especially prisoners held without charge; and

(B) allow full and unfettered access to the Ogaden region by humanitarian aid organizations and international human rights investigators.

(2) TORTURE VICTIM RELIEF — While it is the responsibility of the Government of Ethiopia to compensate the victims of unlawful imprisonment and torture and their families for their suffering and losses, the President shall provide assistance for the rehabilitation of victims of torture in Ethiopia at centers established for such purposes pursuant to section 130 of the Foreign Assistance Act of 1961 (22 U.S.C. 2152).

(c) Sense of Congress — It is the sense of Congress that the Government of the United States should —

(1) encourage the Government of Ethiopia to enter into discussions with opposition political groups interested in reconciliation in order to bring such groups into full participation in the political and economic affairs of Ethiopia, including their legalization as political parties, and provide such assistance as is warranted and necessary to help achieve the goal described in this paragraph; and

(2) provide assistance to promote the privatization of government owned or controlled industries and properties in Ethiopia.

SEC. 6. SUPPORT FOR ECONOMIC DEVELOPMENT IN ETHIOPIA.

(a) Resource Policy Assistance — The President, acting through the Administrator of the United States Agency for International Development and in cooperation with the World Bank and other donors, shall provide assistance, as needed, for sustainable development of Ethiopia's Nile and Awash River resources, including assistance to help Ethiopia with the technology necessary for the construction of irrigation systems and hydroelectric power that might prevent future famine.

(b) Health Care Assistance — The President, acting through the Administrator of the United States Agency for International Development, shall provide material support to hospitals, clinics, and health care centers in Ethiopia, especially hospitals, clinics, and health care centers in rural areas.

SEC. 7. REPORT.

Not later than 180 days after the date of the enactment of this Act, the President shall transmit to Congress a report on the implementation of this Act, including a description of a comprehensive plan to address issues of security, human rights, including in the Ogaden region, democratization, and economic freedom that potentially threaten the stability of Ethiopia.

SEC. 8. AUTHORIZATION OF APPROPRIATIONS.

(a) In General — There are authorized to be appropriated to carry out this Act $20,000,000 for each of the fiscal years 2008 and 2009.

(b) Availability — Amounts appropriated pursuant to the authorization of appropriations under subsection (a) are authorized to remain available until expended.

Passed the House of Representatives October 2, 2007.
Attest:
LORRAINE C. MILLER,
Clerk.
END

APPENDIX VIII. CHRONOLOGY OF ETHIOPIAN INTERNATIONAL RELATIONS

1275
- Emperor Yekuno Amlak dispatched an emissary to Emperor Michael VIII Palaiogos of Byzantine.

1541
- The defeat of the force of Gragn Mohammad, supported by Turkey. Ethiopia was supported by Portugal. This was the first international conflict in the region.

1624–1704
- Hiob Ludolf introduced the first text in Amharic grammar and started Ethiopian studies program in Frankfurt, Germany.

1769
- James Bruce, from Scotland, discovered the source of the Blue Nile.

1776–1941
- A period of US isolationism in international affairs

1784
- The Russian government requested the Patriarch in Antioch, Jerusalem, to translate Russian words into Ethiopian languages.

1808
- Ethiopian merchants and African Americans established the Abyssinian Baptist Church in Lower Manhattan, New York.

1829
- Kharkov University, in Russia, introduced the study of the Amharic language.

1868
- Emperor Theodros committed suicide at the Battle of Makdala between Ethiopia and Britain.
- Henry M. Stanley, a special correspondent for *New York Herald*, covered the Battle of Makdala. The British force was led by Sir Robert Napier.

1871

- Italian–American Treaty of Commerce and navigation signed

1875
- The Battle of Gundet between Ethiopia and Egypt

1876
- The Battle of Gura between Ethiopia and Egypt

1886
- The British controlled northern Somalia and named it British Somaliland.

1888
- The Italians controlled southern Somaliland, Italian Somaliland.

1896
- Ethiopia, under Emperor Menelik, defeated Italy at the Battle of Adwa.

1897
- Benito Sylvain, from Haiti, arrived at the court of Emperor Menelik. Benito Sylvain served as Emperor Menelik's *Aide-de-camp.*
- Dr. Joseph Vitalien, from Guadeloupe, arrived in Ethiopia and served as Emperor Menelik's personal physician. He helped found two early hospitals in Ethiopia.
- Treaty between Ethiopia and Britain over the Ogaden and the Haud regions.

1899
- William H. Ellis, a.k.a. Guillaume Enriques Ellesio, an African-American Wall Street stockbroker, cotton grower in Texas, and an admirer of Emperor Menelik, arrives in Ethiopia.
- Ellis receives permission to grow cotton and establish a textile factory in Southern Ethiopia.
- Ellis convinces Emperor Menelik to enter in a Treaty of Amity and Commerce with the United States.

1900
- The American Consul at Marseilles, France, Robert Peet Skinner, suggested to the US State Department that a commercial mission be dispatched to Ethiopia.

1902
- Treaty regarding the use of the Blue Nile and Lake Tana signed between Ethiopia and Great Britain

1903
- Robert P. Skinner sends a letter to the State Department in May urging that a special mission be dispatched to Ethiopia.
- Skinner meets with President Theodore Roosevelt and presents his case regarding US relations with Ethiopia.
- Francis B. Loomis, Assistant Secretary of State, instructs Skinner to proceed to Ethiopia in June, investigate and report on commercial conditions.
- Assistant Secretary of State Loomis informs Skinner in July that US officials have decided to enter into negotiation with Emperor Menelik II on a "Treaty of Amity, Reciprocal Establishments and Commerce."
- On October 25, Consul Skinner leaves Marseilles for Beirut, Lebanon, takes on board US Marines and proceeds for Ethiopia.
- On December 18, Skinner and his party arrive in Ethiopia.
- On December 27, Emperor Menelik II and Consul Robert P. Skinner sign a Treaty of Amity and Commerce. Ethiopia is extended "Most Favored Nation" (MFN) status. Gifts are exchanged between Emperor Menelik and

President Theodore Roosevelt.
- Dr. Joseph Vitalien helps establish the Ras Mekonnen Hospital in Harar.

1904
- US Senate ratifies on March 17 the treaty between Ethiopia and the United States, claimed to be the most picturesque document of its kind placed before the US Senate foreign relations committee.
- Kent J. Loomis, brother of Assistant Secretary of State Francis B. Loomis, dies on June 20 on his way to Ethiopia to deliver to Emperor Menelik the copy of the treaty signed by President Theodore Roosevelt.
- President Theodore Roosevelt sends Emperor Menelik II a special invitation to attend the World's Fair in St. Louis, Missouri.
- Consul Skinner reports that US trade interest in Ethiopia is greater than any of the European powers trading with Ethiopia.

1905
- The Bank of Abyssinia is founded as a branch of the National Bank of Egypt

1906
- The first US Consul General in Ethiopia, Frank R. Mowrer, is appointed and the US legation established.
- Great Britain, France, and Italy reinforce the General Act of Brussels (1890) and call to exercise "a rigorous supervision over the importation of arms and ammunitions" into Ethiopia.

1907
- The British representative in Ethiopia is in charge of American affairs after the departure of the first US Consul General, Mr. Mowrer.
- Edward Vialle is appointed American Vice-Consul General

1908
- Vice-Consul General Vialle leaves and the British representative once again look after the American interest.

1909
- Dr. Joseph Vitalien helps establish the Menelik II Hospital in Addis Ababa

1913
- Lij Iyasu Michael, grandson of Emperor Menelik, becomes the ruler of Ethiopia (1913–1916)
- US Legation temporarily closed
- Death of Emperor Menelik II
- The Allied Powers (Britain, France, and Italy) and the US complain about Lij Iyasu's penchant for the Central Powers that included Germany and the Ottoman Empire during World War I (1914–1918)

1914
- The Treaty of Amity and Commerce expires on March 7 and John P. Ward is sent to Ethiopia to negotiate its renewal. The treaty is signed between Lij Iyasu and the United States June 27 and ratified by the US Senate and signed by the President in September. Lij Iyasu is notified of ratification in December.
- Guy Love is appointed US Deputy Consul General in Addis Ababa
- Hoffman Philip is appointed Minister Resident and Consul General
- The US National Foreign Trade Council is founded by US companies
- American Field Service Program (AFS) is established

1916

- Lij Iyasu is deposed.
- Empress Zewditu, Emperor Menelik's daughter, becomes Empress of Ethiopia and rules from 1916 to 1930.
- Ras Teferi Mekonnen becomes Crown Prince and Regent.

1917
- Ras Teferi sends a letter to President Woodrow Wilson

1918
- Negadras Afework Gebre Iyesus heads a trade mission to the United States.

1919
- The US Consul General in London sends a telegram to Secretary of State Robert Lansing advising him to accord the Ethiopian delegation appropriate procedure and hospitality.
- The first official Ethiopian delegation, including Dejazmach Nadew Aba Mebrek, Kentiba Gebru Desta, Ato Heruy Wolde Selassie, and Ato Sinke, visit New York and Washington, DC. The group, when asked by an African-American newspaper, *The Chicago Defender*, commented on lynching in the United States.
- Empress Zewditu Menelik sends a letter to President Woodrow Wilson in appreciation of the his efforts to establish world peace, with gifts for President and Mrs. Wilson.

1920
- The treaty of 1914 is proclaimed, after a delay caused by US bureaucratic negligence.

1922
- The Abyssinian Baptist Church, of New York, established by Ethiopian merchants and African-Americans in 1808, is relocated from Lower Manhattan to its current location in Harlem.
- Blatengeta Heruy Wolde Selassie visits the US to purchase munitions.
- 1923
- President Calvin Coolidge delivers a message to the US Congress declaring an isolationist US foreign policy.
- 1925
- President Coolidge nevertheless dispatches Consul General Ralph J. Totten to Ethiopia to express the need for reestablishing a consulate in Addis Ababa.

1927
- Dr. Workeneh Martin, Ethiopian Envoy Extraordinary and Minister Plenipotentiary to the Court of St. James in London, visits the United States and negotiates with J.G. White Engineering Corporation of New York about building a dam on Lake Tana and the Blue Nile.
- Ras Teferi gives a statement to the American press and invites US investors to Ethiopia.
- An article authored by Zewdu Beyene, an Ethiopian residing in the US, appears in the Amharic newspaper, *Berhanena Selam* (Light and Peace), commenting on race relations and discrimination against blacks in the United States. The US Vice-Consul, James Loder Park, dispatches the English translation of the article to the State Department with a cautionary note and suggests that appropriate reception of Ethiopians would be "free from color prejudices."

1928
- The coronation of Prince Regent Teferi Mekonnen
- Addison E. Southard is appointed Minister Resident and Consul General to Ethiopia and serves from 1928 to 1936.
- In response to Ethiopia's earlier request to purchase airplanes and tanks, the State Department reports that the US War Department has no surplus airplanes and tanks to sell. However, in a subsequent letter, the State Department notifies Ethiopia that there is no legal restriction on the exportation of arms and ammunitions to Ethiopia, although the Department professed not to encourage the exportation of arms and ammunitions to any country.

1929
- Officials of J.G. White Engineering Corporation, Gano Dunn and Henry A. Lardner, visit Ethiopia. They meet with Empress Zewditu and King Teferi.
- The Treaty of Conciliation is signed between Ethiopia and the United States.
- The Treaty of Arbitration is signed between Ethiopia and the United States.
- The British *Westminster Gazette* writes articles to arouse British public against importation of arms into Ethiopia from the United States.
- The first Ethiopian airplane, *Nesere Teferi* (Teferi's bird), lands in Addis Ababa from Djibouti.

1930
- The death of Empress Zewditu and the coronation of King Teferi as Emperor Haile Selassie I. The US sends a special delegation to attend the coronation.

1931
- An American, Everett A. Colson, is appointed financial advisor to Ethiopia and serves until 1935.
- Professor Ernest Work, from Muskingum College in Ohio, serves as educational advisor of Ethiopia.
- 1935
- President Roosevelt and Secretary of State Cordell Hull send a message to Benito Mussolini advising Ethiopia and Italy to resolve their disputes without resorting to armed conflict.
- President Roosevelt remarks that their dispute is of no concern to the United States.
- The US prohibits American citizens from travelling as passengers on Ethiopian or Italian vessels.
- Twenty thousand African-Americans demonstrate in New York City in support of Ethiopia against Fascist aggression.

1936
- Fascist Italy attacks Ethiopia.
- The death of Lij Iyasu under suspicious circumstances.
- Everett Colson dies in London while assisting Emperor Haile Selassie during the Italian occupation. Colson had come to Ethiopia in 1933 and served as an advisor to the Ministry of Foreign Affairs.

1941
- With the help of British forces, Ethiopia's occupation by fascist Italy is ended.
- Britain controls Ethiopian communications and currency, introduced the

East African shilling.

- Eritrea becomes a British mandate after the defeat of Italy. The British mandate ends in 1952.
- The Atlantic Charter is signed by President Franklin D. Roosevelt and Prime Minister Winston S. Churchill.

1942

- The US considers resumption of diplomatic relations with Ethiopia.
- An American, George Blowers, becomes Governor of the State Bank of Ethiopia.
- The first Ethiopian paper currency, the *birr*, is introduced.

1943

- Britain contemplates turning Ethiopia into its trustee. The US State Department opposes the idea.
- Lij Yilma Deressa, Vice-minister of Finance, attends the World Food Conference at Hot Springs in Virginia and meets President Franklin Delano Roosevelt.
- President Roosevelt authorized that Ethiopia be qualified for lend-lease program in which allied nations are supplied with war materials.
- Blata Efraim Tewolde Medhin is appointed Ethiopia's first resident Minister in Washington, DC.
- The US War Department orders the "Establishment of a War Department Fixed Radio Station in Africa," leading to the Ethio–US treaty that established the Kagnew communication station in Asmara.

1944

- Emperor Haile Selassie gives the US a building lot for the American Legation in Ethiopia.

1945

- Emperor Haile Selassie meets with President Franklin Roosevelt at Great Bitter Lake in the Suez Canal.
- Ethiopian Airlines (EAL) is established with the assistance of Trans World Airlines (TWA) of the United States.

1946

- EAL makes its first international flight to Cairo.

1949

- President Harry S. Truman calls for a program that assists in the improvement and growth of the people of other countries.
- Ethiopia and the US agrees to raise their diplomatic representation from legation to embassy.
- Ras Imiru Haile Selassie becomes the first Ethiopian ambassador to the United States.
- George Merrill becomes the first US ambassador to Ethiopia.

1950

- The US Congress passes the Act for International Development and establishes the US International Cooperation Administration, also known as Point Four.

1951

- Ethiopia joins the UN force and participates in the Korean War, by providing the Kagnew Battalion, from 1951–1954.

1952

- Ethiopia signs a Point Four technical aid agreement. Herman Kleine directs Point Four Program in Ethiopia.
- The National Foreign Trade Council (founded in 1914) suggests that treaty with Ethiopia be rejected.
- The UN sponsors federation between Ethiopia and Eritrea.
- Col. Nasser comes to power after the overthrow of King Farouk.

1953
- A Treaty of Amity and Commerce and a mutual defense assistance agreement are signed between the two countries.
- A treaty is signed establishing the Kagnew Station communication facility for twenty-five years.

1954
- The Technical Cooperation Special Technical Service is signed.
- The Technical Cooperation in Water Resource Development Program is signed.
- The Technical Cooperation Vocational and Industrial Craft Program are signed.
- The Technical Cooperation Service Joint Fund for Eritrea is signed.
- Emperor Haile Selassie visits the US and addresses the joint session of the US Congress. He visits several cities in the US, including Stillwater, Oklahoma, home of Oklahoma State University (OSU.) OSU is involved in the development of Ethiopia's agricultural institutions
- The Gondar College of Public Health, established by UNICEF, FAO and the US Operations Mission in Ethiopia, becomes operational.

1955
- The Ogaden region, including the Reserved area and Haud, is returned to Ethiopia by Britain.
- The first civil war between North and South Sudan erupts.
- 1956
- Sudan gains independence from Britain.

1957
- The Technical Cooperation Economic Assistance is signed.

1958
- General Ibrahim Abud comes to power in Sudan after a coup d'état.

1959
- The first Ethiopian *Abune* of the Ethiopian Orthodox Church is officiated, thus replacing the Egyptian *Abune* of the Coptic church of Egypt designated by Alexandria, Egypt.

1960
- Coup d'état attempt by the Imperial Bodyguard against Emperor Haile Selassie's government.
- Somalia gains independence.

1961
- ELF is launched.

1962
- Eritrea is federated with Ethiopia.
- US Peace Corps Volunteers (PCV), numbering 279 volunteers, arrives in Ethiopia.

1963

- The OAU is inaugurated.
- A mutual defense pact is signed between Ethiopia and Kenya.
- Ras Assrate Kassa is appointed governor of Eritrea.

1964

- Kenya gains independence.
- Ethiopia and Somalia border war.
- The Congo Civil War.

1972

- The second civil war between North and South Sudan starts.

1973

- At the OAU summit, Libya accuses Ethiopia of being an imperialist state opposed to the realization of Greater Somalia.
- Emperor Haile Selassie makes his last visit to the United States.
- Ethiopia terminates its official diplomatic relationship with Israel.
- Kagnew Station is closed. Communication facilities are moved to Diego Garcia in the Indian Ocean.
- Black September Organization assassinates US diplomat in Khartoum.

1974

- The government of Emperor Haile Selassie is overthrown.
- 62 former government officials are summarily executed
- A military regime called the *Derg* assumes power.

1975

- Kifle Wodajo, Ambassador to the US, opposes the *Derg*'s policy and leaves his post.

1976

- The US Congress pressures the Ford Administration to reduce US military aid to Ethiopia.

1977

- War erupts between Ethiopia and Somalia. The Somali army reaches the city of Harar, 300 miles from the Somali border.
- Ayalew Mandefro, Ambassador to the US, leaves his post and opposes the *Derg*'s policy.
- A period of "Red Terror" in Ethiopia results in the death of 3,000 people and the arrest of 20,000 young urban dwellers.
- Large-scale defection of Ethiopia's officials and the exodus of Ethiopians to neighboring countries.
- The US accuses Ethiopia, Argentina, and Uruguay of human rights abuses.
- The US aid to Ethiopia is cut.
- Soviet military equipment, costing from $100 million to $200 million, starts arriving in Ethiopia.
- Col. Mengistu signs a Declaration of the Basic Principles of Friendly Mutual Relations and Cooperation with the USSR.
- Amnesty International names Ethiopia for human rights abuses.
- US military personnel are expelled from Ethiopia.
- US agencies such as USI, MAAG, and NMRC are closed.
- US Consulate in Asmara is closed.
- US embassy staff in Addis Ababa is reduced.
- About 300 US personnel and dependents at the Kagnew Station are given four days by the Ethiopian government to leave the country before the station

is closed.

- News correspondents from Agence France, the Washington Post, and Reuter's news agency are ordered to leave Ethiopia within 48 hours.
- Ethiopia orders a return of eighty-one army, air force, and navy personnel from training in the United States.
- At a meeting in Ta'izz, North Yemen, Arab countries declare their interest in blocking non–Arab access to the Red Sea.

1979

- 4,000 Ethiopian children orphaned by war are airlifted to Cuba.
- Ethiopia complains about the US escalating subversive activities in the Horn of Africa.
- Members of the Bete Israel are smuggled out of Ethiopia.
- A Treaty of Cooperation and Friendship is signed between Ethiopia and Kenya.

1980

Frederic L. Chapin, Ambassador to Ethiopia, leaves his position at Ethiopia's request.

1982

- The US Department of State announces an end to the policy of blanket protection against deportation of Ethiopians in the United States. The policy is reversed within five months.
- The US Department of State estimates that war against secessionist groups in Eritrea and Tigre as well as Somalia has consumed more than 227% of Ethiopia's GNP.
- The Voice of America Amharic (VOA–Amharic) language program is launched.

1983

- Another conflict between North and South Sudan is started.

1984

- Israel airlifts 8,000 Bete Israelis in a clandestine mission named Operation Moses. Sudanese officials and State Security, the CIA, and the Mossad are involved in the smuggling.
- The Ogaden National Liberation Front (ONLF) is founded. ONLF seeks the Somali-speaking region of the Ogaden to break away from Ethiopia.

1985

- EPLF opens its Washington office.
- US warns the 600-strong American community to leave Ethiopia as the situation in the country remains unpredictable.

1986

- The Soviet Union reduces its support to Ethiopia because of Michael Gorbachev's "new thinking" and the end of the Cold War.
- The US Congress forms the Congressional Caucus for Ethiopian Jews to promote the emigration of the Bete Israelis to Israel.
- The Intergovernmental Agency on Development (IGAD) is established.

1989

- An attempt is made to overthrow Col. Mengistu Haile Mariam.
- Ethiopia renews diplomatic relations with Israel.
- EPRDF is created by the TPLF.

1990

- US Assistant Secretary of State for African Affairs Herman Cohen hosts a luncheon for Issayas Afewerki at the US Department of State Foreign Service Club.
- US-sponsored talks occur between EPLF and the *Derg* representative Ashagre Yigletu.
- Issayas Afewerki meets with Sen. Edward Kennedy and Rep. Howard Wolfe, Chairman, House Foreign Subcommittee on Africa.
- Herman Cohen testifies at a Congressional hearing that Eritrea had a right to self-determination within the Ethiopian framework.
- The US offers to the *Derg* and the EPLF a proposal to settle their differences.
- Ethiopia serves on the UN Security Council and supports the US by voting to condemn Iraq's invasion of Kuwait.

1991
- Former Sen. Rudy Boschwitz (R-Min.), Deputy Assistant Secretary of State for Africa Irvin Hicks, and Director of African Affairs in the National Security Council Robert Frasure visit Ethiopia to negotiate the emigration of the Bete Israelis to Israel.
- President George H.W. Bush sends a letter to Col. Mengistu reaffirming US support for Ethiopia's territorial integrity.
- The American Association of Ethiopian Jews (AAEJ) and the North American Conference on Ethiopian Jewry (NACEJ) pressure the US and Israeli governments to help Ethiopian Jews settle in Israel.
- TPLF/EPRDF advances on Addis Ababa, the *Derg* is overthrown, and TPLF/EPRDF comes to power in Ethiopia.
- In a Bete Israeli airlift 18,000 people leave Ethiopia for Israel
- Colonel Mengistu flees to Zimbabwe.
- Lt. General Tesfaye Gebre-Kidan is named acting president.
- Tesfaye Dinka is named Prime Minister.
- The London Conference of ethnic-based organizations forms a post-*Derg* Transitional Government of Ethiopia (TGE).
- The EPLF enters Asmara.
- TPLF/EPLF enters Addis Ababa.
- Eritrea deports 82,396 former Ethiopian troops and solders and 43,527 civilians from Eritrea.
- Gen. Siad Barre of Somalia falls from power.
- Warlords control Somalia.

1992
- Elections for Regional Council are held in Ethiopia; the OLF accuses the government of rigging the elections.
- OLF withdraws from the 87-member Council of Representatives.
- Mr. Mervyn Dymally, Chairman of the US House Subcommittee on Africa, writes to Meles Zenawi criticizing the election as "shameful and irresponsible."
- The US participates in a UN program, Operation Restore Hope.
- American troops are stationed in Camp Lemonier, Djibouti.
- UN Security Council votes to authorize US-led force to safeguard food shipment to Somalia.
- US Marine Corps lands in Somalia
- UN takes command of international peacekeeping force in Somalia.

- Eritrea attempts to broker peace in the HOA region.

1993

- Eritrea gains its independence.
- Ethiopian opposition groups hold a National Conference for Peace and Reconciliation in Addis Ababa.
- UN program in Somalia, Operation Restore Hope, is ended after two US Black Hawks are downed.
- The US force leaves Somalia.
- Peace between Somali factions is brokered in Addis Ababa. Ethiopia sides with Mohamed Farah Aideed.
- TFG in Somalia is established.

1994

- General election in Ethiopia.
- Ethiopia is divided into nine ethnic-based regions called *kilil*.
- UN ended its operation in Somalia.

1995

- New members of parliament are elected to replace the TGE.
- Mr. Meles Zenawi becomes Prime Minister.
- Former Congressman Harry Johnson tries to mediate between the EPRDF and the opposition political parties. The opposition political parties boycotts elections.
- Dr. Negaso Gidada assumes the ceremonial position of President.
- President Hosni Mubarak of Egypt escapes an assassination attempt in Addis Ababa on his way to an OAU summit. Sudan is blamed.
- Ethiopia engages against fundamentalist Muslim group called *al-Ittihad al-Islami* that seeks the independence of the Ogaden.

1996

- The Voice of America started broadcasting in Afan Oromo and Tigrigna.
- US ambassador to the UN, Madeleine K. Albright, calls Sudan "a viper's nest of terrorists."
- Bombing of civilian targets in Addis Ababa; al-Ittihad al-Islami is suspected by the Ethiopian government.
- *Maariv*, an Israeli newspaper, reports on the discarding of blood donated by Ethiopian-Israelis. Ethiopian-Israelis in Jerusalem protest.
- The Washington Post reported that Ethiopia, Eritrea, and Uganda have received US military equipment to overthrow the government of Sudan.
- Ethiopia sends troops to Somalia to attack Islamic Court Union.

1998

- Border war between Ethiopia and Eritrea.
- US embassies in Nairobi, Kenya and in Dar es Salam, Tanzania, are attacked

1999

- Prime Minister Meles Zenawi deports 52,200 Eritreans from Ethiopia.
- The US State Department orders nonessential employees to leave US embassies in Ethiopia and Eritrea in response to anti-American feeling in both countries.

2000

- US-sponsored African Growth and Opportunity Act (AGOA) is passed.
- National Summit on Africa is held in Washington, DC.
- A new Ethiopian embassy building in Washington, DC, is inaugurated.

- The UN Security Council imposes an arms embargo on both Ethiopia and Eritrea.
- The border war between Ethiopia and Eritrea is ended.
- A peace treaty between Ethiopia and Eritrea is signed.
- UN Security Council sets up UN Mission in Ethiopia and Eritrea (UNMEE).

2001
- The United States makes abrupt changes in foreign and domestic policies in response to attacks of September 11.
- A split emerges within the ruling party, TPLF, in Ethiopia.
- UN members endorse collective efforts against illegal arms circulation.

2002
- Ethiopia's Foreign Minister, Seyoum Mesfin, prematurely announces that the UN Permanent Court of Arbitration has rewarded the border town of Bademe to Ethiopia.

2003
- The Ethiopian government is accused of committing widespread human rights abuses against the Anuak population in the Gambella region.
- The Ethiopian government rejects the UN decision on Bademe that awarded the area to Eritrea.
- Conflict in Darfur, Sudan, starts.

2004
- The attack on the Anuak civilians continued.
- Transitional Federal Government (TFG) of Somalia is created.

2005
- General elections in Ethiopia take place. The opposition parties, United Ethiopian Democratic Forces (UDEF) and Coalition for Unity and Democracy (CUD) won election. CUD is a new political party and becomes popular. CUD leaders are imprisoned for two years. The political leaders accused the government for vote rigging and election improprieties and declined to join the Parliament.
- The government's special force, the *Agazi*, is accused of killing 193 peaceful demonstrators and arresting 30,000 people. Six government troops are reported killed.
- War between North and South Sudan, that started in 1983, ends.
- John Garang, Chairman of the SPLA, dies in helicopter crash.

2006
- Prime Minister Meles Zenawi sends troops to Somalia to support the TFG against the ICU. The Ethiopian and the TFG troops are accused of human rights abuses in Somalia.
- The Ethiopian Human Rights Bill (H.R. 5680), also known as the Ethiopian Freedom, Democracy and Accountability Act, authored by Rep. Chris Smith, is supported by members of Ethiopian diaspora but the Ethiopian government lobbies against the bill. The bill fails to appear on the House floor for vote.

2007
- Members of the Abyssinian Baptist Church made a pilgrimage to Ethiopia in commemoration of the bicentennial anniversary of the church's establishment by Ethiopian merchants and African Americans in 1808.
- A semi-autonomous Puntland state of Somalia is created.

- Congressman Donald Payne, Chairman of the Subcommittee on Africa and Global Health, introduces Ethiopia Democracy and Accountability Act, known as H.R. 2003. The bill went to the Senate in 2009.
- The Ethiopian government jams VOA–Amharic, VOA–Afan Oromo, and Germany's Deutsche Welle (DW) Amharic radio programs.
- Ethiopia fights the Ogaden National Liberation Front (ONLF) in the Ogaden region. Chinese nationals and Ethiopians working in Chinese-run oil fields are attacked by ONLF. The Ethiopian government takes counter insurgency measures and is accused of human rights abuses against civilians in the Ogaden.
- Ethiopia is accused of providing the US with prison cells for interrogating suspected terrorists from other countries.
- Elections are held in Kenya and lead to ethnic-based conflict and political crisis.

2008
- Sudanese army displaced Ethiopian farmers in Western Ethiopia. Meles Zenawi denies the accusation.
- President Omer Hassan Ahmed el Beshir is charged with genocide in Darfur.
- VOA adds a half-hour morning radio program in Amharic.
- P.M. Meles Zenawi hints that he may withdraw Ethiopian troops from Somalia before the Transitional Government controls Somalia.
- Senator Russ Feingold, Chairman of the Subcommittee on African Affairs, introduces a bill, Support for Democracy and Human Rights in Ethiopia Act of 2008, in the US Senate.

2009
- Ethiopia withdrew its troops from Somalia in January

Bibliography

Note: According to patronymic customs, most Ethiopians and Eritreans are not given surnames or family names. Hence, in this bibliography, such persons' names are followed by the fathers' names.

Articles and Book Chapters

Abate Kassa, March 1994. "The unmaking of the great Ethiopian Airlines," *Ethiopian Register*, vol. 1, no. 2.

Addis Tribune. August 13, 1999. "Egypt and the hydro-politics of the Blue Nile River — Part II. Addis Ababa, Ethiopia.

Amare Tekle. September, 1989. "The determinants of the foreign policy of revolutionary Ethiopia," *The Journal of Modern African Studies*, vol. 27, no. 3.

Aregawi Berhe. 2004. "The origins of the Tigray People's Liberation Front," *African Affairs*. Royal African Society, vol. 103, no. 413.

The Economist. May 8, 1999. "Africa's forgotten war."

Bashiron, D. 1958. "Ethiopian philology in Russia." *Ethiopian Observed*, vol. 2, no. 3.

Bereket Habte Selassie. June 1984. "The American dilemma on the Horn." *Journal of Modern African Studies*, vol. 22, no. 2.

Clapham, Christopher S. September/October, 1990. "The political economy of conflict in the Horn of Africa," *Survival*, vol. 32, no. 5.

Dima Noggo Sarbo. 2007. "The Ethiopia-Eritrea conflict: Short sighted solutions and long-term problems." The University of Tennesse, Knoxville. Unpublished article.

Fenyo, Mario. 2002. "Italians in Ethiopia," in Abdul Karim Bangura. *Mario Fenyo on the Third World: A Reader*, New York, NY: Writers Club Press.

Fikru Gebrekidan. July 23, 1999. "Ethiopia and New World Blacks: Part I," *Addis Tribune*, Addis Ababa, Ethiopia.

Getachew Metaferia. 2008."The dynamics of ethnic politics and economic development: The cases of China and Ethiopia," *Journal of South Asian and Middle Eastern Studies.*

_____. 2006. "Africa and the making of U.S. foreign policy in the era of globalization," Alice M. Jackson, ed. *Political Issues in America: A Multidimensional Perspective,* Boston: MA: Pearson Publishing.

_____. Fall 2005. "China: Ethnic politics, nation building and its global role," *Journal of South Asian and Middle Eastern Studies,* vol. 29, no. 1.

_____. 2003. "The Ethiopian and Eritrean border dispute: A critical perspective," *Horn of Africa,* vol. 21.

_____. 1995. "The Ethiopian connection to the Pan-African movement," Journal *of Third World Studies,* vol. 12, no. 2.

Hansberry, Leo. 1965. "Ethiopian ambassadors to Latin Courts and Latin emissaries to Prester John," *Ethiopia Observer.* vol. 4, no. 1.

Horup, Ellen. 1936. "Ethiopia: Member of the League of Nations?" A reprint in *Politiken,* Copenhagen, Denmark.

Henze, Paul B. 1994. "The economic dimensions of federalism in the Horn of Africa," in Peter Wood & Murray Forsyth, (eds.) 1994. *Conflict and Peace in the Horn of Africa — Federalism and its Alternatives,* Brookfield, Vermont: Dartmouth Publishing Company.

Karadawi, Ahmed. 1991. "The smuggling of the Ethiopian Falasha to Israel through Sudan," *African Affairs,* vol. 90.

Keller, Edmond J. 1985. "United States foreign policy on the Horn of Africa: Policy making with blinders on," in Bender, Gerald J., James S. Coleman and Richard L. Sklar. *African Crisis Area and U.S. Foreign Policy.* Berkeley: University of California Press.

Kenyatta, Jomo. September, 1935. "Hands off Abyssinia," *Labour Monthly,* London, vol. 17, no. 9.

Khadiagala, Gilbert M., and Terrence Lyons, (eds.) 2001. Boulder, CO: Lynne Rienner.

Legum, Colin, and Bill Lee. 1977–1978. "Crisis in the Horn: International dimensions of the Somali-Ethiopian conflict," *Africa Contemporary Record: Annual Survey and Documents.*

Levine, Donald N. August 3, 2007. "Ethiopia's missed chances — 1960, 1974, 1991, 1998, 2005-AND NOW:II An Ethiopian dilemma: Deep structures, wrenching processes." Keynote address at the Fourth International Conference on Ethiopian Development Studies, Western Michigan University, Kalamazoo, Michigan.

Lyons, Terrence. 1994. "Crisis on multiple levels: Somalia and the Horn of Africa," in Samatar, Ahmed I. (ed.) 1994. *The Somali Challenge: From Catastrophe to Renewal?* Boulder, CO: Lynne Rienner Publishers.

Mesfin Araya. 1990. "The Eritrean question: An alternative explanation," *Journal of African Studies,* vol. 28, no. 1.

Manheim, Frank J. April 1937. *Journal of Negro History,* vol. 17, no. 2.

Olufemi, Kola. 1983. "Sino-Soviet rivalry in the Horn." *Horn of Africa,* vol. 6, no. 3.

Ottaway, Marina. Summer/Fall 1992. "Nationalism unbound: The Horn of Africa revisited." *School of Advanced International Studies Review*, vol. 12, no. 2.

Pankhurst, Richard. 1999. "Italian fascist war crime in Ethiopia: A history of their discussion, from the league of Nations to the United Nations (1936-1947), *Northeast African Studies*, vol. 6, no 1-2.

_____. 1972. "William H. Ellis — Guillaume Enriques Ellisio: The first Black American Ethiopianist?" *Ethiopia Observer*. Vol. 15 no.2.

Petterson, Donald. Autumn 1986. "Ethiopia abandoned? An American perspective," *International Affairs*, (London), vol. 62, no. 4.

Schwab, Peter. January 1978. "Cold war on the Horn of Africa," *African Affairs*, vol. 77, no. 306.

Shinn, David H. 2005. "Ethiopia: Governance and terrorism," Robert I. Rotberg (ed.), *Battling Terrorism in the Horn of Africa*, Washington, DC: Brookings Institution Press.

_____. 1971. "A survey of American–Ethiopian relations prior to the Italian occupation of Ethiopia," *Ethiopia Observer*, vol. 14, no. 4.

Singer, Audrey and Jill H. Wilson. 2006. "From 'there' to 'here': Refugee resettlement in Metropolitan America," Washington, D.C.: Metropolitan Policy Program, the Brookings Institute.

Swain, Ashok. 1997. "Ethiopia, the Sudan, and Egypt: The Nile river dispute," *The Journal of Modern African Studies*, vol. 35, no 4.

Theodore S. Dagne. Summer 1992. "The Horn of Africa: A region still in crisis," *Mediterranean Quarterly*, vol. 3, no. 3.

Wasserman, Max J. August 1946."The new Ethiopian monetary System," *The Journal of Political Economy*, vol. 54, no. 4.

BOOKS

Abebe Zegeye and Siegfried Pausewang (eds.) 1994. *Ethiopia in Change: Peasantry, Nationalism and Democracy*. New York, NY: British Academic Press.

Adejumobi, Saheed A. 2007. *The History of Ethiopia*. Westport, Connecticut: Greenwood Press.

Andargachew Tiruneh. 1993. *The Ethiopian Revolution 1974–1987* Cambridge, UK. Cambridge University Press.

Baffour, Agyeman-Duah. 1994. *The United States and Ethiopia. Military Assistance and the Quest for Security, 1953–1993*. Lanham: University Press of America.

Bahru Zewde. 2002. *Pioneers of Change in Ethiopia*. Oxford, Ohio: James Currey Ltd.

Bakken, Harokd L. 1984. *United States Strategic Military Access in Northeast Africa*. Monterey, CA.: Naval Postgraduate School.

Balsvik, Randi Ronning. Reprint in 2005. *Haile Selassie's Students: The Intellectual and Social Background to Revolution, 1952–1977*. Addis Ababa, Ethiopia: Addis Ababa University Press.

Bates, Darrell. 1979. *The Abyssinian Difficulty: The Emperor Theodros and the Magdala Campaign, 1867–68*. New York, NY: Oxford University Press.

Bereket Habte Selassie. 2007. *The Crown and the Pen.* Trenton, NJ: The Red sea Press, Inc.

_____. 1980. *Conflict and Intervention in the Horn of Africa.* New York, NY: Monthly Review Press.

Brzezinski, Zbigniew. 1993. *Power and Principle: Memoirs of the National Security Adviser, 1977–1981.* London: Weidenfeld & Nicolson.

Crabites, Pierre. 1938. *Americans in the Egyptian Army,* London: George Routledge & Sons, Ltd.

Chester, Edward W. 1974. *Clash of Titans: Africa and U.S. Foreign Policy.* Maryknoll, NY: Orbis Books

Clapham, Christopher. 1988. *Transformation and Continuity in Revolutionary Ethiopia.* New York, NY: Cambridge University Press.

Clarke, Walter & Jeffrey Herbst. 1997. *Learning from Somalia: The Lessons of Armed Humanitarian Intervention.* Boulder, CO: Westview Press.

Clough, Michael. 1992. *Free At Last? U.S. Policy Toward Africa and the End of the Cold War.* New York, NY: Council on Foreign Relations Press.

Cohen, Herman J. 2000. *Intervening in Africa — Superpower Peacemaking in a Troubled Continent.* New York: St. Martin's Press.

Collier, Paul. 2007. *The Bottom Billion — Why the Poorest Countries are Failing and What Can be Done About It.* Oxford: Oxford University Press.

Connell, Dan. 1997. *Against All Odds: Chronicle of the Eritrean Revolution.* Lawrenceville, NJ: Red Sea Press.

Copson, Raymond W. (ed.) 2007. *United States in Africa: Bush Policy and Beyond.* London, UK: Zed Books.

Crocker, Chester A., 1985. *U.S. Interests in Regional Conflicts in the Horn of Africa.* Washington, DC: US State Department, Bureau of Public Affairs.

Daniel Kendie. 2005. *The Five Dimensions of the Eritrean Conflict 1941-2004: Deciphering the Geo-Political Puzzle.* Gaithersburg, MD: Signature Book Printing, Inc.

De Waal, Alexander. 2004. *Islam and its Enemies in the Horn of Africa.* Bloomington, IN: Indiana University Press.

Diop, Cheikh Anta. 1974. *The African Origin of Civilization.* Mercer Cook, (ed.) Chicago, Ill.: Lawrence Hill & Co.

Dorina, A. Bekoe, (ed.) 2006. *East Africa and the Horn.* Boulder, CO: Lynne Rienner Publishers.

Dougherty, James E. 1982. *The Horn of Africa: A Map of Political-Strategic Conflict.* Special Report. Washington, DC: Institute for Foreign Policy Analysis, Inc.

Du Bois, W.E. Burghardt. 1946/1965. *The World and Africa.* New York, NY: International Publication Co.

Drysdale, John. 2001. *Whatever Happened to Somalia?* London, UK: HAAN Publishing.

Erlich, Haggai. 2002. *The Cross and the River: Ethiopia, Egypt, and the Nile.* Boulder, CO: Lynne Rienner.

_____. 1996. *Ras Alula and the Scramble for Africa,* Lawrenceville, NJ: The red Sea Press, Inc.

_____. 1986. *Ethiopia and the Challenge of Independence*. Boulder, CO.: Lynne Rienner Publishers.

_____. 1983. *The Struggle over Eritrea, 1962–1978. War and Revolution in the Horn of Africa*. Stanford, CA.: Hoover Institute.

Esposito, John L. 1995. *The Islamic Threat: Myth or Reality?* New York, NY: Oxford University Press.

Farer, Tom J. *War Cloud on the Horn of Africa: Crisis for Détente*, Washington, DC: Carnegie Endowment for International Peace.

Farkan, Evelyn N. 2003. *Fractured States and US Foreign Policy: Iraq, Ethiopia, and Bosnia in the 1990s*. New York: Palgrave Macmillan.

Fentahun Tiruneh. 1990, *The Ethiopian Students: Their Struggle to Articulate the Ethiopian Revolution*, Typeset/Edited by Nyala Type, Chicago, Ill.

Fikru Negash Gebrekidan. 2005. *Bond Without Blood: A History of Ethiopian and New World Black Relations 1896–1991*. Lawrenceville, New Jersey: Africa World Press

Francisco, Alvarez. 1881. *Narrative of the Portuguese Embassy to Abyssinia During the Year 1520-1527*. Translated by Edward John Stanley, London.

Franklin, John Hope and Alfred A. Moss, Jr. 1994. *From Slavery to Freedom*. New York: McGraw Hill.

Getachew Metaferia and Maigenet Shifferraw. 1991. *The Ethiopian Revolution of 1974 and the Exodus of Ethiopia's Trained Human Resources*. The Edwin Mellen Press: Lewiston, New York.

Ghelawdewos Araia. 1995. *Ethiopia: The Political Economy of Transition*. Lanham: University Press of America.

Gordon, David F., David C. Miller Howard Wolpe, and American Assembly. 1999. *United States and Africa: A Post-Cold War Perspective*. Norton, WWW & Company, Inc.

Gruber, Ruth. 1987. *The Exodus of the Ethiopian Jews*, New York, NY: Athenuem.

Haile Selassie I. 2007. *My Life and Ethiopia's Progress, 1892–1937*, vol. I. The Autobiography of Emperor Haile Selassie I, King of Kings and Lord of Lords. Translated and annotated by Edward Ullendorff, Chicago, Jamaica, London, Republic of Trinidad and Tobago: Frontline Distribution International, Inc., 4th printing.

_____. 1973. *My Life and Ethiopia's Progress*, vol. II. Edited and annotated by Harold Marcus, Ezekiel Gebissa, and Tibebe Eshete. East Lansing, MI: Michigan State University Press.

Halliday, Fred and Maxine Molyneux. 1981. *The Ethiopian Revolution*. London, UK: Verso editions and NLB.

Hansberry, William Leo. 1981. *Pillars in Ethiopian History: The William Leo Hansberry African History Notebook*. Joseph E. Harris, (ed.) Washington, DC: Howard University Press.

Harris, Joseph E. 1994. *African-American Reactions to War in Ethiopia 1936–1941*. Baton Rouge, Louisiana: Louisiana State University Press.

Hashim, Alice Bettis. 1997. *The Fallen State: Dissonance, Dictatorship, and Death in Somalia*. Lanham, MD: University Press of America.

Heil, Alan L., Jr. 2003. *Voice of America: A History*. New York: Columbia University Press.

Henriksen, Thomas H. (ed.) 2001. *Foreign Policy for America in the Twenty-first Century*. Stanford, California: Hoover Institute.

Henze, Paul B. 1991. *The Horn of Africa: From War to Peace*. London: Macmillan Press.

_____. 1990. *The United States and the Horn of Africa — History and Current Challenge*. Santa Monica, CA: Rand Corporation.

Herbson, John W. 1988. *The Ethiopian Transformation: The Quest for the Post-Imperial State*. Boulder, Co.: Westview Press.

Heslam, David. 2000/01. *Nations of the World, a Political Economy and Business Handbook*. Grey House Publishing: Lakeville, CT.

Holmes, Charles Henry. 1917. *Ethiopia: The Land of Promise*. New York, NY: The Cosmopolitan Press.

Hussey, C. L. March 4, 1904. *Report on the U.S. Diplomatic Expedition to Abyssinia*. Office of Naval Intelligence, Register No.167.

International Institute for Strategic Studies (IISS). September 4, 1979. *The Military Balance, 1979-80*. London: IISS.

_____. 1975. *The Military Balance, 1975–197*. London: IISS.

Jackson, Donna R. 2007. *Jimmy Carter and the Horn of Africa: Cold War Policy in Ethiopia and Somalia*. England: McFarland & Co.

Jackson, John G. 1970. *Introduction to African Civilization*. Secaucus, NJ: Citadel Press.

Jacquin-Berdal, Dominique and Martin Plaut (eds.) 2005. *Unfinished Business: Ethiopia and Eritrea at War*. Trenton, NJ: The Red Sea Press.

Jhazbhay, Iqbal. 2006. *Ethiopia, Somaliland and Somalia amid an Islamist Rising Storm on the Horn: The African Union and the case for Urgent Preventive Diplomacy*. Johannesburg, South Africa: Centre for Policy Studies.

Kaplan, Steven, Tudor Parfitt, and Emanuela Trevisan Semi. 1995. *Between Africa and Zion: Proceedings of the First International Congress of the Society for the Study of Ethiopian Jews*. Jerusalem, Israel: Ben-Zvi Institute.

Khalilzed, Zalmay and Ian O. Lesser. 1998. *Sources of Conflict in the 21ˢᵗ Century — Regional Futures and U.S. Strategy*. Santa Monica, CA.: RAND.

Kinfe Abraham. 1994. *Ethiopia from Bullets to the Ballot Box: The Bumpy Road to Democracy and the Political Economy of Transition*. Lawrenceville, NJ.: The Red Sea Press, Inc.

Klare, Michael T. 2001. *Resource Wars: The New Landscape of Global Conflict*. New York: Henry Holt and Co.

Korn, David. 1986. *Ethiopia, the United States, and the Soviet Union*. London: Croom Helm.

Laidi, Zaki. 1990. *Superpowers in Africa: The Constraints of a Rivalry, 1960–1990*. Chicago, Ill: University of Chicago Press.

Leenco Lata. 2004. *The Horn of Africa as Common Homeland*. Waterloo, Ontario, Canada: Wilfrid Laurier University Press.

Lefebvre, Jeffrey A. 1991. *Arms for the Horn: US Security Policy in Ethiopia and Somalia, 1953–1991*. Pittsburg: University of Pittsburg Press.

Legum, Colin & Bill Lee. 1979. *Horn of Africa in Continuing Crisis*. New York: African Publishing Co.

Levine, Donald N. 2000. (Second edition,) *Greater Ethiopia: The Evolution of a Multiethnic Society*. Chicago, Ill.: The University of Chicago Press.

Makinda, Sam. 1987. *Superpower Diplomacy in the Horn of Africa*. London, UK: Croom Helm.

Marcus, Harold G. 1994. *A History of Ethiopia*. Berkeley: University of California Press.

_____. 1987. *Haile Selassie I The Formative years, 1892–193*. Berkeley, California: University of California Press.

_____. 1983. *Ethiopia, Great Britain and the United States 1941–1974*. Berkley, CA.: University of California Press.

Marsden, Philip. 2007. *The Barefoot Emperor: An Ethiopian Tragedy*. Harper Collins Press.

Mathew, David. 1947 and 1974. *Ethiopia: The Study of a Polity 1540–1935*. London: Eyre and Spultiswoode, 1947. Second reprint in 1974. Westport, Connecticut: Greenwood Press.

Menkhaus, Ken. 2004. *Somalia: State Collapse and the Threat of Terrorism*. New York: Oxford University Press.

Messay Kebede. 2009. *Radicalism and Cultural Dislocation in Ethiopia, 1960–1974*, Rochester, NY: University of Rochester Press.

Naim, Asher. 2003. *Saving the Lost Tribe: The Rescue and Redemption of the Ethiopian Jews*. New York: Ballantine Books.

Nalty, Bernard C. 1903. *Guests of the Conquering Lion: The Diplomatic Mission to Abyssinia*. Marine Corps Historical Reference Service, no. 12, Historical Branch, G-3, Washington, DC: US Marine Corps.

National Democratic Institute for International Affairs and African American Institute. 1992. *An Evaluation of the June 21, 1992 Elections in Ethiopia*. Washington, DC.

Natsoulas, Theodore. 1977. *The Hellenic Presence in Ethiopia: A Study of a European Minority in Africa (1740–1936)*. Athens, Greece.

Negussay Ayele. 2003. *Ethiopia and the United States*. WWW, OCopy.com

Nganda, Benjamin M. 1989. *Superpower Influence in the Horn of Africa*. Carlisle Barracks, PA.: US Army War College.

Njolstad, Olav. 1996. *Peacekeeper and Troublemaker: The Containment Policy of Jimmy Carter, 1977–1978*. Norwegian Institute for Defense Studies.

Okbazghi Yohannes. 1997. *The United States and the Horn of Africa: An Analytical Study of Pattern and Process*. Boulder, CO: Westview Press.

Ottaway, Marina. 1999. *Africa's New Leaders — Democracy or State Reconstruction?*

Washington, DC: Carnegie Endowment for International Peace.

_____. 1982. *Soviet and American Influence in the Horn of Africa*. New York: Praeger.

Ottley, Roi. 1943. *'New World a-coming': Inside Black America*. Boston, Mass.: Houghton Mifflin Co.

Pankhurst, Richard. 2003. *Sylvia Pankhurst: Counsel for Ethiopia*. Hollywood: CA.: Tsehai Publisher.

_____. 2001. *The Ethiopians: A History*. Oxford, UK: Blackwell Publishing

Patman, Robert G. 1990. *The Soviet Union in the Horn of Africa.* New York: Cambridge University Press.

Paulos Milkias and Getachew Metaferia, (eds.) 2005. *The Battle of Adwa — Reflections on Ethiopia's Historic Victory Against European Colonialism,* New York: Algora Publishing.

Rasmuson, John R. 1973. *History of Kagnew Station and American Forces in Eritrea.* Asmara, Ethiopia.

Riley, Ronald G. 1986. *United States' Interests in the Horn of Africa.* Carlisle Barracks, PA: US Army College.

Rosenthal, Eric. 1938. *Stars and Stripes in Africa.* London.

Rothberg, Robert I., ed., 2005. *Battling Terrorism in the Horn of Africa.* Cambridge, Mass.: World Peace Foundation and Washington, DC.: Brookings Institution Press.

Rothchild, Donald and Edmond J. Keller. 2006. *Africa-US Relations: Strategic Encounters.* Boulder, CO.: Lynne Rienner.

Rubenson, Sven (ed.) 1994. *Tewodros and His Contemporaries, 1855–1868.* Lund, Sweden: Bloms Tryckeri.

Samatar, Ahmed I. (ed.) 1994. *The Somali Challenge: From Catastrophe to Renewal?* Boulder, CO: Lynne Rienner Publishers.

Sanceau, Elaine. 1944. *The Land of Prester John: A Chronicle of Portuguese Exploration.* New York: Alfred A. Knopf.

Sauldie, Madan M. 1987. *Superpowers in the Horn of Africa.* New York: APT Books.

Schraeder, Peter J., Steve Smith, and Thomas Biersteker (ed.) 1996. *United States Foreign Policy toward Africa: Incrementalism, Crisis, and Change.* New York: Cambridge University Press.

Scott, William R. 2006. *The Sons of Sheba's Race: African-Americans and the Italo–Ethiopian War, 1935–1941.* Hollywood, CA: Tsehai Publishers.

Schwab, Peter. 1972. *Ethiopia and Haile Selassie.* New York: Facts on File, Inc.

Shepherd, George W. Jr. 1987. *The Trampled Grass: Tributary State and Self-reliance in the Indian Ocean Zone of Peace.* Westport, Connecticut: Greenwood Press.

Shirreff, David. 1995. *Bare Feet and Bandoliers — Wingate, Sandford, the Patriots and the Part they Played in the Liberation of Ethiopia.* London & NY: The Radcliff Press.

Shumet Sishagne. 2007. *Unionists and Separatists, the Vagaries of Ethio–Eritrean Relation, 1941–1991.* Hollywood: Tsehai Publishers.

Skelton, James W., Jr. 1991. *Volunteering in Ethiopia: A Peace Corps Odyssey.* Denver, Co.: Beaumont Books.

Skinner, Robert P. 1963. *Abyssinian Scrapbooks.* U.S.N. Academy, Reel 2900

———. 1906. *Abyssinia of To-Day.* London: Edward Arnold, Publisher to the Indian Office.

———. 1904. *Our Mission to Abyssinia.* Washington, D.C.: Government Printing Office.

Snow, Donald M. and Eugene Brown. 2000. *United States Foreign Policy: Politics Beyond the Water's Edge* (2nd edition.) Boston and New York: Bedford/St. Martin's.

Spector, Stephen. 2005. *Operation Solomon: The Daring Rescue of the Ethiopian Jews.* New York: Oxford University Press.

Spencer, John H. 1984. *Ethiopia at Bay: A Personal Account of the Haile Selassie Year.* Algonac, Michigan: Reference Publishers, Inc.

_____. 1977. *Ethiopia, the Horn of Africa, and the U.S. Policy.* Cambridge Mass.: Institute for Foreign Policy Analysis, Inc.

Steer, George. 1937. *Caesar in Abyssinia.* Boston, Mass.: Little, Brown and Company.

Taye Assefa, ed. 2008. *Academic Freedom in Ethiopia — Perspectives of Teaching Personnel,* Addis Ababa, Ethiopia: Forum for Social Studies.

Teferra Haile-Selassie. 1997. *The Ethiopian Revolution 1974–199.* London: Kagan Paul International.

Tekeste Negash. 1997. *Eritrea and Ethiopia: The Federal Experience.* New Brunswick, NJ: Transaction Publishers.

_____. & Kjetil Tronvoll. 2000. *Brothers at War.* Athens, Ohio: James Currey.

Tesfatsion Medhanie. 2007. *Towards Confederation in the Horn of Africa.* Frankfurt, Germany and London: IKO — Verlag fur Interkulturelle Kommunikation.

Teshome Wagaw. 1993. *For Our Soul: Ethiopian Jews in Israel.* Detroit, MN: Wayne State University Press.

Tecola W. Hagos. 1995. *Democratization? Ethiopia (1991–1994) — A Personal View,* Cambridge, MA: Khepera Publishers.

Tripodi, Paolo. 1999. *The Colonial Legacy in Somalia.* New York: St. Martin's Press, Inc.

Ullendorff, Edward. 1965. *The Ethiopians: An Introduction to Country and People.* London: Oxford University Press.

Varnis, Steven L. 1990. *U.S. Food Aid Policy and Ethiopian Famine Relief.* New Brunswick, NJ.: Transaction Publishers.

Vestal, Theodore M. 1999. *Ethiopia: A Post-Cold War African State.* Westport, CT.: Praeger Publishers.

Warburg, Gabriel. 2003. *Islam, Sectarianism and Politics in Sudan since the Mahdiyya.* Madison, WI: The University of Wisconsin Press.

Ward, Barry J. (ed.) 2002. *Rediscovering the British Empire.* Malabar, Florida: Krieger Publishing Company.

Waterbury, John. 2002. *The Nile Basin: National Determinants of Collective Action.* New Haven: Yale University Press.

Wittkopf, Eugene R., Jr. and J.M. Scott. 2003. *American Foreign Policy.* Wadsworth/ Thomson Learning: Belmont, CA.

Woodward, Peter. 2006. *US Foreign Policy and the Horn of Africa.* Burlington, VT.: Ashgate Press.

_____ & Murray Forsyth (eds.) 1994. *Conflict and Peace in the Horn of Africa — Federalism and its Alternatives.* Brookfield, Vermont: Dartmouth Publishing Company.

_____, 1990. *Sudan 1898–1989: The Unstable State.* Boulder, CO: Lynne Rienner Publishers.

Work, Ernest. 1935. *Ethiopia a Pawn in European Diplomacy.* New York: The Macmillan Company.

BOOKLETS

Ethiopian Student Union of North America. January,1971. "Imperialism in Ethiopia." *Challenge*, New York: Journal of the World Wide Union of Ethiopian Studies, vol. 11, no. 1.

Ministry of Information. 1973. *Ethiopia Today: The Arts*. Addis Ababa, Ethiopia: Commercial Printing Press.

Ratliff, William E. 1986. *Follow the Leader in the Horn: The Soviet-Cuban Presence in East Africa*. Washington, DC: The Cuban American National Foundation.

BOOKS AND JOURNALS IN AMHARIC, AND GOVERNMENT REPORTS

Abyssinian Heritage Development Center. 2004. *Ye Hewat Kewsena ye Zegoch Mebt Regeta*, (TPLF crisis and human rights abuses.) Washington, D.C.: Abyssinian Heritage Development Center.

Daniel Mengistu. March, 2001. "Issayas Afewerki was our agent," *Menelik*.

Dawit Gebru, 1985, *Kentiba Gebru Desta ye Ethiopia Kirse*, Addis Ababa, Ethiopia: Bole Printing House.

Dawit Wolde Giorgis. 2006. *Kehidet Bedem Meret*, (in Amharic), Fredericksburg, VA: Aesop publishers.

Geday Bahreshum. 1992. *Amora*, (in Amharic), publisher not furnished.

Kiflu Tadese. 2005. *Genbot 7*, Silver Spring, MD: K & S Press.

Menelik, (March, 2001).

Merse Hazen Wolde Kirkos. 2008. *Ye hayagnaw Zemen Mebacha ye Zemen Taric Tezetaye 1896-1922* (The Downing of the 20th Century — My recollections 1896-2007.) Addis Ababa, Ethiopia: Addis Ababa University Press.

Ministry of Information. June 10, 2007. *One Ethiopia*. Asmara, Eritrea: Eritrean Ministry of Information.

Ministry of Information. 1973. *Ethiopia Today: The Arts*. Addis Ababa, Ethiopia: Ministry of Information.

Senai, Addis Ababa, 1993, Vol. 1, no. 3.

Tekle Hawariat Tekle Mariam. 2005. *Yehiwete Tarik* (Autobiography), Addis Ababa: Addis Ababa University Press.

Zewde Gabre-Sellassie, 1975, *Yohannes IV of Ethiopia — A Political Biography*, Oxford University Press.

Zewde Reta. 2000. *Ye Eritrea gudie*" (*Eritrea's Case 1941-1963*.) Addis Ababa: Central Printing Press.

JOURNALS, NEWSPAPERS, AND REPORTS

Africa Watch Report. 1991. *Evil days: 30 years of War and famine in Ethiopia*. Washington, D.C.: Human Rights Watch.

"Africa summit 'Bold' policy marshal plan style solutions sought." February 21, 2000. *The Washington Post*.

Alao, Abiodun. 1994. "Anarchy and tranquility in the Horn of Africa." *Brassey's Defence Yearbook*, vol. 104.

Allain, Jean. 2006. "Slavery and the league of nations: Ethiopia as a civilised nation." *Journal of the History of International Law*, vol. 8.

American Journal of International Law. 1909. Supplement, vol. III.

Anderson, Jack. January 2, 1985. "Israel aiding Mengistu in Ethiopia." *The Washington Post*.

Boustany, Nora, May 14, 2005. "Ethiopia defends record on rights," *The Washington Post*.

The Chicago Defender, July 12, 1919. "Abyssinian mission arrives in U.S. 'Representatives of foreign government on way to White House; mission secret'."

Buckley, Stephen, February 2, 1995. "Authorities change face in Africa ... enlightened leaders or savey strongmen?"*The Washington Post*.

Ethiopian Community Center, Inc. Newsletter. Winter, 1985. "Major fundraising for Ethiopian famine victims launched," vol. iv, no. 1.

Fletcher, Michael A. December 31, 2006. "Bush has quietly tripled aid to Africa." *The Washington Post*.

Garland, Gregory L., September, 2009. "Ideals in Action: Africa Bureau Marks 50th Anniversary," *U.S. Department of State Magazine*.

Gettleman, Jeffrey and Mark Mazzetti, April 11, 2007. "Ethiopia holding 41 suspects who fought with Somali Islamists, officials confirm," *The new York Times*.

Ignatius, David, May 13, 2007. "Ethiopia's Iraq," *The Washington Post*.

Kaplan, Robert D. April 2003. "A Tale of Two Colonies." *The Atlantic Monthly*.

Kassebaum, Nancy Landon. Summer 1992. "The United States and the Horn of Africa," *Mediterranean Quarterly*, Vol. 3, no. 3.

Kenyatta, Jomo. September 1935. "Hands off Abyssinia." *Labour Monthly*. Vol. XVII, no. 9.

Makinda, Samuel M. Summer 1992. "Security in the Horn of Africa," *Adelphi Papers*, No. 269.

_____. January/February 1985. "Shifting alliances in the Horn of Africa." *Survival*, Vol. 27, no. 1.

Manheim, Frank J. April 1932. "The United States and Ethiopia: A study in American imperialism. *Journal of Negro History*, Vol. 17, no. 2.

Mesfin Araya. 1990. "The Eritrean question: An alternative explanation." *The Journal of African Studies*, Vol. 28, no. 1.

Morgan, Scott A. July 3 2006. "Ethiopia human rights bill advances through the House." *Los Angeles Chronicle*.

National Democratic Institute for International Affairs and African-American Institute. 1992. *An Evaluation of the June 21, 1992 Elections in Ethiopia*. Washington, DC: National Democratic Institute for International Affairs.

Omang, Joanne. February 9, 1987. "Ex-official says Ethiopia mired in 'no-win' war." *The Washington Post*.

Pankhurst, Richard. June 25, 1999. "Ethiopia, Egypt, and the Nile: An historical fantasy." *Addis Tribune*, Addis Ababa, Ethiopia.

_____. 1972. "William H. Ellis — Guillaume Enriquest Ellesio: The first black American Ethiopianist?" *Ethiopia Observer*, Vol. XV, no. 2.

Petterson, Donald. 1986. "Ethiopia abandoned?: An American perspective." *International Affairs*, Vol. 62, no. 4.

Remnek, Richard B. Autumn 1990. "The strategic importance of the Bab el-Mandeb and the Horn of Africa." *Naval War College Review*, Vol. 43, no 4.

Rodan, Steve. March 9, 1983. "Falashas rebel in Israel — ruling of conversion threatens to alienate Ethiopian Jews in adopted land." *The Washington Post*.

Schwab, Peter. January, 1978. "Cold war on the Horn of Africa." *Journal of the Royal African Society*, Vol. 77, no. 306.

Seeman, Don. June, 1999. "One people, one blood": Public health, political violence, and HIV in an Ethiopian-Israeli setting." *Culture, Medicine and Psychiatry*, Vol. 23, no. 2.

Silverstein, Ken. July 2007. "Lobbying firms blocked action against Ethiopia's tyrant." *Harper's Magazine*.

Swain, Ashok. 1997. "Ethiopia, the Sudan, and Egypt: The Nile River dispute." *The Journal of Modern African Studies*, Vol. 35, no. 4.

Tesfamichael Georgio. 1981. "Ye tegentayochna ye CIA genugenet" (The relationship between separatists and the CIA). *Massawa Symposium*, Asmara: Government Printing Press.

Tesfatsion Medhanie, 2008. *Constitution-Making, Legitimacy and Regional Integration: An Approach to Eritrea's Predicament and relations with Ethiopia*, Denmark: Aalborg University, DIIPER Research Series, Working Paper No. 9.

Tigre People's Liberation Front Foreign Relations Bureau. November, 1982. "The general situation in Tigre."

Tseday Alehegn. April 2005. "Lasting legacies and ties that bind: African-American and Ethiopian relations." *Tadias*.

Vita, Mathew. September 20, 2000. "Senate approves normalized trade with China," *The Washington Post*.

Wondwossen Hailu. January 1971. "Origins of American imperialism in Ethiopia," *Challenge*, Journal of the World Wide Union of Ethiopian Students, New York, NY: The Ethiopian Student Union of North America, Vol. XI, no. 1.

Zewde Gabre Sellassie, 2003. "Ethio–American business relations, 1903-2003." Speech given to African-American entrepreneurs in Addis Ababa, Ethiopia.

"Africa Summit 'Bold' Policy Marshal Plan Style Solutions Sought." February 21, 2000. *The Washington Post*.

Act of International Development Public Law 535, 81st. US Congress, 1950.

"CIA and EPLF at Kagnew Station." 1993. *Senai*, Vol. 1, no. 3.

Financial Times. October 4, 2007.

The Washington Post. August 17, 1991.

The New York Times. August 11, 1991.

NEWSLETTERS

Africa Confidential. Various, 1993–2007.

American Journal of International Law. 1909. Supplement vol. III.

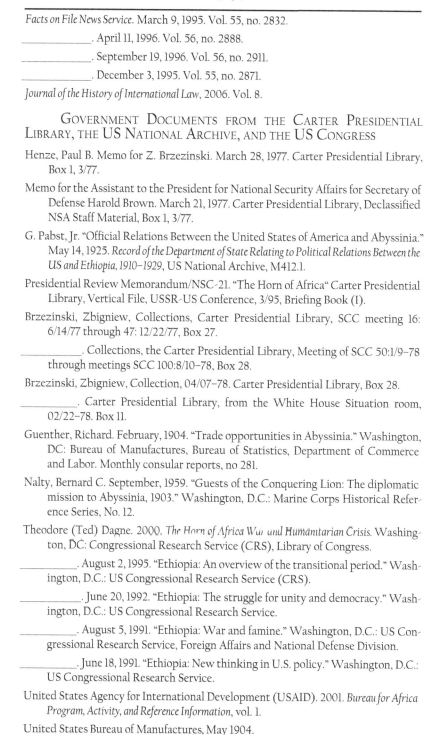

Facts on File News Service. March 9, 1995. Vol. 55, no. 2832.

_____. April 11, 1996. Vol. 56, no. 2888.

_____. September 19, 1996. Vol. 56, no. 2911.

_____. December 3, 1995. Vol. 55, no. 2871.

Journal of the History of International Law, 2006. Vol. 8.

GOVERNMENT DOCUMENTS FROM THE CARTER PRESIDENTIAL LIBRARY, THE US NATIONAL ARCHIVE, AND THE US CONGRESS

Henze, Paul B. Memo for Z. Brzezinski. March 28, 1977. Carter Presidential Library, Box 1, 3/77.

Memo for the Assistant to the President for National Security Affairs for Secretary of Defense Harold Brown. March 21, 1977. Carter Presidential Library, Declassified NSA Staff Material, Box 1, 3/77.

G. Pabst, Jr. "Official Relations Between the United States of America and Abyssinia." May 14, 1925. *Record of the Department of State Relating to Political Relations Between the US and Ethiopia, 1910–1929,* US National Archive, M412.1.

Presidential Review Memorandum/NSC-21. "The Horn of Africa" Carter Presidential Library, Vertical File, USSR-US Conference, 3/95, Briefing Book (I).

Brzezinski, Zbigniew, Collections, Carter Presidential Library, SCC meeting 16: 6/14/77 through 47: 12/22/77, Box 27.

_____. Collections, the Carter Presidential Library, Meeting of SCC 50:1/9–78 through meetings SCC 100:8/10–78, Box 28.

Brzezinski, Zbigniew, Collection, 04/07–78. Carter Presidential Library, Box 28.

_____. Carter Presidential Library, from the White House Situation room, 02/22–78. Box 11.

Guenther, Richard. February, 1904. "Trade opportunities in Abyssinia." Washington, DC: Bureau of Manufactures, Bureau of Statistics, Department of Commerce and Labor. Monthly consular reports, no 281.

Nalty, Bernard C. September, 1959. "Guests of the Conquering Lion: The diplomatic mission to Abyssinia, 1903." Washington, D.C.: Marine Corps Historical Reference Series, No. 12.

Theodore (Ted) Dagne. 2000. *The Horn of Africa War and Humanitarian Crisis.* Washington, DC: Congressional Research Service (CRS), Library of Congress.

_____. August 2, 1995. "Ethiopia: An overview of the transitional period." Washington, D.C.: US Congressional Research Service (CRS).

_____. June 20, 1992. "Ethiopia: The struggle for unity and democracy." Washington, D.C.: US Congressional Research Service.

_____. August 5, 1991. "Ethiopia: War and famine." Washington, D.C.: US Congressional Research Service, Foreign Affairs and National Defense Division.

_____. June 18, 1991. "Ethiopia: New thinking in U.S. policy." Washington, D.C.: US Congressional Research Service.

United States Agency for International Development (USAID). 2001. *Bureau for Africa Program, Activity, and Reference Information,* vol. 1.

United States Bureau of Manufactures, May 1904.

United States Bureau of Statistics, Department of Commerce and Labor. 1904. Monthly consular reports, no. 284.

United States Congress. 1999. *The Ethiopis [sic]- Eritrean War: U.S. Policy Options Hearing before the Subcommittee on Africa of the Committee on International Relations House of Representatives One Hundred Sixtieth Congress First Session*, May 25, 1999. Washington, DC: US Government Printing Press, Serial No. 106-60.

_____. 1992. *The Horn of Africa: Changing Realities and U.S. Response: Hearing Before the Subcommittee on African Affairs of the Committee on Foreign Relations, United States Senate, One Hundred Second Congress, Second Session, March 19, 1992.* Washington, DC: US Government Printing Press.

_____. 1992. *The Political Crisis in Ethiopia and the Role of the United States. Hearing before the Sub-committee on Africa of the Committee on Foreign Affairs House of Representatives One Hundred Second Congress, First session, June 18, 1991.* Washington, DC: Government Printing Press.

_____. 1988. *Human Rights in Ethiopia Hearing, Sib-Committee on Human Rights and International Organizations, International Economic Policy and Trade, and on Africa of the Committee on Foreign Affairs, House of Representatives, September 15 and October 21, 1987. Washington, DC: US* Government Printing Press.

_____. 1976. *Ethiopia and the Horn of Africa Hearing Before the Subcommittee on African Affairs, US* Senate Ninety-fourth Congress, August 4, 5, and 6, 1976. Washington, DC: US Government Printing Press.

_____. 1953. *Hearing Before the Subcommittee of the Committee on Foreign Relations, US Senate Eighty Third Congress.* Washington, DC: US Government Printing Press.

United States Department of States. February 6, 1900. *Instructions to Consuls*, vol. 171, letter no. 61.

_____. January 8, 1900. *Consular Letters from Marseilles*, vol. 18, letter no. 93.

_____. 1904. *Foreign Relations of the United States*. Washington, DC: Government Printing Press,

_____. June 4, 1903. *Instructions to Consuls*, vol. 187, letter no. 178.

United States Library of Congress, Julian W. Witherell (compiler). 1978. *The United States and Africa: Guide to the U.S. Official Documents and Government-Sponsored Publications on Africa, 1785–1975.*

United States Government. 1986. *Israel, Egypt, Sudan, Ethiopia, and Somalia,* Congressional Committee on Foreign Affairs, US House of Representatives, US 99th Congress 1st Session. Washington, DC: US Government Press.

_____. 1927. *Foreign Relations of the United States*, Vol. II. Washington, DC: US Government Printing Press.

_____."Treaties between the United States and Ethiopia," 1914, 1929, and 1955. Washington, DC: US Government Press.

US International Cooperation Administration. 1959. *Fact Sheet: Mutual Security in Action.* Department of State Publication 6801, Public Service Department, Bureau of Public Affairs. Washington DC: US Government Press.

ELECTRONIC-BASED INFORMATION

Alemayehu G. Mariam, October 13, 2008. *Ethiopian Review*, "The political economy of remittances in Ethiopia," http://www.ethiopianreview.com/content/5297/print

Arman, Abukar, October 29, 2008. "Somalia after the Ethiopian occupation," Worldpress. org. http://www.worldpress.org/print_article.cfm?article_id=3431&dont=yes

Binyam Kedir Abdu, February 22, 2007. "Notes taken during meeting between Meles Zenawi and European MPs"on May 13, 2005, http://www.ethiomedia.com/articles/meles_zenawi_and_european_mps...

De Waal, Alex A December 1992. "The Horn of Africa - Howitzer culture," in *New Internationalist*, issue 238, http://www.newint.org/issue238/culture.htm

Druckman, Yaron, May 21, 2008. "State gets failing grade on Ethiopian immigration," *Israel Culture*. http://www.ynet.co.il/english/article/0,7340, L-3545844,00.htm

Ethiomedia, August 29, 2995. "Dr. John H. Spencer (1907–2005): A message from Ethiopians in the Diaspora." www.ethiomedia.com/fastpress/john_spencer.htmlwww.ethiomedia.com/fastpress/john_spencer.html

Marchal, Roland, February 05, 2007. "Somalia: A new front against terrorism," http://hornofafrica.ssc.org/marchal/printable.html

Mitchell, Anthony, September 18, 2006. "Judge says Ethiopian forces killed 193," AP report. http://www.ethiomedia.com/addfile/police_kill_193.html

Mohammed, Abdul, February 20, 2007. Ethiopia's strategic dilemma in the Horn of Africa," http://hornofafrica.ssrc.org/Abdul_Mohammed/printable.html

Negussay Ayele, December 27, 2002. "A Page From a Century of Ethiopia-United States Relations." www.mediaethiopia.com

Terrazas, Aaron Matteo, June 2007. "Beyond regional circularity: The emergence of an Ethiopian diaspora," Migration Policy Institute, http://www.migrationinformation.org/Profiles/print.cfm?ID=604

Vestal, Theodore M. 2005. "Human rights abuses in 'democratic' Ethiopia: Government-sponsored ethnic hatred." www.unb.br/ics/dan/geri/Textos/vestal.htm, www.unb.br/ics/dan/geri/Textos/vestal.htm.

Wachter, Paul, February 14, 2007. "Bush's Somalia strategy enables an Ethiopian despot," *The Nation*, http://www.thenation.com/doc/20070226/wachter

Human Rights Watch, 2008. "Arrest, detention, rendition, and torture," http://hrw.org/reports/2008/eastafrica1008/5.htm#_toc210201068

THESIS/DISSERTATION AND UNPUBLISHED DOCUMENTS

Aregawi Berhe. 2008. "A political History of the Tigray people's Liberation front (1975–1991). Revolt, ideology and mobilization in Ethiopia." Free University of Amsterdam, Faculty of Social Sciences, Ph. D. Dissertation.

Blakey, Leah-Rachel McAnally. 2003. "Making the Hard Choices Between Power and Principle: The Ogaden War, 1977–1978," Saint Louis University, Ph.D. Dissertation.

David, Steven R. 1980. "The Realignment of Third World Regimes from one Superpower to the other: Ethiopia's Mengistu, Somalia's Siad and Egypt's Sadat," Harvard University, Ph.D. Dissertation.

Dawit Toga. 2000. "Superpower Rivalry and Regional Conflicts in the Horn of Africa: Shifting Alliances, Strategic Choice, and Domestic Politics," Columbia University, Ph.D. Dissertation.

Hilletework Mathias. 1988. "Superpowers' Involvement in the Horn of Africa the Ethiopian-Somali Border Conflict," Howard University, Ph.D. Dissertation.

Kilhfner, Donald W. 1968. "The United States and Ethiopia, 1903–1915," Howard University, M.A. Thesis.

Makinda, Samuel. 1985. "Superpower Involvement in the Horn of Africa, 1974–1982," Australian National University, Ph.D. Dissertation.

Merera Gudina. 2002. "Ethiopia: Competing Ethnic Nationalism and the Quest for Democracy, 1960-2000," The Hague, The Netherlands Institute of Social Studies, Ph.D. Dissertation.

Reese, Cynthia M. 1987. "U.S.–Soviet Competition for Influence in the Horn of Africa," American University, M.A. Thesis.

Dima Noggo Sarbo. August, 2007. "The Ethiopia-Eritrea Conflict: Short sighted solution and long term problems," The University of Tennessee, Knoxville.

Yang, Il-Seung. 1985. "United States Foreign Policy Options in Ethiopia and Somalia," Western Illinois University, M.A. Thesis.

INDEX

A

Abreha Deboch, 36

Abune, 10, 21, 36, 177

Abyssinia, 3, 10, 12, 14-18, 23, 30, 36-37, 54, 129, 154, 156, 173, 186, 189-193, 195, 197

Abyssinian Baptist Church, 16, 25, 171, 174, 182

Addis Ababa University, 12, 21, 31, 55, 58, 81, 111, 187, 194

Addis Tedla, 80

Adwa (See also Battle of), 3, 11-13, 54-55, 68, 145, 172, 192

Afan Oromo, 181, 183

Afar, 21, 49, 123-124, 131

Afework Gebre Iyesus, 22, 174

Afghanistan, 114

African-American, 5, 13, 16, 26, 35-36, 39, 54, 57, 120, 172, 174-175, 189, 192, 195-196

African Crisis Response Initiative (ACRI), 82

African Growth and Opportunity Act (AGOA), 7, 100, 181

African Renaissance, 7, 88, 91, 97, 103, 122, 127

African Union (AU) 49, 138

Afro-Caribbean, 13

Afro-Marxist, 67, 69-70

Agame, 127

Agazi, 118, 182

Agence France Presse, 64

Ahmed ibn Ibrahim, 87

Aklilu Habte, 104

Al-Ittihad al-Islami, 82, 93, 135-136, 140, 181

Al-Nimery, Jaffar, 74, 131-132

Al-Qaeda, 82, 93, 102, 133, 136

Al-Turabi, Hassan Abdallah, 82, 92

Albright, Madeleine K., 92, 181

Alemaya Agricultural College, 55

Alexandria, 10, 177

Ambo, 55

American Association of Ethiopian Jewry, 73

American Jewish groups, 75

Amhara, 60, 87, 100, 104

Amharic, 5, 7, 10, 12, 16-17, 25, 27, 69-70, 103-106, 149-151, 157-158, 171, 174, 179, 183, 194

Amnesty International (AI), 64, 178

Andom, Michael, 71

Angola, 67, 69, 127

Arab League, 50-51, 65

Arab States, 46-47, 50, 62, 83-87, 91

Armey, Richard, 93, 109

Ashagre Yigletu, 88, 180

Asia, 28, 57, 102, 137

Asmara, 11, 41, 49, 51, 64, 80, 84-85, 95, 104, 125, 127, 176, 178, 180, 192, 194, 196

Assab, 124, 128

Assrate Kassa, 83-85, 178

Atnafu Abate, 71

Axumite kingdom, 16

Ayalew Mandefro, 63, 66-68, 163, 178

Ayana Biru, 17